The
RED SOX
READER

The
RED SOX
READER

Edited by Dan Riley

REVISED EDITION

A Mariner Book
Houghton Mifflin Company
Boston • *New York*

First Mariner Books edition 1999

For information about permission to reproduce selections from
this book, write to Permissions, Houghton Mifflin Company,
215 Park Avenue South, New York, NY 10003.

Library of Congress Cataloging-in-Publication Data
The Red Sox reader / edited by Dan Riley. — Rev. ed.
      p.   cm.
ISBN 0-395-97999-4
1. Boston Red Sox (Baseball team) — History. 2. Boston Red Sox
(Baseball team) — Humor. I. Riley, Dan.
GV875.B62R43 1991
796.357'64'0974461 — dc20 90-28179 CIP

Printed in the United States of America

Book design by Robert Overholtzer

QUM 10 9 8 7 6 5 4 3

Grateful acknowledgment is made to the following for permission to
reprint previously published material:

The Boston Globe for "Lee Will Be Missed" by Ray Fitzgerald. Copyright © 1978. "Yaz, to the End, True to Himself" by Peter Gammons. Copyright © 1983. "Fenway: From Frazee to Fisk" by Martin F. Nolan. Copyright © 1986. "The Perfect Ending to a Perfect Season" by Michael Blowen. Copyright © 1986. (All articles published courtesy of *The Globe.*)

The Boston Herald for "History's Sad Lesson" by Charles Pierce. Copyright © 1986. (Published courtesy of *The Herald.*)

Doubleday & Company for "The Greatest Game Ever Played" by Thomas Boswell from *How Life Imitates the World Series.* Copyright © 1982 by Washington Post Writers' Group.

Doris Kearns Goodwin for "From Father, with Love" by Doris Kearns Goodwin. Originally published in the *Boston Globe.* Copyright © 1986 by Doris Kearns Goodwin.

David Halberstam for "The Fan Divided" by David Halberstam. Originally published in the *Boston Globe.* Copyright © 1986 by David Halberstam.

George F. Will for "The Pursuit of Excellence" by George F. Will. Originally published in the *Boston Globe*. Copyright © 1987 by George F. Will. (Published courtesy of Mr. Will.)

Geoffrey Wolff for "No El Foldo Foils Fandom" by Geoffrey Wolff. Originally published in the *Boston Globe*. Copyright © 1987 by Geoffrey Wolff.

And thanks to Bill Lee.

To Meagan and Gillian
may their lives be filled with all the things
I tried to get into this book: good writing,
fond memories, and high hopes.

Acknowledgments

This book could not have been written without the help of
   Lorna . . . first, last, and always;
   my late dad, Cliff Riley, who raised me as a Red Sox fan;
   Marie Riley, who instilled in me the patience of Job, a pre-
requisite for all Red Sox fans;
   Bill and Betty, who provided generous, take-it-to-the-bank
support;
   Curt Gowdy and Ned Martin, radio uncles who taught me
all about the game;
   Mike Blowen, who helped keep this Sox-fan-in-exile from
sinking into the lard of Raider-Laker-Dodger hype with relief
packages of sports pages from home.

Contents

PLAYGOERS

NOTICES

Introduction

Dear Reader:

The Boston Red Sox are probably the most amusing team in baseball history. This is not to say that they are or ever have been a funny team with rosters full of zany characters like "Marvelous" Marv or "Uek," Dizzy, Dazzy, or the Ol' Perfesser. Jim Rice was definitely not Bill Cosby in spikes.

No, when we call the Red Sox baseball's most amusing team, we're not invoking the contemporary meaning of the word that's measured in smiles, but in its antecedent definition which comes from the Middle French — *muser* — which, as near as we can figure out, had something to do with the gaping mouths of animals and metamorphosed in time to mean, variously, "distract," "bemuse," "bewilder," "absorb." All of which the Red Sox have done throughout their history with a consistency bordering on the diabolical, leaving more than a few mouths agape up and down the New England landscape.

When the history of twentieth-century baseball is written, it will, without doubt, belong to the New York Yankees — statistically speaking. More pennants, more playoffs, more World Series, most 56-game hitting streaks, most 60-home-run seasons, most players starting 2,130 games in a row, most players' numbers retired, most centerfield monuments, most times managed by Billy Martin, most dollars spent by George Steinbrenner, most Reggie Bars.

Even books. Although this book is dedicated, in part, to the notion that while the Yankees may have always had the better players, the Red Sox have had the better writers, even we have to admit that in terms of sheer numbers of forests felled in bald-faced glorification of one team, the Yankees take the prize there, too. Is there a Yankee alive who hasn't taken his dreary tale of pinstripe servitude to the likes of Peter Golenbock or Dick Schapp to regurgitate for the insatiable Manhattan masses?

But there'll be another side of the game for future historians to deal with, and that side will belong to the Boston Red Sox, whose grip on the baseball imagination defies so much of the statistical logic upon which the game is built. Not a single world championship in 68 years. Yet, has there ever been an also-ran in history that's inspired as much sympathetic passion as the Red Sox? Maybe Robert E. Lee. Maybe the Spanish Loyalists.

And why is that? As a lifelong New England sports fan, I've been witness to that full range of emotions sports fans are heir to — the old thrill of victory/agony of defeat refrain, as ABC puts it. The victory, of course, is always most thrilling when it's least expected, and the defeat always most agonizing when least deserved. In years of watching the Celtics routinely accumulate NBA championships or watching, in years mercifully past, the Patriots routinely mocked as patsies of the NFL, it's been my experience that simple winning and losing both engender a similar sense of thudding finality. Neither Celtic victories nor Patriot defeats have ever been as emotionally exquisite as the many memorable wins and losses of the Red Sox, and I don't think this is merely a question of the difference between baseball and basketball or baseball and football. I think it's because no team — in any American sport — has spent so long a time in that Purgatory that exists between Ultimate Victory and Utter Defeat as the Red Sox have. Theirs is an ongoing saga, spanning decades, of unexpected wins giving way to undeserved losses, leaving legions of fans to muse — to ponder — to reflect . . . *what if.*

They're the greatest *what if* team in sports, and that's what makes them baseball's most amusing team. Their power to divert, bemuse, bewilder, and absorb lies in their ability to engage us long after the final out of any season. The *what if*'s cascade upon the mind like raindrops on a field of seedlings giving bloom to a thousand radiant imaginings. What if Buckner makes the play at first? What if Piniella doesn't come up with Remy's drive to right? What if Doyle turns the double play on Bench? What if Aparicio doesn't slip rounding third? What if it rains and Lonborg gets another day of rest? What if Pesky doesn't hold the ball? What if The Kid never goes to Korea? What if Frazee doesn't sell The Babe?

There have been so many allusions made to the Red Sox as modern-day Greek heroes, tragically flawed by an Achilles' heel of far more mythic dimension than any mere lack of a left-handed stopper out of the bullpen could ever possibly explain, that one would think there are more classics professors running around Boston than Kennedys. The most thoroughly Homeric version of this metaphor holds that all the countless *what if*'s in Red Sox history flow from the first. What if Harry Frazee, too dully human to recognize the great gift granted him by the gods that was Babe Ruth, had not sold the wondrous Bambino down the slime river to the loathsome New York Yankees. In doing so, of course, he insulted the gods to such a degree that a curse has been visited upon the Sox from that day forward resulting in an endless series of ennobling but ultimately futile ascents to the pinnacle of the baseball world. (Was that a hot dogger named Sisyphus seen tumbling down after Lonborg on the ski slope that day? We wonder.)

That's how the Greeks would've figured it anyway, and we haven't seen any scientific evidence to refute their maddeningly rational view of the world. Certainly it's as credible as any worldview promulgated by your neighborhood cult leader or visiting ayatollah. The Red Sox surely haven't become as fascinating a team as they have by mere human design. The ownership has been no more enlightened than any other, and oftentimes considerably less so. And the players don't appear to have been cut out of any special mold. Yet with rousing regularity Red Sox teams seem to rally themselves and their followers to these improbable Olympian heights of anticipation . . . then a two-out pop to third and another winter of bittersweet remembrances is upon us.

All this curse of the gods stuff may be just plain Greek to Joe Fan, who would gladly trade all the mythic musings of a dozen modern-day Homers for one four-game thrashing of a National League rival in October. Maybe so. Maybe *The Red Sox Reader* is sorry consolation for a World Championship flag flying over Fenway. But take heart, Sox fans. A world championship is a transitory prize. You win it one year, and the next year you lose it to a bunch of whozits from Cleveland or Pittsburgh. But mythology, like the mythology woven through the history of our team and recorded in these pages, renews itself and is ours forever.

D.R.
February 1987

Introduction to the Revised Edition

Since *The Red Sox Reader* first appeared in the spring of 1987, the Red Sox themselves have appeared in two more postseason series — in '88 and '90. Stretching back to the fateful October of 1986 then, that makes three postseason appearances in five years. Our boys have practically become regulars — Team October!

Unfortunately, their play in these two series, consisting of eight straight forgettable losses, has been about as inspiring as watching a cow walk through a Chicago stockyard. It's enough to make one long for the days of two-out, two-strike losses in the bottom of the tenth. Cry all you want about that ball going through Buckner's legs, but at least that was losing on a grand scale. That was losing to write home about . . . or at least write about. What's to be said about Clemens getting thrown out in the second inning of a mercifully last playoff game in Oakland? Even an Updike would be hard-pressed to weave memorable prose out of that one.

Needless to say, not much good writing has come out of recent Sox history. So *The Red Sox Reader* has more or less been revised backward. We've added two pieces here on the Sox of the '40s from recent, successful books by Dan Shaughnessy and David Halberstam.

Red Sox teams from here on out, of course, are now saddled with a dual burden. They either have to win it all, or

they have to find a way to lose more dramatically, more tragically, more unbelievably than their predecessors.

Frankly, as the pages ahead reveal, winning it all would be
a whole lot easier.

D.R.
October 1990

THE PLAYHOUSE

Among the verities of the age, has any been as reliable as "no lead is safe in Fenway"? The capricious nature of Fenway has probably contributed more to the storied history of the team than any fact readily obtainable by the minds of ordinary men or sabermetricians. (As to the facts of mythology, there's still an argument to be made that the gods won't let us win it all until the Babe's body is returned to its rightful resting place somewhere at the foot of the 420 sign in center.) There is, to be sure, that malcontented segment of the populace, generally located at points southwest of Bridgeport, who scream "Enough already!" when Garagiola or Kubek goes in to explaining for the umpteenth time how the shortstop has to watch for the carom on balls hit down the left field line. Well, let them complain. It's no more possible to overdo the finer attributes of Fenway than it is to overdo discussion of the Sistine Chapel or Beethoven's Fifth. Surely what one is to art and the other is to music, Fenway is to ballparks. As Martin F. Nolan of the *Boston Globe* says in the essay that kicks things off here, the park has always been the star. Even in bad seasons, we know The Green Monster is going to make for some mighty entertaining baseball. And, on rare occasions, when the game's a stinker, the recollections are redolent of richer times, as writer-historian Doris Kearns Goodwin warmly reminds us in her piece.

Martin F. Nolan

From Frazee to Fisk

Park Is Unique, so Is Its History

Boston Globe, October 6, 1986

The ballpark is the star. In the age of Tris Speaker and Babe Ruth, the era of Jimmie Foxx and Ted Williams, through the empty-seats epoch of Don Buddin and Willie Tasby and unto the decades of Carl Yastrzemski and Jim Rice, the ballpark is the star. A crazy-quilt violation of city planning principles, an irregular pile of architecture, a menace to marketing consultants, Fenway Park works. It works as a symbol of New England's pride, as a repository of evergreen hopes, as a tabernacle of lost innocence. It works as a place to watch baseball.

It is a ballpark, not a stadium. The Big A in Anaheim, the Astrodome in Houston and Shea Stadium in Queens are all planned, programmed and enclosed in neat off-ramp packages designed by demographic studies and traffic engineers. Fenway Park laughs at traffic engineers. It is cozy, yes, but it is cantankerous, not cute.

The Red Sox are beloved nationwide (to the delight of television ad salesmen) because for decades Bostonians and New Englanders have departed in search of economic opportunity elsewhere. This exodus had begun to reverse itself only since the last World Series here in 1975.

Shake a tree in Orange Country and a half-dozen Dorchester émigrés fall out. In Baltimore, Earl Weaver used to complain that Oriole partisans at Memorial Stadium were outnumbered by Red Sox fans who had motored north from nearby Washington. Ex-Bostonians are plentiful in the capital because Boston's greatest natural resource and chief export has been politics.

Fenway has been a talisman for the poetically inclined. It is old, it is idiosyncratic and a frequent citadel of dashed hopes — all enduring themes of literature. Fenway is the ultimate protagonist of the lit'ry life, a survivor.

"All literary men are Red Sox fans," John Cheever told Diane White a few weeks after the exquisite agony of 1978. "To be a Yankee fan in literary society is to endanger your life." The late author saw the Yankee–Red Sox rivalry as the Trojan War, with the Red Sox as the tragic Trojans (broad-backed Yaz in a noble frieze, his poignant popup soaring beyond the topless towers of Ilium before the dream is dashed by the grit-gloved Graig Nettles).

The Red Sox may resemble Trojans, but as Gov. William Bradford wrote in "Of Plimoth Plantation," the first New England literary work, "they knew they were Pilgrims." The franchise was known as the Boston Pilgrims after having been variously nicknamed the Plymouth Rocks, the Speed Boys (it was a long time ago) and the Boston Puritans. The new owner, John I. Taylor, put red stockings on the team in 1907 to exploit the lingering fame of the old 19th-century National League franchise. "From now on, we'll wear red stockings and I'm grabbing that name Red Sox," Taylor said.

The team's popularity outgrew its Huntington Avenue grounds (now the site of Northeastern University), and Taylor oversaw construction of the new ballpark. With the same directness with which he baptized the team, Taylor, whose family also owned the *Globe,* said "It's in the Fenway section, isn't it? Then name it Fenway Park."

The Fens was the centerpiece of the "Emerald Necklace" of parks designed by Frederick Law Olmsted, a planned environment of babbling brooks and green vistas, a design that held out a peaceful vision for urban America. But the stronger influence upon Fenway Park — and of its literary destiny — was the unplanned, antipastoral engine of haphazard growth that butchered Boston's landscape, the railroad.

Lansdowne Street necessitated the improbable Wall because Lansdowne Street was squeezed by the multilined pathway of the Boston and Albany railroad, the tracks that transported Boston's wealth and innocence westward. These roaring lines (now hemmed to a modest ribbon by the Massachusetts Turnpike) defined "the other side of the tracks."

Fenway Park is funky because of an odd circumstance of geographical neglect. *The Late George Apley* explains why the Back Bay historically has lorded over the South End (and Fenway). Although South End houses were as grand and substantial as their counterparts in the Back Bay, Apley discovered a man sitting *in shirtsleeves* on a South End stoop. He sold his property, and the South End was degentrified for almost a century. Had Fenway not been on the other side of the tracks, it might have been bulldozed and replaced with boutiques. Fans would not have sat in shirtsleeves in the bleachers, the team would have fled to suburbia, and would the Framingham Red Sox have as much appeal?

The tracks also symbolized another enduring literary theme, treason. On one treacherous day in 1920, Babe Ruth was sold to the New York Yankees by the new Red Sox owner, Harry Frazee. New York, the symbol of capitalist crassness, that day lost future generations of poets.

Fenway, the vestibule of approach avoidance, would win any literary plebiscite over Yankee Stadium, a self-confident garage for a juggernaut. The arrogance of easy winners against the charm of the underdog? New York neon vs. New England pewter? Trendy vulgarity vs. traditional serenity? No contest. Now playing right field for Nathaniel Hawthorne, John Updike. Now at first base for William Dean Howells, David Halberstam.

Babe Ruth's betrayal was based on Frazee's longing for the bright lights of Broadway. He needed money to finance a new musical, *No, No, Nanette,* and had already sold several Sox players, all of whom took the train to join the Yankees. The Babe had just ended a fabulously successful career as a pitcher ($29\frac{2}{3}$ consecutive scoreless World Series innings) to begin to make history with his bat. In the 1919 season, he had 29 home runs, 112 RBIs and still managed to pitch in 17 games, winning 9.

Frazee's Boston roots were notoriously shallow, and he became a New York prototype, what the tabloids meant when they said "playboy socialite." Frazee's name in our household ranked somewhere between Judas Iscariot and Benedict Arnold. (My father was involved in show business in the 1920s and played banjo in New York bands.) Frazee died in a Park Avenue apartment in 1929 with New York Mayor Jimmy Walker at his bedside.

Pinstripe paranoia has been a Boston curse ever since. Since Ruth was sold, the Yankees' lead over the Red Sox in winning World Series is 22–0. When Joe Page lumbered out of the Yankee bullpen in the late '40's, he resembled King Kong and the Red Sox performed like Fay Wray. Tommy Henrich always made the clutch hit, or Gene Woodling did, or Yogi Berra. Although we all earnestly sang, "He's better than his brother Joe, Dom-in-ic DiMaggio!" we didn't believe it. Manhattan's mark of Cain was stamped upon Boston's brow indelibly by Bucky Dent in 1978.

New York literati have more recently rooted for the Red Sox because of the antics of George Steinbrenner, the principal owner of the Yankees. Steinbrenner's "pennant-buying" has caused acute embarrassment for even the most loutish Yankee fans, and several transferred their allegiance to the Red Sox. To root against big, rich, bustling Yankee Stadium and to cheer for elegant, wan, near-miss Fenway Park was politically popular, if not imperative among literati.

This switch is hugely ironic because Steinbrenner's open wallet was modeled on the original Daddy Warbucks of baseball, Thomas Austin Yawkey. In 1933, the 30-year-old Yawkey inherited a textile fortune and spent part of it buying the Boston Red Sox. He brightened the Depression years in Boston with a million-dollar renovation of Fenway Park — concrete bleachers, new left-field stands. Yawkey also began a talent-buying spree that brought Lefty Grove, Jimmie Foxx and Joe Cronin to Boston. Later, with farm products like Ted Williams, Dom DiMaggio and Bobby Doerr, the Red Sox restoration had begun. Yawkey was more of a gentleman fan than a field marshal.

In 1946, the American League pennant returned to Fenway after an absence of 28 years. A major factor was a trade with Detroit that brought Rudy York and his 117 RBIs to first base. Although he was with the team less than two seasons, York became the prototype of Fenway sluggerdom. Instead of first basemen, the Sox favored power forwards. For decades, Red Sox policy built a row of condominiums down the right-field line — Foxx, Walt Dropo, Vic Wertz, Dick Gernert, Mickey Vernon, Norm Zauchin, Dick Stuart, Lee Thomas, George Scott, Tony Perez. (Bill Buckner's modest size and immodest talent is a bright sign.)

The team's strategy has been a prisoner of Fenway, or at least of the Wall. Big-boom righthanded hitters were always courted (many of whom dented the Wall for singles), even though the most productive hitters at Fenway have been lefthanded — Williams, Yastrzemski, Wade Boggs. The hit-and-run remains a rarity and the stolen base a sacrilege. Lefty hero Mel Parnell once explained the southpaw's enemy at Fenway was the smallness of foul territory, not the Wall, but management's patience has been historically short with lefties (adios, Bill Lee, John Tudor, Bobby Ojeda).

Red Sox philosophy defies logic as the park defies geometry. The kaleidoscope of contrariness only adds to the charm. The park is not the only enticement for loyal Bosox rooters; so is the tradition of almost winning, the September–October malady of *gonfalonia interruptus*.

The major difference between Bosox rooters and adherents of the Chicago Cubs is not the difference between Fenway and Wrigley Field. Sox fans are used to the near miss. Cub fans inhabit the limbo between buffoonery and the quiescence of Adlai Stevenson Democrats — it doesn't matter if you lose eloquently or lose poignantly as long as you lose.

Since World War II, the Red Sox have brought their disciples to the foothills of glory a half-dozen times. Each approach and each disappointment is documented in the minds and hearts of New England:

Oct. 15, 1946 — Enos Slaughter scores from first on a single in the seventh game and St. Louis wins the game and the Series. In his only World Series, Ted Williams is outhit by a rookie catcher for the Cardinals, Joe Garagiola.

Oct. 4, 1948 — The first American League playoff ends early as the Cleveland Indians pummel starter (at 8–7) Denny Galehouse and win the pennant, 8–3.

Oct. 2, 1949 — A team bulging with .300 hitters and two 20-game winners heads into Yankee Stadium needing one victory out of two. They lose twice, 5–4 and 5–3.

Sept. 26, 1950 — Again with steady hitters and two 144-RBI sluggers, the Sox challenge, but the Yankees eliminate them a week early.

Oct. 12, 1967 — After the "Impossible Dream" pennant, a tired Jim Lonborg starts the seventh game, which a fresh Bob Gibson wins by scattering three hits for the Cardinals.

Oct. 2, 1972 — Two future Hall of Famers find themsleves occupying third base, but Luis Aparicio wasn't supposed to be when Yaz tripled. The Sox lose the game and the pennant to the Tigers, 3–1.

Oct. 22, 1975 — The anticlimax to the great 12-inning Sixth Game as Perez takes Bill Lee downtown. The Cincinnati Reds win the game and the World Series, 4–3.

Oct. 2, 1977 — The Sox get close again, but fade in the rain, tied for second with Baltimore.

Oct. 2, 1978 — In the second-ever AL playoff, Yaz' heroics, Piniella's blind catch, Dent's poke off Torrez end with another Yankee victory, 5–4.

Oct. 2, 1981 — Yet another tease into the "final weekend" before finishing 2½ out, eliminated by the Indians, 11–4.

T. S. Eliot, an undergraduate at Harvard when the Red Sox received their current name, wrote that "April is the cruelest month . . . mixing memory and desire." Yet desire has not fled the souls of Red Sox fans, not while they can maintain hope this late in the season. October in New England remained in the memory of an Amherst native who went west. Helen Hunt Jackson could have written this anthem of hope for every survivor of a Fenway season:

> O suns and skies and clouds of June,
> And flowers of June together,
> Ye cannot rival for one hour
> October's bright blue weather.

This offer not available for Series games played in the Astrodome.

Doris Kearns Goodwin

From Father, with Love

Baseball Bonds Three Generations

Boston Globe, October 6, 1986

The game of baseball has always been linked in my mind with the mystic texture of childhood, with the sounds and smells of summer nights and with the memories of my father.

My love for baseball was born on the first day my father took me to Ebbets Field in Brooklyn. Riding in the trolley car, he seemed as excited as I was, and he never stopped talking; now describing for me the street in Brooklyn where he had grown up, now recalling the first game he had been taken to by his own father, now recapturing for me his favorite memories from the Dodgers of his youth — the Dodgers of Casey Stengel, Zach Wheat, and Jimmy Johnston.

In the evenings, when my dad came home from work, we would sit together on our porch and relive the events of that afternoon's game which I had so carefully preserved in the large, red scorebook I'd been given for my seventh birthday. I can still remember how proud I was to have mastered all those strange and wonderful symbols that permitted me to recapture, in miniature form, the every movement of Jackie Robinson and Pee Wee Reese, Duke Snider and Gil Hodges. But the real power of that scorebook lay in the responsibility it entailed. For all through my childhood, my father kept from me the knowledge that the daily papers printed daily box scores, allowing me to believe that without my personal renderings of all those games he missed while he was at work, he would be unable to follow our team in the only proper way a team should be followed, day by day, inning by inning. In other words, without me, his love for baseball would be forever incomplete.

To be sure, there were risks involved in making a commitment as boundless as mine. For me, as for all too many Brooklyn fans, the presiding memory of "the boys of summer" was the memory of the final playoff game in 1951 against the Giants. Going into the ninth, the Dodgers held a 4–1 lead. Then came two singles and a double, placing the winning run at the plate with Bobby Thomson at bat. As Dressen replaced Erskine with Branca, my older sister, with maddening foresight, predicted the forever famous Thomson homer — a prediction that left me so angry with her, imagining that with her words she had somehow brought it about, that I would not speak to her for days.

So the seasons of my childhood passed until that miserable summer when the Dodgers were taken away to Los Angeles by the unforgivable O'Malley, leaving all our rash hopes and dreams of glory behind. And then came a summer of still deeper sadness when my father died. Suddenly my feelings for baseball seemed an aspect of my departing youth, along with my childhood freckles and my favorite childhood haunts, to be left behind when I went away to college and never came back.

Then one September day, having settled into teaching at Harvard, I agreed, half reluctantly, to go to Fenway Park. There it was again: the cozy ballfield scaled to human dimensions so that every word of encouragement and every scornful yell could be heard on the field; the fervent crowd that could, with equal passion, curse a player for today's failures after cheering his heroics the day before; the team that always seemed to break your heart in the last week of the season. It took only a matter of minutes before I found my-

self directing all my old intensities toward my new team —
the Boston Red Sox.

I am often teased by my women friends about my obsession, but just as often, in the most unexpected places — in
academic conferences, in literary discussions, at the most
elegant dinner parties — I find other women just as crazily
committed to baseball as I am, and the discovery creates an
instant bond between us. All at once, we are deep in conversation, mingling together the past and the present, as if the
history of the Red Sox had been our history too.

There we stand, one moment recollecting the unparalleled
performance of Yaz in '67, the next sharing ideas on how the
present lineup should be changed; one moment recapturing
the spendid career of "the Splendid Splinter," the next
complaining about the manager's decision to pull the pitcher
the night before. And then, invariably, comes the most vivid
memory of all, the frozen image of Carlton Fisk as he rounded
first in the sixth game of the '75 World Series, an image as
intense in its evocation of triumph as the image of Ralph
Branca weeping in the dugout in its portrayal of heartache.

There is another, more personal memory associated with
Carlton Fisk, for he was, after all the years I had followed
baseball, the first player I actually met in person. Apparently,
he had read the biography I had written on Lyndon Johnson
and wanted to meet me. Yet when the meeting took place, I
found myself reduced to the shyness of childhood. There I
was, a professor at Harvard, accustomed to speaking with
presidents of the United States, and yet, standing beside this
young man in a baseball uniform, I was speechless.

Finally, Fisk said that it must have been an awesome
experience to work with a man of such immense power as
President Johnson — and with that, I was at last able to
stammer out, with a laugh, "Not as awesome as the thought
that I am really standing here talking with you."

Perhaps I have circled back to my childhood, but if this is
so, I am certain that my journey through time is connected in
some fundamental way to the fact that I am now a parent

myself, anxious to share with my three sons the same ritual I once shared with my father.

For in this linkage between the generations rests the magic of baseball, a game that has defied the ravages of modern life, a game that is still played today by the same basic rules and at the same pace as it was played 100 years ago. There is something deeply satisfying in the knowledge of this continuity.

And there is something else as well which I have experienced sitting in Fenway Park with my small boys on a warm summer's day. If I close my eyes against the sun, all at once I am back at Ebbets Field, a young girl once more in the presence of my father, watching the players of my youth on the grassy field below. There is magic in this moment, for when I open my eyes and see my sons in the place where my father once sat, I feel an invisible bond between our three generations, an anchor of loyalty linking my sons to the grandfather whose face they never saw but whose person they have already come to know through this most timeless of all sports, the game of baseball.

PLAYERS

The collection of player profiles that follows is, admittedly, an odd one. The obvious choices are there, of course — Updike's classic on The Kid's last at-bat and Peter Gammons's heartfelt report on Yaz's farewell. But there's also a vintage Red Smith piece on one of the Splendid Splinter's not so glorious days. There's an excerpt from Robert W. Creamer's excellent biography of Babe Ruth — hopefully its inclusion will irritate Yankee fans enough to compensate for the anguish it'll rekindle in Bosox bosoms. Then, just to remind us that not all our heroes played their minor league ball with Olympus of the Far Hellenic League, there's a largely irreverent assortment of snapshots from Brendan C. Boyd and Fred C. Harris, who've enshrined the dubious legacies of Guido Grilli, Pumpsie Green et al. for posterity. Leonard Shecter offers up a demythologized view of the Sox of '68, but somehow his incisive detailing of the daily drudgery of major league life seems to heighten our appreciation of those flashes of brilliant play that transcend it all. George Will is not a Red Sox fan, but he loves self-discipline, so who better to pen an appreciation of that most willfully successful of Red Sox — Wade Boggs? Bill Lee was not the greatest Red Sox ever, but he certainly was among the most interesting, so we've indulged our fondness for The Spaceman here with two views, one by Lee himself in interview, and one through the eyes of the late Ray Fitzgerald. That makes for some glaring omissions among The Spaceman's contemporaries of course — Elegant Lynn, Stalwart Fisk, Dazzling Tiant, Simmering Rice. Red Sox fans of the late '70s, like Sox fans of the late '40s, probably saw more great players win fewer world championships than humanly possible — our point exactly.

Robert W. Creamer

Departure from Boston: Sold Down the River

Babe: The Legend Comes to Life, 1974

Johnny Igoe arranged a postseason tour for Ruth that took him through the west and eventually to Los Angeles, where he appeared in exhibition games with other major leaguers, played golf with Buck Weaver and reportedly hit a drive 340 yards. He was also supposed to make a series of movie shorts with such gripping titles as *Home Sweet Home, Touch All Bases, The Dough Kiss, The Bacon,* and even *Oliver Twist.* Frazee posed for a publicity picture, doling out porridge with a spoon while Ruth supposedly said, "please, sir." The films were postponed but money was pouring in, and, prompted by Igoe, Ruth began to complain that his three-year contract with Frazee at $10,000 a year was grossly inadequate. He wanted $20,000 a year, he said, or he might not play at all in 1920. Since 1919 had been the best year baseball had ever had in terms of crowds and revenues, Babe had a pretty good argument. But Frazee was in a financial bind with Joe Lannin, from whom he had bought the Red Sox after the 1916 season and who still held Frazee's notes for a substantial portion of the purchase price. Lannin was calling for payment, and Frazee was having difficulty complying with his demands. His credit in Boston was becoming shaky.

Frazee and Colonel Huston, Ruppert's partner, were both convivial party types and got along well. Huston was a self-made man, an engineer who had grown up in Ohio and made a fortune in construction in Cuba after the Spanish-American War. He was a big heavy man, a careless dresser, open and friendly, who considered the ballplayers and sportswriters his friends. In contrast, Ruppert was a New York aristocrat whose father had been a millionaire brewer. Ruppert owned horses, was a member of the Jockey Club, exhibited show dogs, dressed meticulously, had a valet, collected objets d'art and moved easily in New York society. He served four terms in Congress from Manhattan's Silk Stocking District and, while a ladies' man, was discreet. He never married, but his will provided generously for a "friend." Ruppert, who carried on the family business of brewing beer, had a faint trace of a German accent (our hero was always Babe Root to Ruppert) and never called anyone by his first name.

He and Huston had nothing in common but money, a keen interest in the Yankees and the appellation "Colonel." Ruppert got his at twenty-two when he was made an honorary colonel on the personal staff of Governor Hill of New York. Huston, who was a captain of engineers in the Spanish-American War (his nickname was Cap), served overseas in World War I and became a colonel. The two had become acquainted because of their rooting interest in the New York Giants. John McGraw learned that the Yankees were for sale and suggested that Ruppert and Huston get together and buy the club. The pair put up $460,000, and in 1915 the Yankees, then a chronic second-division team, became theirs.

Despite his fastidiousness and the dilettante impression he gave, Ruppert was a hard, practical businessman. Huston was much more sentimental and impulsive. Huston liked Wild Bill Donovan, whom they had hired as manager, but Ruppert was impatient with the slow progress toward respectability the team was making. When Huston went to France, Ruppert decided it was time to hire a new manager. He asked Ban Johnson, with whom he was still on good terms, if he could suggest a replacement.

"Get Miller Huggins," Johnson said. Huggins was a tiny man — five feet six and a half inches tall, barely 140 pounds in weight — who had been managing the St. Louis Cardinals for five years without spectacular success, but Johnson was always a shrewd judge of talent. "He's a fine manager, and we'll take a good man away from the National League."

Ruppert wired Huston about the proposed change and Huston instantly replied negatively. He did not want the unimpressive little Huggins. He suggested instead that Ruppert hire the Dodger manager, big fat Wilbert Robinson, a jolly crony of Huston's. As a courtesy to his partner, Ruppert interviewed Robinson, but his mind was already made up. Impressed with Huggins, he hired him and told Huston about it after it was a fait accompli. Huston was furious, and the relationship between the two colonels, never close, was always uneasy after that.

Still, on some things they worked together well, and when Frazee indicated that Ruth was available, Huston was quick to discuss with Ruppert the possibility of getting him. The Yankees had been acquiring ballplayers aggressively during 1918 and 1919, and Ruppert was heartily in favor of obtaining an obvious star and drawing card in Ruth. The only drawback was money. Ruppert had ample wealth, but he was a practical man. Prohibition was about to go into effect, and Ruppert knew it was going to cause a precipitous decline in the revenue of his Manhattan brewery. Too, he was aware that McGraw and the Giants might at any time terminate the arrangement that permitted the Yankees to play in the Polo Grounds (and particularly so if Ruth joined the club). The vague plans he and Huston had tossed around about building their own ballpark might have to be implemented, and great quantities of cash would be needed for that. So a lump cash payment for Ruth was out. Nonetheless, the colonels met with Frazee and worked out a deal satisfactory to both sides.

The Yankees agreed to buy Ruth for $100,000, which was double the largest amount ever paid for a ballplayer before that. No other players were involved — it was a straight purchase — but the financial arrangements were complex. According to the contract of sale signed on Friday, December 26, 1919, Ruppert and Huston gave Frazee $25,000 in cash and three promissory notes for $25,000 each, one payable November 1, 1920, the second November 1, 1921, the third November 1, 1922. The notes were at 6 per cent, so the total amount the Yankees paid was nearer to $110,000. The cash-hungry Frazee moved at once to sell (discount) the notes, and the amiable Huston acted as an agent for him, writing to the Royal Bank of Canada on December 30 on Frazee's behalf. He sent a letter to Ruppert that day (local mail service was much faster and more efficient a half century ago than it is today) asking him to endorse the note to facilitate discounting. "As you will remember," Huston wrote Ruppert, "I told Mr. Frazee that I would try to get him a short-time loan at my bank, with one of the notes we gave the Boston Club as collateral."

Two months later, in February 1920, Huston again sent a message to Ruppert, this time saying, "Mr. Harry Frazee is asking us to aid him in getting three $25,000 notes discounted. He says events with Mr. Lannin made it impossible to follow his original intention of having the notes discounted in Boston. As you will remember, I had one of his notes of $25,000 discounted at my bank in New York. Although I only asked for a temporary accommodation of 90 days, which was all that Mr. Frazee wanted at that time, I can possibly have the note renewed. . . . However, the balance I carry with my bank hardly places me in a position to ask for a larger accommodation, and, frankly, I must keep my credit absolutely green there, so as to utilize same in case we are called upon to build new grounds. . . . I don't know whether or not you are in a position to further Mr. Frazee's desires, but he feels we should help him out some way, as he could have sold the fellow for cash."

For along with the $100,000 for Ruth, Frazee wanted a substantial loan. This was the crux of the deal, and Ruth came to the Yankees because Ruppert agreed to it. He gave Frazee a letter on December 26 that said, "I hereby offer to loan or cause to be loaned to you $300,000. . . . to be secured by a first mortgage [upon the] land now used as a baseball playing field by the Boston American League Baseball Club." In other words, Ruppert, co-owner of the New York Yankees, would hold a mortgage on Fenway Park, the Boston team's home field. Ruppert's letter said the loan offer would expire if it were not acted upon in ninety days. Frazee's continuing financial difficulties were evident in a letter he sent to Ruppert in April 1920:

Dear Colonel,

You remember that I phoned you about ten days before the expiration of your agreement to make a loan of $300,000 on Fenway Park and asked you to extend the time, which you advised me you would tell Mr. Grant to do. However, I have received no word from Mr. Grant. I telephoned Col. Huston today, as I could not reach you on the phone, asking the Colonel to see you and advise that I have cleaned up all matters upon the preferred Stock which your Attorney wanted before making the loan and I am now ready to accept it on May 15.

You can understand how important this is to me as my plans have all been based on my ability to secure this loan. There-fore, will you please send me signed agreement, copy of which Mr. Grant has, stating that you will advance the $300,000 . . . and if possible make the date May 20th. . . . I need this agreement signed by you here very badly to complete the balance of my negotiations.

Frazee sent a copy of the letter to Huston, who was much more accessible than Ruppert, with a scribbled note saying, "Dear Col, This is copy of letter just mailed to Col Ruppert after my phone to you. Wire or phone me quick."

The loan was made and relations between the two clubs continued to be cordial, with Frazee sending player after player to the Yankees over the next few seasons for more and more cash. The Red Sox soon became a baseball disaster area, finishing dead last nine times in eleven seasons, but Frazee survived, eventually sold the Boston team and in 1925 hit the jackpot financially in New York with the enormously successful *No, No, Nanette.*

In all, then, counting the initial payment, notes, interest and loan, the Yankees put up more than $400,000 in cash and credit to obtain Ruth. They knew what they were getting, in more ways than one. The contract of sale clearly reveals that Ruppert and Huston were well aware of Ruth's discontent with his $10,000-a-year contract with Frazee and the likelihood that he would demand a substantial increase when he learned of his transfer to New York. The second clause in the agreement said if Ruth did not report before July 1, the deal was off and Frazee would return the cash and the notes. The third clause said if Ruth demanded an increase in salary and the Yankees "deem it necessary to increase the salary in order to retain the services of said player," the Yankees would pay the increase as long as it did not raise Ruth's salary beyond $15,000. If they had to go beyond $15,000, the Red Sox would be obliged to pay "such excess up to the sum of Twenty-five Hundred ($2,500) for each of the years 1920 and 1921." The fourth clause said if Ruth did not ask for a salary increase but did demand a bonus for agreeing to play with the Yankees, the New York club would spring for the first $10,000 of the bonus, but the Red Sox would have to pay anything over that up to $15,000.

In brief, the Yankees anticipated trouble with Ruth. To allay it, they hurriedly dispatched the diminutive Huggins to California to find him and discuss things. Announcement of the deal was to be delayed until Huggins met with the Babe.

Meanwhile, a day or so after signing the contract of sale, Frazee phoned Barrow, who lived on Riverside Drive in New York City.

"I want to talk to you," he said. "Meet me at the Knickerbocker Hotel."

When Barrow arrived at the Knickerbocker, Frazee was having a drink with an actor. After perfunctory hellos, he wasted no time.

"I'm going to make you mad as hell with what I have to tell you. I'm going to sell Ruth to the Yankees."

"I thought as much," Barrow said. "I felt it in my bones. You're making a mistake, Harry. You know that, don't you?"

"Maybe I am, but I can't help it. Lannin is after me to make good on my notes. My shows aren't going so good. Ruppert and Huston will give me $100,000 for him, and Ruppert has agreed to loan me $300,000. I can't turn that down."

In California Huggins had some trouble tracking down the restless Ruth but eventually found him playing golf in Griffith Park. When Ruth came off the course, Huggins introduced himself. "I'm Miller Huggins of the Yankees, Babe. I'd like to talk to you."

"Sure," Babe said, shaking hands. I've been traded to the Yankees, he said to himself.

They found a quiet place and made small talk for a few minutes. Then the manager said, "Babe, how would you like to play for the Yankees?"

"Have I been traded?"

Huggins hesitated. "Well, the deal hasn't been made yet. I'd like to find out a few things. I want to know if you'll behave yourself if you come to New York."

"I'm happy with the Red Sox," Ruth said, bridling a bit. "I like Boston. But if Frazee sends me to the Yankees, I'll play as hard for them as I did for him."

"Babe, you've been a pretty wild boy in Boston. In New York you'll have to behave. You'll have to be strictly business."

Ruth became irritated. "I already told you I'll play the best I can. Let's get down to business. How much are you going to pay me?"

Huggins mentioned the two years left on Ruth's $10,000 contract. "I want a lot more dough than that," said Babe.

"All right," Huggins said. "If you promise to behave yourself, Colonel Ruppert will give you a new contract."

"For how much?"

Huggins mentioned $15,000 a year and then $17,500. Ruth said no. He repeated what he had told Frazee during the autumn. He wanted his salary doubled to $20,000. He also wanted a piece of the money the Red Sox would be getting for him. Huggins shook his head. He would have to get in touch with New York. They shook hands and parted. When they met again there was more haggling, but they came to terms and Ruth signed an agreement. Technically, he would continue under his old contract — $10,000 a year for 1920 and 1921 — but he would also receive an immediate bonus of $1000 and then $20,000 more over the next two years, to be paid in $2500 lumps at regular intervals during each season. The Yankees could do nothing about giving him a percentage of the money they were paying Frazee.

In sum, then, Ruth received $41,000 from the Yankees for the 1920 and 1921 seasons. Huggins wired Ruppert, and in New York the press was called in and told the startling news that the Red Sox had sold Babe Ruth to the Yankees. It was Monday, January 5, 1920.

In Boston the story created consternation. A cartoon appeared in one of the newspapers showing Faneuil Hall and the Boston Public Library decked with For Sale signs. Frazee faced the criticism coolly and blandly blamed Ruth for Boston's sixth-place finish in 1919. "It would be impossible to start next season with Ruth and have a smooth-working machine," he said. "Ruth had become simply impossible, and the Boston club could no longer put up with his eccentricities. I think the Yankees are taking a gamble. While Ruth is undoubtedly the greatest hitter the game has ever seen, he is likewise one of the most selfish and inconsiderate men ever to put on a baseball uniform."

Sportswriters dutifully echoed that theme, arguing that the sale of Ruth would benefit the Red Sox. One school of thought held that Ruth would never again be the player he was in 1919.

Fans generally were more realistic. "For the love of Mike," one said in disgust, "I give up." Another prescient follower of Boston baseball said succinctly, "I figure the Red Sox is ruined." A policeman commented, "From what I can see, there no longer is any sentiment in baseball."

During the season that followed, Frazee had posters put up in Fenway Park advertising a show of his called *My Lady Friends*. A disgusted fan jerked his thumb at the poster and said, "Those are the only friends that son of a bitch has."

In California Ruth was a bit taken aback by Frazee's comments and the sensation the news of the sale created. For some reason, perhaps sentiment, perhaps with the idea of strengthening his hand with Ruppert and Huston, perhaps with an eye on cigar sales, he sent a wire to Boston saying, WILL NOT PLAY ANYWHERE ELSE. MY HEART IS IN BOSTON. A cynic said, "He means that's where his cigar factory is."

New York felt a lot better about the whole thing, although the *New York Times* ran an editorial called "The High Price of Home Runs," comparing the money that was paid for Ruth to the salary being paid a visiting professor at a city university. In New Jersey, where he was working in a shipyard, Ping Bodie, the incumbent Yankee left fielder, said, "I suppose this means I'll be sent to China."

Ruth stayed in California another month before returning to Boston. Late in February he said goodbye to Helen and left for New York to join his new club on its trip south to spring training. The Yankee dynasty was about to begin.

Brendan C. Boyd and Fred C. Harris

From *The Great American Baseball Card Flipping, Trading and Bubble Gum Book*

Eddie Bressoud

There are certain ballplayers who are so colorless in their habits, so commonplace in their demeanor, so totally lacking in the essential dramatic fire of athletic combat that the best that anyone, even their most ardent admirers, can think to say about them is that they are steady. This means that they do not make too many errors, hit around .275, are always on time for the team bus and never forget their mother's birthday. Being considered steady is such a vaguely insulting characterization — somewhat akin to being thought of as "safe" by all the girls down at the bowling alley — that you might occasionally expect one of these sluglike individuals to resent it. They never seem to mind though. They're too steady.

The fifties were fraught with steady infielders — the infield being a particularly fertile breeding ground for steadiness — of all heights, weights, dispositions, and, curiously enough, abilities. Some of my favorites were Andy Carey, who was married to a beauty queen; Bobby Doerr, who was from Los Angeles; Billy Goodman, whose middle name was Dale and who slouched; Ray Boone, who took over from Lou Boudreau and had bad knees; Woodie Held, who should have been an outfielder; Johnny Pesky, who batted in front of Ted Williams; Billy Martin, whose real name was Marchilengelo; Marty Marion, who was the world's tallest shortstop; Gene Mauch, who had a bad temper; Al Smith, who had beer poured on his head in the World Series; Jerry Lumpe, who had an unfortunate name; Norm Siebern, who was boring; Chuck Schilling, who was Carl Yastrzemski's roommate; George Kell, who batted over .300 nine times without anybody finding out; Johnny Lipon, whose nickname was "Skids"; and Jerry Adair who was nice.

But my favorite all-time imperturbable infielder was Eddie Bressoud, an itinerant shortstop of modest pretensions and equally modest accomplishments whose performances were so lacking in variation and whose character was so unflappable in crisis that he was finally gifted by his hordes of enthusiastic admirers with a nickname commensurate with his stress rate.

Yes, I'm afraid you're right — Steady Eddie.

Don Buddin

In addition to looking like every clean-cut, square-shooting, Sunday School–attending, devoted to his family, straight A student and Eagle Scout who ever took an ax to his grandmother, Don Buddin had one other cross to bear during his brief and disastrous major league tenure.

He was a professional goat.

Now your professional goats come in all sizes, shapes and dispositions. There is your small-time goat like Elio Chacon, a moderately gifted shortstop for the Reds and the Mets in the early sixties, who could never seem to do anything quite right. There is your big-time goat like Ozzie Virgil, an itinerant utility infielder of blessed memory whose entire big league career was characterized by a pristine and diamond-hard propensity for mishandling the basics. There are your part-time goats like Ralph Branca or Mickey Cochrane, admirable athletes whose otherwise distinguished careers were

RED SOX

EDDIE BRESSOUD   SS

DON
BUDDIN
HOUSTON COLTS   SS

marred by a single catastrophic happenstance, the notoriety of which will live on long after them. And there is your full-time goat like Lu Clinton, who was so bad that I don't even want to go into it.

Don Buddin was a little different from all these.

For Don Buddin was a creative goat.

He was the sort of guy who would perform admirably, even flawlessly, for seven or eight innings of a ball game, or until such time as you really needed him. Then he would promptly fold like Dick Contino's accordion. Choke. Explode. Disinte-grate. Like a cheap watch or a '54 Chevy. He would give up the ghost and depart. Don Buddin would make 40 errors a year and 38 of them would lose ballgames. He would get 130 hits during a season, only 6 of which would come with men on. He would neglect to touch a base during a rally, lose pop-ups in the sun in extra innings, forget the count and try to bunt with 2 strikes. If there was a way to make the worst out of a situation, Don Buddin could be counted on to find it. There is a little bit of this in many of us, of course, and quite a bit of it in fact in most, but then again we aren't being paid big league salaries are we, or being interviewed by *Collier's* magazine?

Dick Stuart

Dick Stuart could fill a book by himself. Being the legitimate cookoo king of the era. He hit 66 home runs one year in the minors and campaigned vigorously each season for the All Star team. He had a television show in each city that he played in and was the first American star to play in Japan. He refused to bunt no matter what the situation and seemed to endorse any product that would pay him fifty bucks. He never stopped talking during his entire career and carried on feuds with almost everyone but the ushers. He might not have been the greatest natural eccentric of the decade but he definitely got the most out of what he had to work with. It was his inability to field his position, however, that gained him his string of unflattering nicknames — "Stonefingers," "The

DICK
STUART
BOSTON RED SOX   16

VERN STEPHENS

Boson Strangler," "Doctor Strangeglove." Highly insulting but all richly deserved. Dick Stuart's fielding had to be seen to be believed. He charted new dimensions in defensive ineptitude. He dropped foul pop-ups, misplayed grounders, bobbled bunts. He missed pick-off throws, dropped relays, messed up force plays. He fell down while covering the bag on easy rollers, knocked his teammates down while circling under flies. Every ball hit his way was an adventure, the most routne play a fresh challenge to his artlessness. It is hard to describe this to anyone who has not seen it. Just as it is hard to describe Xavier Cugat or Allan Ludden.

Stu once picked up a hot dog wrapper that was blowing toward his first base position. He received a standing ovation from the crowd. It was the first thing he had managed to pick up all day, and the fans realized that it could very well be the last.

Vern Stephens
Vern Stephens hit pop-ups.

High pop-ups. Major league pop-ups. Neck straining pop-ups.

Pop-ups which often disappeared from sight. Pop-ups which on occasion brought rain.

For this reason he was known as Pop-Up Stephens, logically and concisely enough.

Except to those who already knew him as Junior.

Vern Stephens, it has often been said, could have played his entire career in a stovepipe.

If they could have found a stovepipe wide enough to hold him.

Pumpsie Green
Pumpsie Green was the first black player on the Boston Red Sox, the last team to admit a black player to its major league roster. In 1959 irate fans paraded around Fenway Park for three days protesting the Red Sox refusal to bring Pumpsie up from the minors. When he was finally brought up in the

PUMPSIE
GREEN
BOSTON RED SOX SS

OUTFIELD
RED
SOX
KEN
HARRELSON

middle of the year, he disappointed even his most ardent supporters by being unable to either hit major league pitching or field major league hitting, thus achieving immediate and total equality with the rest of the Red Sox lineup. He disappointed no one, however, with his bizarre behavior. One summer weekend in 1962, when after a particularly humiliating defeat at the hands of the New York Yankees, he and Gene Conley, the erratic 6'8" basketball-playing pitcher, walked off the team bus in the middle of a traffic jam in the Bronx and disappeared into the postgame crowd. They were not encountered again until nearly three days later, when an alert *New York Post* sports reporter spotted them standing in line at Idlewild International Airport attempting to board a plane for Israel — with no luggage, no passport, and in what in all candor must be described as a markedly inebriated condition. Needless to say, they did not make it onto the plane. No explanation was ever given for their behavior. Green was returned to Louisville shortly thereafter. Conley was given his release at the beginning of the next season.

Ken Harrelson
Ken Harrelson was referred to affectionately as The Hawk. A check of his profile will supply you with the reason. Harrelson introduced long hair and outrageous attitudes to the Sporting World. He was the first of the Athletic Free Spirits. He was also the only one of these self-indulgent postadolescents with enough presence to carry it off. Derek Sanderson and Duane Thomas please note.

Harry Agganis
The Golden Greek. An All American quarterback at Boston University, a fancy fielding, home-run-hitting first baseman for the Boston Red Sox, a tall, handsome, clean-cut son of immigrant parents, a good student, an all-around athlete, a youth leader and a teenage idol, Harry Agganis was the epitome of the American dream. The day that he died of leukemia at age 25, in 1955, I was attending a performance of the *Big Brother Bob Emery* television program with a group

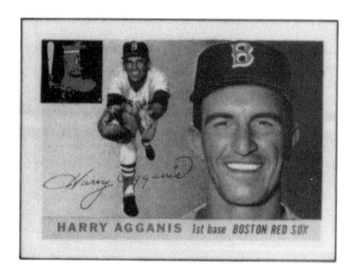

HARRY AGGANIS *1st base BOSTON RED SOX*

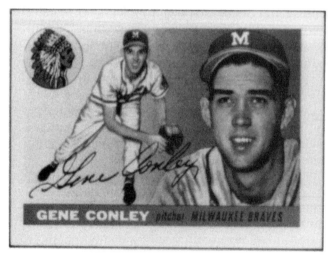

GENE CONLEY *pitcher MILWAUKEE BRAVES*

of my fellow Cub Scouts. I can still remember the oversized headline in the Boston newspapers and the feeling of stunned incredulity they aroused in all of us — our first encounter with the underlying frailty of the human condition. Up until then death had been something that only happened to animals or in the movies or to bank robbers or people who had fires in their houses or to the old. But Harry Agganis? If something like this could happen to Harry Agganis then what was to become of us?

What indeed?

Gene Conley
Funny, he doesn't look Jewish.

Carroll Hardy
Carroll Hardy holds the singular distinction of being the only man ever to pinch hit for Ted Williams, which on the face of it might seem ridiculous unless you stop to consider that Williams was injured at the time and that the Red Sox didn't have anybody better they could put up to bat. No, on second thought I take it all back. It is ridiculous.

Mike Fornieles
In 1960 Mike Fornieles was one of the premier relief pitchers in the American League — fireman of the year, 10–5 record, 14 saves, 70 appearances, 2.64 earned run average, voted overwhelmingly to the American League All Star team.

The next year he hurt his arm and his earned run average almost doubled.

In 1963 he went to spring training with the Red Sox, tried to throw hard, couldn't, was sent down to the minors, hit hard, and released.

Two months later I watched him pitch for the Supreme Diner Saints, a Boston semi-pro pickup team whose maximum salary was $25 a night.

The moral of the story is

(1) it's a tough life

CARROLL
HARDY
HOUSTON COLT .45s   OF

MIKE FORNIELES
pitcher CHICAGO WHITE SOX

(2) save your money

(3) and, as my old friend Angelo Cartolucci used to tell me, when reflecting on the gyrating intricacies of the New York stock and bond markets — kid, in this business you got to wear your tennis shoes.

Gene Stephens

Gene Stephens was the ultimate caddy, or scrub — which is the baseball equivalent of the fag (if you'll pardon the expression), or new boy, in the English public school system. It is the caddy's sole function in life to come in as a substitute in the late innings of a hopelessly lopsided game, to act as a defensive replacement for an aging power hitter, or to pinch run for a slow-witted, second-string catcher with varicose veins. For accomplishing these varied and undemanding assignments with a minimum of carping and a maximum of efficiency, the caddy is permitted by management to sit at the back of the team bus, to have his uniform cleaned by the assistant to the assistant equipment manager, and to dream on unencumbered of one day working his way into the starting lineup himself. Caddies are generally fleet-footed, weak-hitting outfielders whose ambitions far outstrip their abilities. Being human, they desire to be stars. And, being human, they are never quite realistic enough to realize the hopelessness of their situation. Some notable caddies of the preceding era were: Jim Pyburn, Al Pilarcik, and Sam Bowens with Baltimore; Chuck Essegian, Al Luplow, and Don Dillard with Cleveland; Fred Valentine, Bud Zipfel, and Dan Dobbek with Washington; and Joe Nossek, Chuck Diering, and Gary Geiger with just about everybody. Gene Stephens held Ted Williams' glove for seven long, humiliating seasons during the Splinter's splendid decline. This is indeed a long term of servitude, even for a caddy. He finally got his big shot at the limelight in 1960 when he was traded to the Baltimore Orioles and proceeded, in the manner of all caddies, to blow it. (Play me or trade me.) During the late fifties the Red Sox had two other full-time caddies of note — Marty Keough for Jim

gene stephens

BOSTON RED SOX
OUTFIELD

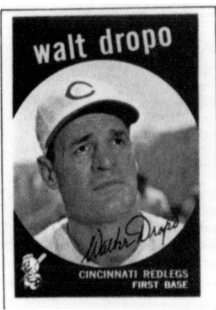

walt dropo

CINCINNATI REDLEGS
FIRST BASE

Piersall, and Faye Throneberry for Jackie Jensen. It was
Throneberry's extra burden in life to be the brother, in spirit
as well as in flesh, to Marvelous Marv Throneberry, the non
plus ultra of New York Mets first basemen.

Fabulous Faye!

Walt Dropo

Walt Dropo, big Moose from Moosup, Connecticut, was one
of my special favorites, although I never saw him play.
Actually, the only time I ever thought of him was when I
opened a pack of cards and saw that I had gotten another card
of him, probably my twentieth, and couldn't trade any of them
to any of my friends because they too already had nineteen
more than they needed. Moose, in the Kluszewski tradition,
was a first baseman, put there where he wouldn't be called
upon to move around much, because in Moose's case, at 6'5"
and 220 pounds (which was his weight as a rookie, I'm sure,
or maybe back in the early days of his youth at Moosup), it
wasn't all that easy to move around.

Tracy Stallard

Tracy Stallard threw the pitch that Roger Maris hit for his
sixty-first home run in 1961. This act and the resulting
publicity that surrounded it saved Stallard's career from the
profound and perpetual anonymity it so richly deserved. His
final major league won–lost totals were 30 games won and 57
lost.

Guido Grilli (et al.)

Some things are just funny in and of themselves. They require
little or no explanation, and are in fact most often beyond
analysis. In this category I would place — the Edsel, Sonny
Tufts, the prune danish, Dr. Joyce Brothers, Orange Julius,
Metrecal, Keye Luke, Levittown, Wayne Newton, the wom-
bat, the Hadassah, Guam, Tony Leonetti, Gatorade, Mrs.
Paul's Fish Sticks, Bosco, Kate Smith, Carmen Lombardo,
gerbils, Robby the Robot, Latvia, Geritol, Earl Scheib, Phila-

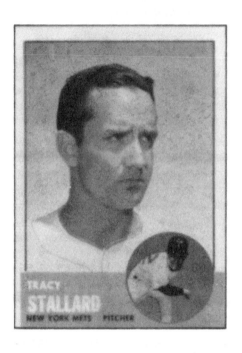

TRACY
STALLARD
NEW YORK METS   PITCHER

RED SOX   1966 ROOKIE STARS

GUIDO GRILLI   PETE MAGRINI   GEORGE SCOTT

delphia, Harold Stassen, Grossinger's, the Flugel horn, Tidy Bowl, and Costa Rica.

The list of ballplayers in this category is just about limitless. But Guido Grilli is certainly a good beginning. Then there was Nelson Chitholm, Ernio Fazio, Purnal Goldy, Stuffy Sternweiss, Buster Narum, and Bobo Osborne. Not to mention the Chicago Cubs of 1952. And the entire National League in 1957. I'm sure you have some favorite of your own. Arlan Bockhorn? Bruno Horvath? Ralph Guglielmi?

Bill Consolo

Someday I'd like to sit down and have a long talk with a major league scout about how and why he makes a decision to sign a particular juvenile prospect. Around about 1952 the Red Sox shelled out 90,000 balloons, which at that time was a record for them, for the services of a hot-shot kid third baseman from Cleveland named Billy Consolo who was supposed to be the greatest thing since sliced bread. The story on him was that he could hit, run, field, throw, bunt, slide, had power, and was smart. Well, he was smart all right, smart enough to get 90 grand out of Tom Yawkey, but as far as the other qualities were concerned, I'm afraid the realities of the situation did not quite live up to the expectations. He could hit, but not breaking pitches. He could run, but seldom got the chance. He had a great glove but was extremely erratic, and his arm was so highly undisciplined that most of his throws ended up at least six rows into the boxes behind the first base bag. About his bunting and sliding prowess I'll have to suspend judgment. It seems to me that any twelve-year-old kid with an ounce and a half of common sense could have told you after fifteen minutes of watching Billy in action that, although he possessed a stunning array of native athletic abilities, he was never going to be a halfway decent major league ballplayer because all of those attributes were deeply and irrevocably flawed and because there was no sense of balance or coordination between the flawed and the unflawed components. Which is to say that if you are starting out to

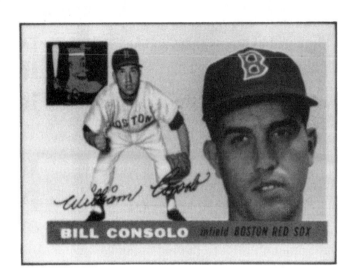

BILL CONSOLO *Infield* **BOSTON RED SOX**

BILLY
KLAUS
PHILA. PHILLIES   INF.

construct a large cantaloupe, the best thing to have is a small cantaloupe and not a collection of large cantaloupe parts. More often than not the parts don't fit.

Billy Klaus

One summer when I was about twelve years old and not particularly wise, as I am today (God help me) in the ways of the world, some supermarket chain or other in the greater Boston area ran a promotion wherein they invited prospective customers to come in and meet a couple of the less luminous lights in the lavish Red Sox galaxy in the friendly, unhurried atmosphere of the Saturday morning checkout counter — somewhere in between the chocolate-covered fish cakes and the curried bananas. When I arrived on the scene with my friends, Tony Werra and Steve Gladdis, hot, dirty, and exhausted after a 6 mile walk in 90° heat, we were informed that only those privileged members of the consuming public who were prepared to pop for five skins worth of Cocoa Puffs, Ex-Lax, Mallomars, and Barcolean were entitled to enter the premises, peruse the assembled dignitaries, and hustle and autograph or two.

In other words — no kids.

I carry three memories of that day to the present.

First is the vivid recollection of our long, discouraging walk home through the grimy summertime haze of North Dorchester.

Second is the image of little Billy Klaus, the Red Sox scrappy second baseman, sitting somewhere in the vicinity of the cash register, his $65 hand-sewn Gucci loafers propped up on a stack of strawberry Yoo-Hoo, gazing out through the Thermopane at the assembled hordes of unwelcome children with what can only be described as a benevolently malicious grin.

And third is a dislike, bordering on disgust, for the commercial proclivities of well-known athletes such as Bobby Hull, Tom Seaver, and Walt Frazier, who, it has often seemed to me, would be sorely tempted to shill diseased blankets to the Indians if they thought there was a buck in it for them.

JIM PIERSALL
Outfield
Cleveland
Indians

FELIX
MANTILLA
BOSTON RED SOX   INF-OF

Jimmy Piersall

Jimmy Piersall squirted home plate with water pistols, heaved equipment bags out of dugouts, watered down the infield between innings, ran into walls trying to catch fly balls, threw baseballs at scoreboards and bats at pitchers, practiced sliding during batting practice, slept on the clubhouse floor, bunted with two out and his team six runs behind in the last of the ninth, ran around the bases backward after hitting homers, did sitting-up exercises in the outfield to distract batters, had nervous breakdowns, made comebacks, starred in the movie version of Anthony Perkins' life story, fathered nine children, and in general made life interesting for seventeen of my first twenty-two major-league seasons. I miss him.

Felix Mantilla

There is a saying around the racetrack — horses for courses — which translates roughly: every dog has his day, given the proper environment. The horse (or dog) in question here is Felix Mantilla, a tall, spindly legged Puerto Rican infielder with limited range and an even more limited throwing arm, who after eight lackluster years in the National League (29 career home runs, .245 lifetime batting average), spent most of the 1964 and 1965 seasons lofting lazy fly balls up, off and over the friendly left-field wall at Fenway Park. If ever there was a swing that was tailor-made for a ball park, it was Felix's that was made for Fenway. Of course, eventually the opposing pitchers started spotting him low and away on the outside part of the plate, and Felix's Green Monster swing began to lose some of its highly artificial luster, but before it had gone sour completely the deleterious Boston flesh peddlers who had secured his services during a mid-winter trade with the Mets for three snow tires and a bottle of Roquefort dressing had managed to unload him at the top like an overinflated growth stock on the latest expansionist patsies — the Houston Colt 45s. Somehow or other Felix never quite got the hang of the Astrodome.

MAURICE McDERMOTT

MOST VALUABLE PLAYER — 1958
AMERICAN LEAGUE

JACKIE JENSEN

Maurice McDermott

Maurice McDermott was Ellis Kinder's drinking partner and the only person in the history of the Poughkeepsie, New York, public school system to be chosen unanimously by his high school graduating class as the man most likely to be found dead in a motel room.

Jackie Jensen

Jackie Jensen, on the other hand, was up there to take his cuts. Because of this he perennially led the Red Sox, and sometimes even the majors, in RBIs and double plays. The double plays were another matter entirely.

Some other things that annoyed me about Jackie were his florid skin and pale kinky locks which made him look for all the world like a miniature Sonny Tufts, his inability to take any razzing at all from the cheap seats, which struck me as totally immature and unprofessional, his oversolicitous concern with his wife's well-being (he retired in 1960 just to be with her), and his well-publicized and self-admitted fear of flying, which seemed an indication of circumspection bordering on cowardice.

Now that I have had thirteen or fourteen years to grow up and reflect on a number of these attitudes, I find that my feelings about most of them have changed markedly, have in fact reversed themselves almost entirely. The things that I despised Jackie Jensen for in 1957 I now respect him for in 1973. Whether this is due to some newfound maturity on my part or is simply a result of the fact that I too have grown older and softer with the years, I do not know. I suspect it is a combination of the two.

Dave Sisler

To be an athlete's brother is a trial. To be an athlete's son is a sorrow. To be a famous athlete's brother or son is a tragedy. But to be a famous athlete's brother AND son who tries to become a famous athlete himself is just plain foolhardy. Dave Sisler was the son of George Sisler, a Hall of Famer and one

DAVE SISLER
BOSTON RED SOX PITCHER

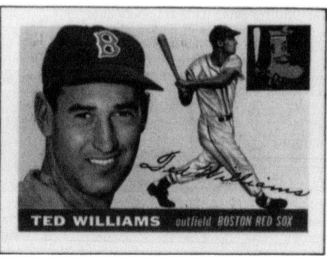

TED WILLIAMS outfield BOSTON RED SOX

of the two or three greatest first basemen who ever lived, and brother of Dick Sisler, whose home run in the last game of the 1950 season clinched the National League Pennant for the Phillies. Do you imagine that there were ever fifteen seconds during the waking existence of Dave Sisler that he was able to forget these facts? What would drive a kid like this to become a ballplayer anyway? Wouldn't he have been happier as a lawyer or a clamdigger or something along that line? He must have known that no matter how good he was he was never going to be good enough. He seemed bright, too. He graduated from Princeton, wore glasses, and was very analytical in postgame interviews. Look at his face in this card — serious, intelligent, taut — the face of an early suicide. Richard Michael Sisler, son of George Harold Sisler, brother of Richard Allan Sisler, possessor of a 38–44 lifetime record, retired from baseball at age thirty-one, wherever you are now, at age forty-two, I only hope that you have made a lot of money in the stock market or are about to discover a cure for cancer.

For your sake.

Ted Williams

In 1955 there were 77,263,127 male American human beings.

And every one of them in his heart of hearts would have given two arms, a leg, and his collection of Davy Crockett iron-ons to be Teddy Ballgame.

Red Smith

Ted Williams Spits

New York Times, 1958

By now some modern Dickens, probably in Boston, must surely have brought out a best seller entitled *Great Expecto-rations*. It was a $4,998 mistake when Ted Williams chose puritanical and antiseptic New England for his celebrated exhibition of spitting for height and distance. In easygoing New York's insanitary subway the price is only $2.

It was bush, of course. There is no other way to character-ize Williams' moist expression of contempt for fans and press, even though one may strive earnestly to understand and be patient with this painfully introverted, oddly immature thirty-eight-year-old veteran of two wars.

In his gay moods, Williams has the most winning disposition and manner imaginable. He can be charming, accommodating and generous. If Johnny Orlando, the Red Sox maître de clubhouse and Ted's great friend, wished to violate a confi-dence he could cite a hundred instances of charities that the fellow has done, always in deep secrecy.

This impulsive generosity is a key. Ted is ruled by impulse and emotions. When he is pleased, he laughs; in a tantrum, he spits. In Joe Cronin's book, this falls $5,000 short of con-duct becoming a gentleman, officer and left fielder.

The price the Boston general manager set upon a minute quantity of genuine Williams saliva, making it the most expen-sive spittle in Massachusetts, suggests that the stuff is rarer than rubies. However, this is one case where the law of supply and demand does not apply.

Actually the $5,000 figure is a measure of Cronin's disapproval of his employee's behavior and an indication of Ted's economic condition. Rather than let the punishment fit the crime, Cronin tailored it to the outfielder's $100,000 salary. As it is, considering Williams' tax bracket, chances are the federal government will pay about $3,500 of the fine, though it may cause some commotion around the Internal Revenue Bureau when a return comes in with a $5,000 deduction for spit.

Baseball has indeed put on company manners since the days when pitchers like Burleigh Grimes, Clarence Mitchell and Spittin' Bill Doak employed saliva as a tool of the trade and applied it to the ball with the ceremonious formality of a minuet.

Incidentally, the penalty was applied after Williams drew a base on balls which forced home the winning run for Boston against the Yankees. He must have realized that a few more victories at those prices would leave him broke, yet the next night he won another game with a home run. With Ted, money is no object.

Nobody has ever been able to lay down a rule determining how much abuse a paid performer must take from the public without reciprocation. It was either Duffy or Sweeney, of the great old vaudeville team, who addressed an audience that had sat in cold silence through the act:

"Ladies and gentlemen, I want to thank you for giving us such a warm and encouraging reception. And now, if you will kindly remain seated, my partner will pass among you with a baseball bat and beat the bejabbers out of you."

Baseball fans consider that the price they pay for admission entitles them to spit invective at a player, harass him at his work and even bounce a beer bottle off his skull. It is not recalled that Williams' hair was ever parted by flying glassware, but verbal barbs from Fenway Park's left-field seats have been perforating his sensitive psyche for years.

There are those of a sympathetic turn who feel it was high time Williams be permitted to spit back. Miss Gussie Moran, trained in the gentle game of tennis, remarked on the radio that she approved, "as long as he didn't spray anybody." As in tennis, Gussie believes, marksmanship and trajectory count.

All the same it is a mark of class in a performer to accept cheers and jeers in stride. One of the soldier citizens of the Boston press — it could have been Johnny Drohan — pointed this out to Williams years ago. Ted was a kid then, a buff for Western movies.

Hoots and jeers were a part of the fame, the man said, and everybody in the public eye had to learn to accept them.

"Take actors, for instance, Ted. You see one in a good show and you applaud and go around talking about how great he is. Then you see him in a bad vehicle and you say, 'He stinks. Whatever gave me the idea he could act?'"

"Oh, no, Johnny," Ted protested, "not that Hoot Gibson. He's *always* great!"

John Updike

Hub Fans Bid Kid Adieu

The New Yorker, 1960

Fenway Park, in Boston, is a lyric little bandbox of a ballpark. Everything is painted green and seems in curiously sharp focus, like the inside of an old-fashioned peeping-type Easter egg. It was built in 1912 and rebuilt in 1934, and offers, as do most Boston artifacts, a compromise between Man's Euclidean determinations and Nature's beguiling irregularities. Its right field is one of the deepest in the American League, while its left field is the shortest; the high left-field wall, three hundred and fifteen feet from home plate along the foul line, virtually thrusts its surface at right-handed hitters. On the afternoon of Wednesday, September 28th, 1960, as I took a seat behind third base, a uniformed groundkeeper was treading the top of this wall, picking batting-practice home runs out of the screen, like a mushroom gatherer seen in Wordsworthian perspective on the verge of a cliff. The day was overcast, chill, and uninspirational. The Boston team was the worst in twenty-seven seasons. A jangling medley of incompetent youth and aging competence, the Red Sox were finishing in seventh place only because the Kansas City Athletics had locked them out of the cellar. They were scheduled to play the Baltimore Orioles, a much nimbler blend of May and December, who had been dumped from pennant contention a week before by the insatiable Yankees. I, and 10,453 others, had shown up primarily because this was the Red Sox's last

home game of the season, and therefore the last time in all
eternity that their regular left fielder, known to the headlines
as TED, KID, SPLINTER, THUMPER, TW and, most cloy-
ingly, MISTER WONDERFUL, would play in Boston. "WHAT
WILL WE DO WITHOUT TED? HUB FANS ASK" ran the
headline on a newspaper being read by a bulb-nosed cigar
smoker a few rows away. Williams' retirement had been
announced, doubted (he had been threatening retirement for
years), confirmed by Tom Yawkey, the Red Sox owner, and
at last widely accepted as the sad but probable truth. He was
forty-two and had redeemed his abysmal season of 1959 with
a — considering his advanced age — fine one. He had been
giving away his gloves and bats and had grudgingly consented
to a sentimental ceremony today. This was not necessarily
his last game; the Red Sox were scheduled to travel to New
York and wind up the season with three games there.

I arrived early. The Orioles were hitting fungos on the
field. The day before, they had spitefully smothered the Red
Sox, 17–4, and neither their faces nor their drab gray visiting-
team uniforms seemed very gracious. I wondered who had
invited them to the party. Between our heads and the low-
ering clouds a frenzied organ was thundering through, with
an appositeness perhaps accidental, "You *maaaade* me love
you, I didn't wanna do it, I didn't wanna do it. . . ."

The affair between Boston and Ted Williams was no mere
summer romance; it was a marriage composed of spats,
mutual disappointments, and, toward the end, a mellowing
hoard of shared memories. It fell into three stages, which
may be termed Youth, Maturity, and Age; or Thesis, Antithesis, and Synthesis; or Jason, Achilles, and Nestor.

First, there was the by now legendary epoch* when the
young bridegroom came out of the West and announced, "All

---

*This piece was written with no research materials save an outdated record
book and the Boston newspapers of the day; and Williams' early career

I want out of life is that when I walk down the street folks will say 'There goes the greatest hitter who ever lived.'" The dowagers of local journalism attempted to give elementary deportment lessons to this child who spake as a god, and to their horror were themselves rebuked. Thus began the long exchange of backbiting, bat-flipping, booing, and spitting that has distinguished Williams' public relations.* The spitting

---

preceded the dawning of my *Schlagballewusstsein* (Baseball-consciousness). Also for reasons of perspective was my account of his beginnings skimped. Williams first attracted the notice of a major-league scout — Bill Essick of the Yankees — when he was a fifteen-year-old pitcher with the San Diego American Legion Post team. As a pitcher-outfielder for San Diego's Herbert Hoover High School, Williams recorded averages of .586 and .403. Essick balked at signing Williams for the $1,000 his mother asked; he was signed instead, for $150 a month, by the local Pacific Coast League franchise, the newly created San Diego Padres. In his two seasons with this team, Williams hit merely .271 and .291, but his style and slugging (23 home runs the second year) caught the eye of, among others, Casey Stengel, then with the Boston Braves, and Eddie Collins, the Red Sox general manager. Collins bought him from the Padres for $25,000 in cash and $25,000 in players. Williams was then nineteen. Collins' fond confidence in the boy's potential matched Williams' own. Williams reported to the Red Sox training camp in Sarasota in 1938 and, after showing more volubility than skill, was shipped down to the Minneapolis Millers, the top Sox farm team. It should be said, perhaps, that the parent club was equipped with an excellent, if mature, outfield, mostly purchased from Connie Mack's dismantled A's. Upon leaving Sarasota, Williams is supposed to have told the regular outfield of Joe Vosmik, Doc Cramer, and Ben Chapman that he would be back and would make more money than the three of them put together. At Minneapolis he hit .366, batted in 142 runs, scored 130, and hit 43 home runs. He also loafed in the field, jabbered at the fans, and smashed a water cooler with his fist. In 1939 he came north with the Red Sox. On the way, in Atlanta, he dropped a foul fly, accidentally kicked it away in trying to pick it up, picked it up, and threw it out of the park. It would be nice if, his first time up in Fenway Park, he had hit a home run. Actually, in his first Massachusetts appearance, the first inning of an exhibition game against Holy Cross at Worcester, he did hit a home run, a grand slam. The Red Sox season opened in Yankee Stadium. Facing Red Ruffing, Williams struck out and, the next time up, doubled for his first major-league hit. In the Fenway Park opener, against Philadelphia, he had a single in five trips. His first home run came on April 23, in that same series with the A's. Williams was then twenty, and played right field. In his rookie season he hit .327; in 1940, .344.

*See *Ted Williams,* by Ed Linn (Sport Magazine Library), Chapter 6, "Williams vs. the Press." It is Linn's suggestion that Williams walked into a circulation war among the seven Boston newspapers, who in their competitive

incidents of 1957 and 1958 and the similar dockside courtesies that Williams has now and then extended to the grandstand should be judged against this background: the left-field stands at Fenway for twenty years have held a large number of customers who have bought their way in primarily for the privilege of showering abuse on Williams. Greatness necessarily attracts debunkers, but in Williams' case the hostility has been systematic and unappeasable. His basic offense against the fans has been to wish that they weren't there. Seeking a perfectionist's vacuum, he has quixotically desired to sever the game from the ground of paid spectatorship and publicity that supports it. Hence his refusal to tip his cap* to the crowd or to turn the other cheek to newsmen. It has been a costly theory — it has probably cost him, among other evidences of good will, two Most Valuable Player awards, which are voted by reporters† — but he has held to

---

zeal headlined incidents that the New York papers, say, would have minimized, just as they minimized the less genial side of the moody and aloof DiMaggio and smoothed Babe Ruth into a folk hero. It is also Linn's thought, and an interesting one, that Williams thrived on even adverse publicity, and needed a hostile press to elicit, contrariwise, his defiant best. The statistics (especially of the 1958 season, when he snapped a slump by spitting in all directions, and inadvertently conked an elderly female fan with a tossed bat) seem to corroborate this. Certainly Williams could have had a truce for the asking, and his industrious perpetuation of the war, down to his last day in uniform, implies its usefulness to him. The actual and intimate anatomy of the matter resides in locker rooms and hotel corridors fading from memory. When my admiring account was printed, I received a letter from a sports reporter who hated Williams with a bitter and explicit immediacy. And even Linn's hagiology permits some glimpses of Williams' locker room manners that are not pleasant.

*But he did tip his cap, high off his head, in at least his first season, as cartoons from that period verify. He also was extravagantly cordial to taxi-drivers and stray children. See Linn, Chapter 4, "The Kid Comes to Boston": "There has never been a ballplayer — anywhere, anytime — more popular than Ted Williams in his first season in Boston." To this epoch belong Williams' prankish use of the Fenway scoreboard lights for rifle practice, his celebrated expressed preference for the life of a fireman, and his determined designation of himself as "The Kid."

†In 1947 Joe DiMaggio and in 1957 Mickey Mantle, with seasons inferior to Williams', won the MVP award because sportswriters, who vote on ballots with ten places, had vengefully placed Williams ninth, tenth, or nowhere at

it. While his critics, oral and literary, remained beyond the reach of his discipline, the opposing pitchers were accessible, and he spanked them to the tune of .406 in 1941.* He slumped to .356 in 1942 and went off to war.

In 1946, Williams returned from three years as a Marine pilot to the second of his baseball avatars, that of Achilles, the hero of incomparable prowess and beauty who nevertheless was to be found sulking in his tent while the Trojans (mostly Yankees) fought through to the ships. Yawkey, a timber and mining maharajah, had surrounded his central jewel with many gems of slightly lesser water, such as Bobby Doerr, Dom DiMaggio, Rudy York, Birdie Tebbetts, and Johnny Pesky. Throughout the late forties, the Red Sox were the best paper team in baseball, yet they had little three-dimensional to show for it, and if this was a tragedy, Williams was Hamlet. A succinct review of the indictment — and a fair sample of appreciative sports-page prose — appeared the very day of Williams' valedictory, in a column by Huck Finnegan in the *Boston American* (no sentimentalist, Huck):

> Williams' career, in contrast [to Babe Ruth's], has been a series of failures except for his averages. He flopped in the only World Series he ever played in (1946) when he batted only .200. He flopped in the playoff game with Cleveland in 1948. He flopped in the final game of the 1949 season with the

---

all. The 1941 award to Joe DiMaggio, even though this was Williams' .406 year, is more understandable, since this was also the *annus miraculorum* when DiMaggio hit safely in 56 consecutive games.

*The sweet saga of this beautiful decimal must be sung once more. Williams, after hitting above .400 all season, had cooled to .39955 with one double-header left to play, in Philadelphia. Joe Cronin, then managing the Red Sox, offered to bench him to safeguard his average, which was exactly .400 when rounded to the third decimal place. Williams said (I forget where I read this) that he did not want to become the .400 hitter with just his toenails over the line. He played the first game and singled, homered, singled, and singled. With less to gain than to lose, he elected to play the second game and got two more hits, including a double that dented a loudspeaker horn on the top of the right-field wall, giving him six-for-eight on the day and a season's average that, in the forty years between Rogers Hornsby's .403 (1925) and the present, stands as unique.

pennant hinging on the outcome (Yanks 5, Sox 3). He flopped in 1950 when he returned to the lineup after a two-month absence and ruined the morale of a club that seemed pennant-bound under Steve O'Neill. It has always been Williams' records first, the team second, and the Sox non-winning record is proof enough of that.

There are answers to all this, of course. The fatal weakness of the great Sox slugging teams was not-quite-good-enough pitching rather than Williams' failure to hit a home run every time he came to bat. Again, Williams' depressing effect on his teammates has never been proved. Despite ample coaching to the contrary, most insisted that they liked him. He has been generous with advice to any player who asked for it. In an increasingly combative baseball atmosphere, he continued to duck beanballs docilely. With umpires he was gracious to a fault. This courtesy itself annoyed his critics, whom there was no pleasing. And against the ten crucial games (the seven World Series games with the St. Louis Cardinals, the 1948 playoff with the Cleveland Indians, and the two-game series with the Yankees at the end of the 1949 season, when one victory would have given the Red Sox the pennant) that make up the Achilles' heel of Williams' record, a mass of statistics can be set showing that day in and day out he was no slouch in the clutch.* The correspondence columns of the Boston papers now and then suffer a sharp flurry of arithmetic on this score; indeed, for Williams to have distributed all his hits so they did nobody else any good would constitute a feat of placement unparalleled in the annals of selfishness.

Whatever residue of truth remains of the Finnegan charge those of us who love Williams must transmute as best we

---

*For example: In 1948, the Sox came from behind to tie the Indians by winning three straight; in those games Williams went two for two, two for two; and two for four. In 1949, the Sox overtook the Yankees by winning nine in a row; in that streak, Williams won four games with home runs.

can, in our own personal crucibles. My personal memories of Williams began when I was a boy in Pennsylvania, with two last-place teams in Philadelphia to keep me company. For me, "W'ms, lf" was a figment of the box scores who always seemed to be going 3-for-5. He radiated, from afar, the hard blue glow of high purpose. I remember listening over the radio to the All-Star Game of 1946, in which Williams hit two singles and two home runs, the second one off a Rip Sewell "blooper" pitch; it was like hitting a balloon out of the park. I remember watching one of his home runs from the bleachers of Shibe Park; it went over the first baseman's head and rose methodically along a straight line and was still rising when it cleared the fence. The trajectory seemed qualitatively different from anything anyone else might hit. For me, Williams is the classic ballplayer of the game on a hot August weekday, before a small crowd, when the only thing at stake is the tissue-thin difference between a thing done well and a thing done ill. Baseball is a game of the long season, of relentless and gradual averaging-out. Irrelevance — since the reference point of most individual contests is remote and statistical — always threatens its interest, which can be maintained not by the occasional heroics that sportswriters feed upon but by players who always care; who care, that is to say, about themselves and their art. Insofar as the clutch hitter is not a sportswriter's myth, he is a vulgarity, like a writer who writes only for money. It may be that, compared to such managers' dreams as the manifestly classy Joe DiMaggio and the always helpful Stan Musial, Williams was an icy star. But of all team sports, baseball, with its graceful intermittences of action, its immense and tranquil field sparsely settled with poised men in white, its dispassionate mathematics, seems to me best suited to accommodate, and be ornamented by, a loner. It is an essentially lonely game. No other player visible to my generation concentrated within himself so much of the sport's poignance, so assiduously refined his natural skills, so constantly brought to the plate that intensity of competence that crowds the throat with joy.

By the time I went to college, near Boston, the lesser stars Yawkey had assembled around Williams had faded, and his rigorous pride of craftsmanship had become itself a kind of heroism. This brittle and temperamental player developed an unexpected quality of persistence. He was always coming back — back from Korea, back from a broken collarbone, a shattered elbow, a bruised heel, back from drastic bouts of flu and ptomaine poisoning. Hardly a season went by without some enfeebling mishap, yet he always came back, and always looked like himself. The delicate mechanism of timing and power seemed sealed, shockproof, in some case deep within his frame.* In addition to injuries, there was a heavily publicized divorce, and the usual storms with the press, and the Williams Shift — the maneuver, custom-built by Lou Boudreau of the Cleveland Indians, whereby three infielders were concentrated on the right side of the infield.† Williams could easily have learned to punch singles through the vacancy on his left and fattened his average hugely. This was what Ty Cobb, the Einstein of average, told him to do. But the game had changed since Cobb; Williams believed that his value to the club and to the league was as a slugger, so he went on pulling the ball, trying to blast it through three men,

---

*Two reasons for his durability may be adduced. A non-smoker, non-drinker, habitual walker, and year-round outdoorsman, Williams spared his body the vicissitudes of the seasonal athlete. And his hitting was in large part a mental process; the amount of cerebration he devoted to such details as pitchers' patterns, prevailing winds, and the muscular mechanics of swinging a bat would seem ridiculous, if it had not paid off. His intellectuality, as it were, perhaps explains the quickness with which he adjusted, after the war, to the changed conditions — the night games, the addition of the slider to the standard pitching repertoire, the new cry for the long ball. His reaction to the Williams Shift, then, cannot be dismissed as unconsidered.

†Invented, or perpetrated (as a joke?) by Boudreau on July 14, 1946, between games of a doubleheader. In the first game of the doubleheader Williams had hit three homers and batted in eight. The shift was not used when men were on base and, had Williams bunted or hit late against it immediately, it might not have spread, in all its variations, throughout the league. The Cardinals used it in the lamented World Series of that year. Toward the end, in 1959 and 1960, rather sadly, it had faded from use, or degenerated to the mere clockwise twitching of the infield customary against pull hitters.

and paid the price of perhaps fifteen points of lifetime average. Like Ruth before him, he bought the occasional home run at the cost of many directed singles — a calculated sacrifice certainly not, in the case of a hitter as average-minded as Williams, entirely selfish.

After a prime so harassed and hobbled, Williams was granted by the relenting fates a golden twilight. He became at the end of his career perhaps the best *old* hitter of the century. The dividing line falls between the 1956 and the 1957 seasons. In September of the first year, he and Mickey Mantle were contending for the batting championship. Both were hitting around .350, and there was no one else near them. The season ended with a three-game series between the Yankees and the Sox, and, living in New York then, I went up to the Stadium. Williams was slightly shy of the four hundred at-bats needed to qualify; the fear was expressed that the Yankee pitchers would walk him to protect Mantle. Instead, they pitched to him. It was wise. He looked terrible at the plate, tired and discouraged and unconvincing. He never looked very good to me in the Stadium.* The final outcome in 1956 was Mantle .353, Williams .345.

The next year, I moved from New York to New England, and it made all the difference. For in September of 1957, in the same situation, the story was reversed. Mantle finally hit .365; it was the best season of his career. But Williams, though sick and old, had run away from him. A bout of flu had laid him low in September. He emerged from his cave in the Hotel Somerset haggard but irresistible; he hit four successive pinch-hit home runs. "I feel terrible," he confessed, "but every time I take a swing at the ball it goes out of the park." He ended the season with thirty-eight home runs and an

---

*Shortly after his retirement, Williams, in *Life,* wrote gloomily of the Stadium, "There's the bigness of it. There are those high stands and all those people smoking — and, of course, the shadows. . . . It takes at least one series to get accustomed to the Stadium and even then you're not sure." Yet his lifetime batting average there is .340, only four points under his median average.

average of .388, the highest in either league since his own .406, and, coming from a decrepit man of thirty-nine, an even more supernal figure. With eight or so of the "leg hits" that a younger man would have beaten out, it would have been .400. And the next year, Williams, who in 1949 and 1953 had lost batting championships by decimal whiskers to George Kell and Mickey Vernon, sneaked in behind his teammate Pete Runnels and filched his sixth title, a bargain at .328.

In 1959, it seemed all over. The dinosaur thrashed around in the .200 swamp for the first half of the season, and was even benched ("rested," Manager Mike Higgins tactfully said). Old foes like the late Bill Cunningham began to offer batting tips. Cunningham thought Williams was jiggling his elbows;* in truth, Williams' neck was so stiff he could hardly turn his head to look at the pitcher. When he swung, it looked like a Calder mobile with one thread cut; it reminded you that since 1954 Williams' shoulders had been wired together. A solicitous pall settled over the sports pages. In the two decades since Williams had come to Boston, his status had imperceptibly shifted from that of a naughty prodigy to that of a municipal monument. As his shadow in the record books lengthened, the Red Sox teams around him declined, and the entire American League seemed to be losing life and color to the National. The inconsistency of the new super-stars — Mantle, Colavito, and Kaline — served to make Williams appear all the more singular. And off the field, his private philanthropy — in particular, his zealous chairmanship of the Jimmy Fund, a charity for children with cancer — gave him a civic presence matched only by that of Richard Cardinal

---

*It was Cunningham who, when Williams first appeared in a Red Sox uniform at the 1938 spring training camp, wrote with melodious prescience: "The Sox seem to think Williams is just cocky enough and gabby enough to make a great and colorful outfielder, possibly the Babe Herman type. Me? I don't like the way he stands at the plate. He bends his front knee inward and moves his foot just before he takes a swing. That's exactly what I do just before I drive a golf ball and knowing what happens to the golf balls I drive, I don't believe this kid will ever hit half a singer midget's weight in a bathing suit."

Cushing. In religion, Williams appears to be a humanist, and a selective one at that, but he and the abrasive-voiced Cardinal, when their good works intersect and they appear in the public eye together, make a handsome pair of seraphim.

Humiliated by his '59 season, Williams determined, once more, to come back. I, as a specimen Williams partisan, was both glad and fearful. All baseball fans believe in miracles; the question is, how many do you believe in? He looked like a ghost in spring training. Manager Jurges warned us ahead of time that if Williams didn't come through he would be benched, just like anybody else. As it turned out, it was Jurges who was benched. Williams entered the 1960 season needing eight home runs to have a lifetime total of 500; after one time at bat in Washington, he needed seven. For a stretch, he was hitting a home run every second game that he played. He passed Lou Gehrig's lifetime total, and finished with 521, thirteen behind Jimmy Foxx, who alone stands between Williams and Babe Ruth's unapproachable 714. The summer was a statistician's picnic. His two-thousandth walk came and went, his eighteen-hundredth run batted in, his sixteenth All-Star Game. At one point, he hit a home run off a pitcher, Don Lee, off whose father, Thornton Lee, he had hit a home run a generation before. The only comparable season for a forty-two-year-old man was Ty Cobb's in 1928. Cobb batted .323 and hit one homer. Williams batted .316 but hit twenty-nine homers.

In sum, though generally conceded to be the greatest hitter of his era, he did not establish himself as "the greatest hitter who ever lived." Cobb, for average, and Ruth, for power, remain supreme. Cobb, Rogers Hornsby, Joe Jackson, and Lefty O'Doul, among players since 1900, have higher lifetime averages than Williams' .344. Unlike Foxx, Gehrig, Hack Wilson, Hank Greenberg, and Ralph Kiner, Williams never came close to matching Babe Ruth's season home-run total of sixty.* In the list of major-league batting records, not one is

---

*Written before Roger Maris's fluky, phenomenal sixty-one.

held by Williams. He is second in walks drawn, third in home runs, fifth in lifetime average, sixth in runs batted in, eighth in runs scored and in total bases, fourteenth in doubles, and thirtieth in hits.* But if we allow him merely average seasons for the four-plus seasons he lost to two wars, and add another season for the months he lost to injuries, we get a man who in all the power totals would be second, and not a very distant second, to Ruth. And if we further allow that these years would have been not merely average but prime years, if we allow for all the months when Williams was playing in sub-par condition, if we permit his early and later years in baseball to be some sort of index of what the middle years could have been, if we give him a right-field fence that is not, like Fenway's, one of the most distant in the league, and if — the least excusable "if" — we imagine him condescending to outsmart the Williams Shift, we can defensibly assemble, like a colossus induced from the sizable fragments that do remain, a statistical figure not incommensurate with his grandiose ambition. From the statistics that are on the books, a good case can be made that in the *combination* of power and average Williams is first; nobody else ranks so high in both categories. Finally, there is the witness of the eyes; men whose memories go back to Shoeless Joe Jackson — another unlucky natural — rank him and Williams together as the best-looking hitters they have seen. It was for our last look that ten thousand of us had come.

Two girls, one of them with pert buckteeth and eyes as black as vest buttons, the other with white skin and flesh-colored hair, like an underdeveloped photograph of a redhead, came and sat on my right. On my other side was one of those frowning chestless young-old men who can frequently be seen, often wearing sailor hats, attending ball games alone. He did not once open his program but instead tapped it, rolled

---

*Again, as of 1960. Since then, Musial may have surpassed him in some statistical areas.

up, on his knee as he gave the game his disconsolate attention. A young lady, with freckles and a depressed, dainty
nose that by an optical illusion seemed to thrust her lips
forward for a kiss, sauntered down into the box seat right
behind the roof of the Oriole dugout. She wore a blue coat
with a Northeastern University emblem sewed to it. The
girls beside me took it into their heads that this was Williams'
daughter. She looked too old to me, and why would she be
sitting behind the visitors' dugout? On the other hand, from
the way she sat there, staring at the sky and French-inhaling,
she clearly was *somebody*. Other fans came and eclipsed her
from view. The crowd looked less like a weekday ballpark
crowd than like the folks you might find in Yellowstone
National Park, or emerging from automobiles at the top of
scenic Mount Mansfield. There were a lot of competitively
well-dressed couples of tourist age, and not a few babes in
arms. A row of five seats in front of me was abruptly filled
with a woman and four children, the youngest of them two
years old, if that. Someday, presumably, he could tell his
grandchildren that he saw Williams play. Along with these
tots and second-honeymooners, there were Harvard fresh-
men, giving off that peculiar nervous glow created when a
sufficient quantity of insouciance is saturated with enough
insecurity; thick-necked Army officers with brass on their
shoulders and steel in their stares; pepperings of priests;
perfumed bouquets of Roxbury Fabian fans; shiny salesmen
from Albany and Fall River; and those gray, hoarse men —
taxi drivers, slaughterers, and bartenders — who will continue to click through the turnstiles long after everyone else
has deserted to television and tramporamas. Behind me, two
young male voices blossomed, cracking a joke about God's
five proofs that Thomas Aquinas exists — typical Boston
College levity.

The batting cage was trundled away. The Orioles fluttered
to the sidelines. Diagonally across the field, by the Red Sox
dugout, a cluster of men in overcoats were festering like
maggots. I could see a splinter of white uniform, and Williams'

head, held at a self-deprecating and evasive tilt. Williams'
conversational stance is that of a six-foot-three-inch man
under a six-foot ceiling. He moved away to the patter of flash
bulbs, and began playing catch with a young Negro outfielder
named Willie Tasby. His arm, never very powerful, had
grown lax with the years, and his throwing motion was a kind
of muscular drawl. To catch the ball, he flicked his glove hand
onto his left shoulder (he batted left but threw right, as every
schoolboy ought to know) and let the ball plop into it
comically. This catch session with Tasby was the only time all
afternoon I saw him grin.

A tight little flock of human sparrows who, from the
lambent and pampered pink of their faces, could only have
been Boston politicians moved toward the plate. The loudspeakers mammothly coughed as someone huffed on the
microphone. The ceremonies began. Curt Gowdy, the Red
Sox radio and television announcer, who sounds like everybody's brother-in-law, delivered a brief sermon, taking the
two words "pride" and "champion" as his text. It began.
"Twenty-one years ago, a skinny kid from San Diego, California. . ." and ended, "I don't think we'll ever see another like
him." Robert Tibolt, chairman of the board of the Greater
Boston Chamber of Commerce, presented Williams with a
big Paul Revere silver bowl. Harry Carlson, a member of the
sports committee of the Boston Chamber, gave him a plaque,
whose inscription he did not read in its entirety, out of
deference to Williams' distaste for this sort of fuss. Mayor
Collins, seated in a wheelchair, presented the Jimmy Fund
with a thousand-dollar check.

Then the occasion himself stooped to the microphone, and
his voice sounded, after the others, very Californian; it
seemed to be coming, excellently amplified, from a great
distance, adolescently young and as smooth as a butternut.
His thanks for the gifts had not died from our ears before he
glided, as if helplessly, into "In spite of all the terrible things
that have been said about me by the knights of the keyboard
up there. . . ."

He glanced up at the press rows suspended behind home plate. The crowd tittered, appalled. A frightful vision flashed upon me, of the press gallery pelting Williams with erasers, of Williams clambering up the foul screen to slug journalists, of a riot, of Mayor Collins being crushed. ". . . And they were terrible things," Williams insisted, with level melancholy, into the mike. "I'd like to forget them, but I can't." He paused, swallowed his memories, and went on, "I want to say that my years in Boston have been the greatest thing in my life." The crowd, like an immense sail-going limp in a change of wind, sighed with relief. Taking all the parts himself, Williams then acted out a vivacious little morality drama in which an imaginary tempter came to him at the beginning of his career and said, "Ted, you can play anywhere you like." Leaping nimbly into the role of his younger self (who in biographical actuality had yearned to be a Yankee), Williams gallantly chose Boston over all the other cities, and told us that Tom Yawkey was the greatest owner in baseball and we were the greatest fans. We applauded ourselves lustily. The umpire came out and dusted the plate. The voice of doom announced over the loudspeakers that after Williams' retirement his uniform number, 9, would be permanently retired — the first time the Red Sox had so honored a player. We cheered. The national anthem was played. We cheered. The game began.

Williams was third in the batting order, so he came up in the bottom of the first inning, and Steve Barber, a young pitcher born two months before Williams began playing in the major leagues, offered him four pitches, at all of which he disdained to swing, since none of them were within the strike zone. This demonstrated simultaneously that Williams' eyes were razor-sharp and that Barber's control wasn't. Shortly, the bases were full, with Williams on second. "Oh, I hope he gets held up at third! That would be wonderful," the girl beside me moaned, and, sure enough, the man at bat walked and Williams was delivered into our foreground. He struck the pose of Donatello's David, the third-base bag being

Goliath's head. Fiddling with his cap, swapping small talk with the Oriole third baseman (who seemed delighted to have him drop in), swinging his arms with a sort of prancing nervousness, he looked fine — flexible, hard, and not unbecomingly substantial through the middle. The long neck, the small head, the knickers whose cuffs were worn down near his ankles — all these clichés of sports cartoon iconography were rendered in the flesh.

With each pitch, Williams danced down the baseline, waving his arms and stirring dust, ponderous but menacing, like an attacking goose. It occurred to about a dozen humorists at once to shout "Steal home! Go, go!" Williams' speed afoot was never legendary. Lou Clinton, a young Sox outfielder, hit a fairly deep fly to center field. Williams tagged up and ran home. As he slid across the plate, the ball, thrown with unusual heft by Jackie Brandt, the Oriole center fielder, hit him on the back.

"Boy, he was really loafing, wasn't he?" one of the collegiate voices behind me said.

"It's cold," the other voice explained. "He doesn't play well when it's cold. He likes heat. He's a hedonist."

The run that Williams scored was the second and last of the inning. Gus Triandos, of the Orioles, quickly evened the score by plunking a home run over the handy left-field wall. Williams, who had had this wall at his back for twenty years,* played the ball flawlessly. He didn't budge. He just stood still, in the center of the little patch of grass that his patient footsteps had worn brown, and, limp with lack of interest, watched the ball pass overhead. It was not a very interesting game. Mike Higgins, the Red Sox manager, with nothing to lose, had restricted his major-league players to the left-field line — along with Williams, Frank Malzone, a first-rate third baseman, played the game — and had peopled the rest of the terrain with unpredictable youngsters fresh, or not so fresh,

---

*In his second season (1940) he was switched to left field, to protect his eyes from the right-field sun.

off the farms. Other than Williams' recurrent appearances at the plate, the *maladresse* of the Sox infield was the sole focus of suspense; the second baseman turned every grounder into a juggling act, while the shortstop did a breathtaking impersonation of an open window. With this sort of assistance, the Orioles wheedled their way into a 4–2 lead. They had early replaced Barber with another young pitcher, Jack Fisher. Fortunately (as it turned out), Fisher is no cutie; he is willing to burn the ball through the strike zone, and inning after inning this tactic punctured Higgins' string of test balloons.

Whenever Williams appeared at the plate — pounding the dirt from his cleats, gouging a pit in the batter's box with his left foot, wringing resin out of the bat handle with his vehement grip, switching the stick at the pitcher with an electric ferocity — it was like having a familiar Leonardo appear in a shuffle of *Saturday Evening Post* covers. This man, you realized — and here, perhaps, was the difference, greater than the difference in gifts — really desired to hit the ball. In the third inning, he hoisted a high fly to deep center. In the fifth, we thought he had it; he smacked the ball hard and high into the heart of his power zone, but the deep right field in Fenway and the heavy air and a casual east wind defeated him. The ball died. Al Pilarcik leaned his back against the big "380" painted on the right-field wall and caught it. On another day, in another park, it would have been gone. (After the game, Williams said, "I didn't think I could hit one any harder than that. The conditions weren't good.")

The afternoon grew so glowering that in the sixth inning the arc lights were turned on — always a wan sight in the daytime, like the burning headlights of a funeral procession. Aided by the gloom, Fisher was slicing through the Sox rookies, and Williams did not come to bat in the seventh. He was second up in the eighth. This was almost certainly his last time to come to the plate in Fenway Park, and instead of merely cheering, as we had at his three previous appearances, we stood, all of us, and applauded. I had never before heard pure applause in a ballpark. No calling, no whistling, just an ocean of handclaps, minute after minute, burst after burst, crowding and running together in continuous succession like the pushes of surf at the edge of the sand. It was a sombre and considered tumult. There was not a boo in it. It seemed to renew itself out of a shifting set of memories as the Kid, the Marine, the veteran of feuds and failures and injuries, the friend of children, and the enduring old pro evolved down the bright tunnel of twenty-two summers toward this moment. At last, the umpire signalled for Fisher to pitch; with the other players, he had been frozen in position. Only Williams had moved during the ovation, switching his bat impatiently, ignoring everything except his cherished task. Fisher wound up, and the applause sank into a hush.

Understand that we were a crowd of rational people. We knew that a home run cannot be produced at will; the right pitch must be perfectly met and luck must ride with the ball. Three innings before, we had seen a brave effort fail. The air was soggy, the season was exhausted. Nevertheless, there will always lurk, around the corner in a pocket of our knowledge of the odds, an indefensible hope, and this was one of the times, which you now and then find in sports, when a density of expectation hangs in the air and plucks an event out of the future.

Fisher, after his unsettling wait, was low with the first pitch. He put the second one over, and Williams swung mightily and missed. The crowd grunted, seeing that classic swing, so long and smooth and quick, exposed. Fisher threw the third time, Williams swung again, and there it was. The ball climbed on a diagonal line into the vast volume of air over center field. From my angle, behind third base, the ball seemed less an object in flight than the tip of a towering, motionless construct, like the Eiffel Tower or the Tappan Zee Bridge. It was in the books while it was still in the sky. Brandt ran back to the deepest corner of the outfield grass, the ball descended beyond his reach and struck in the crotch where the bullpen met the wall, bounced chunkily, and vanished.

Like a feather caught in a vortex, Williams ran around the square of bases at the center of our beseeching screaming. He ran as he always ran out home runs — hurriedly, unsmiling, head down, as if our praise were a storm of rain to get out of. He didn't tip his cap. Though we thumped, wept, and chanted "We want Ted" for minutes after he hid in the dugout, he did not come back. Our noise for some seconds passed beyond excitement into a kind of immense open anguish, a wailing, a cry to be saved. But immortality is nontransferable. The papers said that the other players, and even the umpires on the field, begged him to come out and acknowledge us in some way, but he refused. Gods do not answer letters.

Every true story has an anticlimax. The men on the field refused to disappear, as would have seemed decent, in the smoke of Williams' miracle. Fisher continued to pitch, and escaped further harm. At the end of the inning, Higgins sent Williams out to his left-field position, then instantly replaced him with Carrol Hardy, so we had a long last look at Williams as he ran out there and then back, his uniform jogging, his eyes steadfast on the ground. It was nice, and we were grateful, but it left a funny taste.

One of the scholasticists behind me said, "Let's go. We've seen everything. I don't want to spoil it." This seemed a sound aesthetic decision. Williams' last word had been so exquisitely chosen, such a perfect fusion of expectation, intention, and execution, that already it felt a little unreal in my head, and I wanted to get out before the castle collapsed. But the game, though played by clumsy midgets under the feeble glow of the arc lights, began to tug at my attention and I loitered in the runway until it was over. Williams' homer had, quite incidentally, made the score 4–3. In the bottom of the ninth inning, with one out, Marlin Coughtry, the second-base juggler, singled. Vic Wertz, pinch-hitting, doubled off the left-field wall, Coughtry advancing to third. Pumpsie Green walked, to load the bases. Willie Tasby hit a double-play ball to the third baseman, but in making the pivot throw

Billy Klaus, an ex–Red Sox infielder, reverted to form and threw the ball past the first baseman and into the Red Sox dugout. The Sox won, 5–4. On the car radio as I drove home I heard that Williams, his own man to the end, had decided not to accompany the team to New York. He had met the little death that awaits athletes. He had quit.

Leonard Shecter

Baseball:
Great American Myth

Life, August 9, 1968

A sensational event was changing from the brown suit to the
gray the contents of his pockets. He was earnest about these
objects. They were of eternal importance, like baseball or
the Republican Party.
   Babbitt by Sinclair Lewis

The Boston Red Sox are in Detroit for the first game of their
season and Carl Yastrzemski, a small-faced, large-shouldered
man who is the world's most valuable baseball player, is
autographing a ball for an open-mouthed, runny-nosed little
boy. He writes:
   To Hal
   "Work Hard"
   Carl Yastrzemski
To those who take baseball seriously, those who make
their living from it and those who hope to, it is never a game.
It is always "Work Hard." Initially a pastime for "white gentlemen" with an excess of leisure, baseball has grown into a
nerve-grinding business populated by intense men who are
stalked always by failure. The .300 hitter, an increasingly
rare breed, is a failure seven times out of 10. The most
successful team, the one that wins the pennant, will lose two
games out of every five. In baseball, as just about nowhere

else in life, there is a decision each day, a *final* score; if the game is won, the demon of the day has been defeated. For the professional ball player, the result is an emotional roller coaster — high highs, low lows; the life of the paranoid. Anyone who does not come to the game wearing callouses upon his sensitivities, upon his civilization even, develops them quickly or follows a different calling. And all the time it is required to wear an "I Love Baseball" button and a jolly facade.

Baseball is indulgent about facades, preferring them to reality. The game has surrounded itself with euphemisms, like a junkyard with an ivy-covered fence. Baseball is peanuts and hot dogs and heart and team spirit and camaraderie and good feeling and a way of life second in wholesomeness only to the Boy Scouts. Of course, it is none of these things, and one only has to examine the fortunes and personnel of a single team over a period of time to understand how shimmery this facade is.

The Red Sox are a good example because the insane pressures of baseball were magnified for them by the winning of a pennant last season. The team that finished ninth in the American League in 1966 and, with great flare and drama, first in 1967 came to spring training this year acutely aware that behind the facade baseball is a game of what-have-you-done-lately? And what they had done lately was lose Jim Lonborg, their best pitcher. Ignoring the Boston general manager's warning not to go skiing, Lonborg tore up a knee on the slopes. This led one of his friends on the team to remark, "That son of a bitch is taking bread off my table."

In addition, Tony Conigliaro, an extraordinary young power hitter, who had been hit in the face by a pitched ball last season, was complaining that he could not see well enough to hit. He returned to Boston, where doctors told him that heavy physical exertion might cause him to lose the vision he had left in his eye and that he had to give up baseball altogether. Not yet aware of the doctors' diagnosis, Dick Williams, the hard-driving manager with the unregenerate scalp-showing crewcut, was telling the press: "As far as I know there's nothing wrong with Conigliaro." Nor did he seem particularly concerned that there might be. The result? "The next time I see him," Conigliaro told a friend, "I'm going to punch him in the head."

The Red Sox players were not sanguine about their chances of winning a pennant again. Besides the injuries, there was the nagging thought that last year they caught lightning in a bottle, that they didn't so much win it as the other teams lost it. Before a pre-season exhibition game, Jim Bouton, who was then pitching for the Yankees, asked several Boston players, "How you gonna do?"

"They all put thumbs down," Bouton reported. "Nothing."

In baseball, however, logic can be an orange Day-Glo skip rope. The euphoria of winning conquers all. So, when the Red Sox defeat Detroit on opening day, pessimism is as hard to find around the club as a shelf of the world's greatest books.

Yastrzemski, who had a bewilderingly poor spring, has hit two home runs against Detroit. It is a continuation of the marvelous élan with which he almost singlehandedly took the Red Sox to the pennant in 1967, and there is great glee in the clubhouse. Yastrzemski explains that he used spring training merely to relax from a taxing winter devoted to trophies, bromides and Bromo. For the past few days, he says, he has been hitting the ball well in practice, and, well, there you are, two home runs.

Another reason for the good feeling is the successful debut of 20-year-old Joe Lahoud. Joe, a rookie with only two years in baseball and a broken ankle which has never healed properly, has been installed in right field ahead of Ken Harrelson, who has a history of hitting the long ball in the major leagues. Harrelson is nicknamed "The Hawk" in honor of the magnificent proportions of his nose. He has a Beatle haircut, likes to wear "love beads," Nehru jacket and dark glasses, and every time Williams sees him in one of those startling getups the crewcut manager looks as though he has just bitten into a lemon.

There is some pleased discussion, too, about Dick Ellsworth, a National League cast-off pitcher the Red Sox acquired over the winter. Ellsworth has pitched nine innings to beat Detroit, and Williams says, "He impressed me back in '63 and '64 when he won 22 and 14 games. You don't get any dumber as the years go by."

Williams also finds it in his bursting breast to say, "Losing Conigliaro and Lonborg has drawn this club closer together." The next game Yastrzemski gets no hits, Lahoud fails to put down a bunt in a vital bunt situation and John Wyatt, the relief pitcher, gives up a game-winning home run. Ebullience gives way to depression. The Red Sox are on the roller coaster.

There are certain forms expected of a baseball player in depression and he deviates from them at great risk. Rigid conformity is the order in baseball: the rebel is usually sent to Coventry — or to Winston-Salem in the Carolina League. After a losing game a player is required to file into the clubhouse as though he were a member of a silent order of monks. As long as he remains grave he is permitted to indulge in the buffet the clubhouse man has prepared. The player may break the silence by gurgling down a beer or munching potato chips, although if the loss of the game can be laid directly at his feet he is better off eating bologna, which is not so noisy. There are those who stare into lockers and those who stare out of them; some, like Yastrzemski, take an inordinate amount of time to get out of their uniforms and into a shower. When Latin American players first came into the major leagues, there was serious trouble because their culture did not call for what they considered "excessive mourning." They thus were branded as "those guys who don't care whether they win or lose."

Williams is a staunch advocate of the black-crepe losing clubhouse. "It shows everybody is disappointed in losing," he says this day. "I don't think we should have a sing-song in the clubhouse."

Once, early last season, Williams climbed aboard a bus after losing a game and there was a burst of laughter from a player in the rear. "He thought it was me," says Lee Stange, a cocky-looking right-handed pitcher. "So, I didn't pitch for two months. I went to him and told him it wasn't me, but it didn't do any good."

Of course, Williams is a stubborn man. A few days after the team leaves Detroit, he is having a conversation with a reporter.

Reporter: "You hear about the Mets and Houston? One to nothing, Houston, in 24 innings."

Williams: "Twenty-six."

Reporter: "I heard on the radio it was 24."

Williams: "It was 26."

It was 24.

Baseball men are constantly involved in such cosmic discussions. They talk about what they do, which is very little. The game they play is a slow one, designed to be played on soft summer days when time hangs heavy. It may be the only game which can be enjoyed while reading a newspaper. And despite the length of the game, which is pushing steadily toward an average of three hours, the action is but a twinkling in the soporific life of a player. Since games are rarely played in the daytime anymore, the players spend hours at afternoon movies or watching game shows on television when they are on road trips. Usually there is a congealed clump of them in the hotel lobby, gossiping and cutting people up. The glamour of baseball is in the eye of the non-beholder. The season goes on and it becomes obvious that Yastrzemski is getting special attention from opposing pitchers. Almost every time he comes to bat, one looks up from one's newspaper to discover him sprawled in the dirt, legs and arms akimbo, batting helmet askew. This is the position a man assumes after avoiding a baseball that has been thrown straight at him with great velocity. But Yastrzemski, continuing his role as a firm-jawed, uncomplaining sportsman, does not accuse the pitchers of using him for target practice.

"They pitch me in and out," he says day after day, "and they get a little wild. So I go down."

But there comes a game in which Yastrzemski is frightened. The whole team is. The players live with the sound the ball made when it struck Conigliaro — like a grapefruit dropped off a roof. Gary Peters is the White Sox pitcher. With the score 2–0 in favor of Boston in the eighth inning and the game slipping away, there is a man on first and Peters' pitch to Yastrzemski is high and tight. Yastrzemski spins around as the ball arrives, throwing up his shoulder to guard his head. The ball hits his shoulder and he falls, twitching in pain. After a moment he is still, and at last he arises and leaves the game.

In the clubhouse he is angry and pale under his baseball tan, which stops at the base of the neck. "I turned to protect my face," he says. "The ball was four, five feet off the plate. Blank him, he's got better control than that. I'm getting damn tired of this every blanking day."

When the reporters have left, Yastrzemski turns to Rico Petrocelli, who has the next locker. Petrocelli is a dark, sad-eyed young man who responds to the stresses of baseball by talking about giving it all up. He is a close friend of Conigliaro and recent events have hit him hard. On the road he wanders around a lot, alone, looking forlorn. "Look at that," Yastrzemski says to Petrocelli. He has a huge bruise on his shoulder and it is still turning new colors. "Blanking right at me," he says. "Blanking right at my head."

There is a deep pain on Petrocelli's long face. He shakes his head, conveying both sadness and revulsion. "Somebody's got to stop it," he says. "Not afterward. Now. It's no good afterward."

This is the fear baseball players live with. It is as much a part of their working day as getting to the park on time or batting practice or taking orders through the long season from a tyrannical manager. But they hate to be afraid. Elston Howard, once of the Yankees, now a catcher for the Red Sox, says what they are all thinking. "Suppose it hit him in the head. The man's got three kids. *I* got three kids. Who's gonna take care of my family if I get hit in the head and can't do nothing?"

Nobody, that's who. And baseball players know that as well as they understand how swiftly time diminishes their talent, how easily their bodies succumb to injury, how eager the young men behind them are to shove them out of jobs, how soon — and at what a young age — they will be through and looking for another way to make a living. They know, most of them, that despite what people on the outside may think, there will be no job in baseball or broadcasting waiting for them, no successful restaurant eager to make them partners. They can capitalize only on the skills they have. It is shocking how many end up in overalls.

The next day the White Sox are gone and Cleveland is in Boston. There were some minor mutterings about close pitches the last time these teams played, and now in the first inning Reggie Smith, the Boston center fielder, is hit on the arm by Sonny Siebert. When Siebert comes to bat in the second inning Gary Waslewski, the Red Sox pitcher, plunks *him* on the arm. It's not the pitching arm, however. There *is* a bond of sorts between pitchers.

Afterward, Waslewski is asked how it feels to stand out there on the mound and throw what could be a lethal missile at a man. "That depends," he says, "on whether you're trying to hit him or not. If you're trying not to hit him, well, it's as bad as giving up a walk. If you are, you feel satisfied." As the season moves its inexorable way, like a train in a long tunnel, the Red Sox are able to win only about half their games. Williams pushes all the buttons, turns all the wheels, screams at mistakes the moment they are made, chewing out players in full if embarrassing view of the whole team. A baseball player's humiliation is often public; he spends much of his career thinking about digging a deep hole and climbing into it.

Williams gives up on Lahoud and sends him down to the minor leagues, installing Harrelson in right field. The Hawk begins to hit right away. "You notice," Williams says, "that his hair is shorter." At the same time George Scott, who hit .300 last year, can't bring his 1968 average to .200. Soon, Scott is on the bench and Harrelson is playing first base. Williams is a bold manager who believes in the hit-and-run, the stolen base and the principle of going with the hot player, the one who can do it *now*. This lineup-churning keeps players alert and battling for their position all the time; you can't make money if you don't play. Williams exploits each nuance of pride and ambition. In some ways he is the perfect manager — dynamic, involved, austere, single-minded, as intense as he is insensitive. Managers are popularly thought of as brainy, brawny handlers of men; they are more often manipulators, adept in the art of sly coercion. The player, like the private in the Army, must learn to endure.

When Williams was hired as manager in 1967, the Red Sox were known as a "country club." Under managers Billy Jurges, Mike Higgins, John Pesky and Billy Herman the team had failed to finish higher than sixth in seven years, but nobody had seemed to care. Williams had played for the Red Sox a couple of seasons as a utility man and knew exactly where to apply the brakes when he took over. He called a meeting and said, "On this club, the rules will be strictly enforced, and if you break them it will be $500. If you want to take a chance, it's up to you."

In the finest traditions of the game, Williams not only can coerce, he can be pointedly cruel. "Talking to Scott," he says one day, "is like talking to cement."

Williams is not liked by his players. "There is no way you can like that man," Harrelson says as he sits near his locker. "He doesn't give you a chance to like him."

"I heard Williams say many times to the players: 'I don't care if you don't like me,'" Pitcher Don McMahon says before a ball game. "Bull. A guy can give you 100% if he hates your guts. But you can get 110% out of him if he likes you."

McMahon has been in baseball 19 years, and early last season he was traded from the Red Sox to the White Sox. Now he is sitting in the Chicago dugout and pointing out at the Boston manager. "Williams is a sarcastic son of a bitch," he says. "If you had a bad game, here came the wisecracks. He'd never let up. I dropped a double-play ball in the eighth inning of one game, they tied it up and we lost in the 18th. He got an expression on his face like I smelled bad or something and he had it all the time I was there."

Through this season, Williams has used that expression on Pitcher John Wyatt. Wyatt did important relief work for the Red Sox through most of 1967, but at the very end he faltered, giving up several game-winning home runs. Over the winter Williams disparaged Wyatt's talents in the public prints, and Wyatt countered with a letter to Larry Claflin of the Boston *Record-American* in which he defended his contribution.

Williams has been angry over Wyatt's letter. Predictably, it is announced one day that Wyatt has been sold — to the Yankees. "I've played for about 11 managers," Wyatt says, "and I never saw one like that. I been sold not because of my ability, but because of a personal thing. If that man is your enemy, forget it."

As Wyatt leaves the clubhouse, Elston Howard, a man not given to roiling troubled waters, says of him: "He can still throw the ball, throw it good, good as anybody around. But he and Williams. . . ." He shrugs. He does not want to get involved.

Late that day, when Williams is at last alone in his office with his usual bulging postgame sandwich and paper beer cup full of potato chips, he is asked whether it isn't unusual in this day, when expansion clubs are paying more than $5 million to be stocked with 30 mediocre players, to give up a pitcher of Wyatt's skill for a pittance and not even get a player in return.

Williams opens his eyes wide, the way he does when he's angry, which is often. A lot of white is suddenly visible around the hazel pupils. "We do a lot of unusual things here," he says. "Like coming from ninth place to win the pennant. That's unusual. Last year we ran and we didn't have a fast ball club and we played in a band-box. *That's* unusual. Me," he thumps himself on the chest, "*me,* managing an All-Star team after 13 years of not making one. If you think that isn't unusual. . . ." He turns his back and walks out of the room. On one cross-country road trip the first stop is Anaheim, where in 1967 the Red Sox lost seven out of nine games to the California Angels. "Ah Anaheim," says one of the players. "Lose a game, win a dame." It does not, however, appear to be one of the team's favorite cities. Anaheim is Disneyland surrounded by motels. The motels are surrounded by parking lots. You need a car to go for a walk. The players sit in their rooms and watch TV, or in the lobby and read newspapers. There is a swimming pool, but it is off limits. They might get sunburned or pull a muscle or something.

Rico Petrocelli sits on a plastic chair on the concrete lawn and talks about the game. "When you're a kid," he says, "you dream. All you see is the glory, the home run, winning, the World Series, the Yankees. This is great, this is baseball. Then you find out about the heartaches, the bad days, the losing. Things happen at home and you have to leave anyway; the kids are growing up without you and you miss your wife something fierce. You hang around hotel lobbies all day long. Hours and days of your life — wasted. I ask myself, 'What am I doing here?' and I haven't got any good answers."

There are answers, of course. "You play," says Harrelson, "for money."

Upstairs in his room, Third Baseman Joe Foy lies in bed dressed only in chain and medallion. The TV set is tuned to an old war movie. It is very noisy and Foy remarks that he has seen it four times, at least. But it is company. "I thought baseball would be all glamour and fame and glory," Foy says. "I never thought of it as a job, just a job. But that's what it is. You're not a baseball star, you're just an employee. I never thought it would be so much work."

"Could you be making as much money at anything else?" he is asked.

Foy laughs. "If I got lucky," he says, "and became a thief."

Foy, however, can see an advantage in not being a baseball player. "If I wasn't a player," he says, "I wouldn't go to a game. I enjoy watching it on TV. I wouldn't break my neck to spend money to see the game."

Most professional baseball players feel this way. To them, baseball is something you *do*. They are always surprised at big crowds.

That night the Red Sox lose. The game illustrates how some of Williams' boldness as a manager, which won a pennant last year, can suddenly begin to look like costly gambling. The Red Sox have two runners on base and none out in the ninth and are trailing by two runs. With two strikes on Scott, Williams signals for the hit-and-run. Scott swings and misses and a runner is thrown out at third. Two out. Petrocelli follows with a home run to tie the score but the Red Sox lose in the 11th inning. Last year Scott would not have missed the ball and the Sox would have wound up with a big inning. Everybody on the team knows it. So does Williams.

His problems are multiplying. As many people feared, Lonborg, threatened with the loss of his year's salary if he could not pitch this season, has probably pushed himself too hard and has come up with a sore shoudler. In the morning after the year of the impossible dream this is only to be expected. Williams is tight-lipped and grim.

The manager has a three-year contract, but there is no coasting for him. For one thing, it would be contrary to his personality. For another, the noisy Boston sporting press, which Williams has not treated gently, is poised for the opportunity to return some old insults. While he was winning the pennant, he was largely immune from criticism. But now it has become apparent that 1968 is going to be a very human year for him.

The next day in the coffee shop Williams sits at a counter and tells the waitress, "And I'll have a scoop of ice cream on that."

There is a raised eyebrow in the waitress's voice. "*On chocolate cream pie?*"

"Whatsamatter?" Williams says. "Is it illegal or something?"

Losing seems to make Williams frantic. He zips players in and out of the lineup. Only Yastrzemski can feel certain he will not be benched. The Red Sox lose for the second straight night. Harrelson, who had one hit in five at-bats the first game, has none in four at-bats this time. He is anxious and fretful. His 2-year-old son Rick has been suffering from a rare kidney ailment and Harrelson says: "I didn't get much sleep for three days. I'm not hitting the ball well." The morning of the third day he is out taking extra batting practice, but it doesn't seem to help. He is red-faced and sweaty. "If I don't hit the ball any better in batting practice before the game tonight," he says, "I'll really be worried."

No need. That night, his name is not in the starting lineup. When he goes up to the batting cage to hit with the substitutes he is furious. He bangs his bat against the batting cage and the bat breaks. Williams turns hard eyes on him. "Next time," Williams says, "it comes out of your paycheck."

The Red Sox win the third game of the series. No game is scheduled for the next day, only a plane ride to Minneapolis, so Williams raises his voice in the clubhouse and says, "Fellas, just make sure you make the bus in the morning." He means that curfew is off.

In the plane the next day there don't seem to be many purple eyeballs. Young bodies recoup fast. Besides, California bars close early — 2 A.M. Casey Stengel always used to say that it isn't the girls that hurt baseball players. It's the hours spent and the whiskey drunk chasing them.

The players are a noisy, happy bunch. Williams is not on the airplane. He has remained behind for some dental work. Gene Oliver, the catcher who never plays and is soon to be sold — largely because, as the Boston press points out regularly, he has an arm like the Venus de Milo — borrows the stewardess's blond wig and dances in the aisle. Oliver makes up in exuberance what he lacks in talent. In the bullpen he's always pretending he's a broadcaster and describes the action, often in obscene terms. "He's something," Al Lakeman, the coach, tells Williams on the bench one day. "You know what I said to him? I said, 'Hey Oliver, you a Jew?' And he said, you know, surprised, 'No, I'm a Catholic.' And I said, 'That's funny, you talk just like a Jew. Talking all the time, just like a Jew.'" Lakeman is pleased with himself.

Another time, Williams is talking about the small crowds the Chicago White Sox are drawing at their home ball park, which is in the South Side Negro ghetto. "It's not really bad around the park," a young reporter from Chicago says. "The riots are miles away. It just has a bad rap."

Williams guffaws. "You kidding? Where'd they move that park to? You sure you're talking about the same one?" He guffaws again. "I remember when I played for Kerby Farrell. We lost a tough game and he just sat around the clubhouse until the bus was ready to go. He said, 'Hell, let it go. I'll walk back.'" Guffaw again. "Imagine if he tried walking from the Chicago ball park! They'd have to go out looking for him all over the place — an ear here, a leg there."

The Red Sox coaches nod wisely. They know you can't walk on the South Side. They know because they have never tried. Baseball is like that. The people in it have only a filmy understanding of the world outside the game. Stereotypes are their only connection with life out there. There is less prejudice in baseball than there is outside of it, yet a baseball man will refer to Willie Mays as a "nigger," mean none of the implications of the word, yet cling to it emotionally as he does to all his stereotypes. In Minneapolis there are two games that tell a lot about the Red Sox and what kind of season this has been for them. In the eighth inning of the first game, with the score 0–0, the Minnesota Twins' second baseman, Rod Carew, gets to first on an error by Petrocelli, is sacrificed to second, then foolishly tries to reach third when Harmon Killebrew hits a ground ball right at Third Baseman Foy. All Foy has to do is reach out and make the tag, but he doesn't move and, slithering like an eel, Carew runs around him. Umpire Al Salerno signals that Carew is safe.

This brings Williams dashing from the dugout. He insists Carew is out. "He ran out of the baseline!" Williams screams.

"You're a vernacular for sexual function liar," says Salerno, who is suffering from a boil on the back of his neck.

"And you are a practitioner of an unnatural sexual act," Williams says.

Salerno throws him out of the game.

"The trouble is," Salerno says later, "there's no more sportsmanship in baseball."

With two out and Carew on third, Tony Oliva, one of the 10 best hitters in baseball, is the batter. It is a polite fiction of the sport that when a manager is thrown out of a game he ceases managing. In fact, he merely runs the game from some other vantage. So it is Williams who now decides that the Red Sox pitcher, José Santiago, is not to walk Oliva purposely even though:

(1) It is a left-handed hitter against a right-handed pitcher, a situation any manager, including Williams, will often go to implausible lengths to avoid; (2) walking Oliva purposely would set up a possible force play at second base, desirable when it is vital to choke off a run; and (3) a right-handed hitter, Rich Rollins, is up next.

Santiago pitches, Oliva chops the ball over the pitcher's head, and Carew scores. The Red Sox lose, 1–0.

The clubhouse is just as quiet as Williams likes it. Except for the whispering. And in it one can detect a tone of gleefulness. Why the hell, the players want to know, would Williams choose to pitch to Oliva with first base open?

The next night is even worse. It is the kind of game that's like having your fingers slammed in a door. The Red Sox have a four-run lead in the fourth, largely the result of a three-run home run by Harrelson who is beginning to move up among the league's leading hitters. The Twins whittle at the lead, but going into the ninth it is still 4–3, Red Sox. Sparky Lyle is the Boston pitcher, and Killebrew leads off with a home run to tie the score. Two outs later, the Twins center fielder, Ted Uhlaender, hits a home run and the game is over. When they talk about shocking defeats in baseball, this is what they mean.

In the airplane to Oakland the next day Lyle still has a numbed look on his face. He says that he has made up his mind. After a bad game like that the only thing he can do, he says, is go up to Williams and demand that he be pitched right away. He is driven to atone for his sins. But at the ball park

Lyle approaches Williams, looks into those eyes with the white all around the pupils and changes his mind. He says nothing. Nor does he pitch. Reggie Smith, the young center fielder, has been making foolish throws — to the wrong base or over the head of the cut-off man. Yastrzemski has tried to help him, telling him to charge the ground balls so his throws will not have to be so hasty. But in a game in Oakland, Smith forgets and his hurried, wild throw lets in a run.

Jerry Adair, the Red Sox utility infielder, who is an old 31 and tough, gets sore and lets it show. "The attitude isn't here," he says, "not the way it was last year. They don't seem to mind losing. They make a lot of mistakes, mental mistakes. The kid in center has a ton of ability and about an ounce of brains. And every time we make a mistake it costs us a game.

"They're young, sure, but they shouldn't make those mistakes. They've had a year, they've had a pennant race. And the pitching. You have to wonder about guys who make pitches as bad as that."

Frustration piles on frustration, hopelessness upon hopelessness. But then the Red Sox go on a winning streak and passion beats in the breast of Boston again. The day the Red Sox win their eighth straight game Yastrzemski hits two home runs and announces that this is the first time all season he has felt comfortable at bat. "Just like last year," he says. Williams is delighted, too. "I'll say this," the manager tells reporters. "I'm quite optimistic. I think we've jelled." And even Massachusetts's Governor John Volpe, on hand because it is Massachusetts Day, decides that this, by heaven, is the *second* year of the impossible dream.

But the season is only half gone, and as it goes on players will make more mistakes and Williams will again have to defend his current and past decisions. He will sit for two hours in his clubhouse office, giving his alligator shoes a spit shine, a copy of *Male* magazine on his desk, and he will tell people who ask that he didn't walk Oliva that day in Minneapolis because Oliva hadn't been hitting Santiago, and Rollins, who was up next, had. The evidence won't bear him out but no one will say so because Williams' eyes turn white so easily on losing days.

The season will go on and Elston Howard's friends on the Yankees will run on his old arm and steal a game and afterward Howard will turn the talk around to the mistakes he says the pitcher made. "I told him and I told him to keep the ball down and he threw it up. What the hell? You can't throw it for him."

The season will go on and the players will talk in the lobbies about what it's all about and it will always come to the same thing — money. The young players will listen to Pitcher Gary Bell because he has been around a long time. "A ballplayer," Bell will tell them, "has to be an individualist. If you aren't, you're not going to make the money. If I win 20 games and we end up sixth place I still get a good raise. If another pitcher wins 15 and his team wins the pennant he won't get as good a raise as I do. If you hit .300, you'll come out on top of the guy who bunts and sacrifices himself and hits to right field. That's the way the game is," and if a young player says, "Yeah, but the manager . . ." everybody will laugh.

The season will go on and Foy will ritualistically kid Yastrzemski, whose income from endorsement of bread, mayonnaise, hot dogs, hot dog rolls, batting gloves, batting helmets, slacks, blue jeans and T-shirts will double his baseball salary. "Yaz," Foy will say, "Yaz, you're my idol. I want my son to be just like you — rich."

The Bill Lee Interview

This interview was conducted for Oui *magazine in the summer of 1978, Bill Lee's last with the Red Sox. The first session with Lee was held in Anaheim while he was still a member of the Sox starting rotation. The second session was held in Fenway after he had been "buried" in the bullpen by Sox manager Don Zimmer.*

Q. Let's start with a standard men's magazine question — do you have lust in your heart?

A. No, I've got about four valves and an aorta coming out and a superior vena cava and a lot of other things. No one has lust in his heart.

Q. Do you have lust anywhere?

A. I have pituitary secretions which effect my progesterone level at certain times, therefore you think on a physical level, as Gurdjieff put it. That would be considered a sex drive and would definitely be synonymous with what Jimmy Carter calls lust. Actually it's a biological reaction to mental input of some kind.

Q. About ten years ago, in his book *Ball Four,* Jim Bouton described the practice of "beaver watching" common among major league ball players who, he says, use binoculars to surveil female crotches in the stands. Have ball players advanced beyond such voyeuristic activities?

A. No, I'd say everything has stayed at that vicarious level. That communication's always going to be there, whether it be ball players or executives in high office buildings. It's the same thing. I think that ball players are in a high state of anxiety all the time, and that's a way of relieving some of the tension. That's probably why athletes and sex are always equated in our speeded up society. We live with more tension.

Q. Bouton also wrote about "Baseball Annies," the groupies who go after ball players rather than rock stars, are they still part of the scene?

A. Oh yeah. There are tons of people hanging around the hotels, and Annies are there to get some kind of vicarious thrill.

Q. Making it with a ball player?

A. Yeah. Usually nothing comes of it. She really just creates a problem for herself. She's not establishing any meaningful relationships, and the ball players are just out for the physical gratification. Teams should go on two month road trips, and the players' families should travel with them. It would eliminate a lot of problems, like divorce. Divorce is rampant in professional sports, one of the major problems.

Q. Because of the separation?

A. Yeah. The problem with ball players is that they grow at a different rate of speed than their wives. They don't bring their wives along with them. They meet for all the wrong reasons, at the wrong time, and all they ever know is personality. They never get to know one another's essence. You know, he's a ball player . . . dut . . . da . . . dut, but the right questions never get asked — are you happy? What are your goals in life? What do you think would be right for the planet earth? You know, get it on a sound basis.

Q. So most players marry too young?

A. Exactly. Then they put their wives at home and they develop at these different rates. You learn things, you feel things, you experience things, and a ball player gets much more experience than the average person simply because he travels so much more and comes in contact with so many more people. When my wife and I first met, it was nice. I always wanted to know everything about her and she always wanted to know everything about me. We were never telling each other "I am this" or "I am that." The problem with people is that they're egocentric. We're centered around ourselves instead of being centered around others. Never talk about yourself. Think about others and let others think about you. Stop thinking that your ego is the most important thing. De-emphasis of the ego is what I'm striving for. It's contrary to our belief. We believe in a pyramid theory of getting to the top. I believe the pyramid should be inverted.

Q. You're into Eastern thought, aren't you?

A. I'm into blending it with Western thought and trying to get harmony between the two. Western man is not content wherever he is, Eastern man is content all the time. It's the duality of our planet. The Chinese have never gone outside their borders to conquer. They've always been conquered. People have come in and the Chinese have absorbed a variety of cultures. Everyone is fearful of what they call the "Red Chinese mind," but the Chinese have never gone outside their own borders.

Q. You visited Red China, didn't you? After the '75 World Series with the Cincinnati Reds you said you were off to see the *real* Big Red Machine.

A. Yeah. That's right, the Big Red Machine. Didn't see much red there, though, except maybe some nice little red cheeks.

Q. Was that just for a vacation?

A. No, I went with a sports group, a lot of people I didn't agree with. I got sick and Dr. Harry Edwards said it was my politics that got me sick.

Q. Harry Edwards the black militant?

A. Yeah, Dr. Harry Edwards, who organized the protests at the '68 Olympics in Mexico City.

Q. When he said it was your politics that made you sick, was he attacking your politics?

A. No, it was because I was out jogging every morning, and, you know, they have a lot of coal dust over there. They burn soft coal because they haven't perfected hydroelectric yet. They're in the early stages of their electric development. I just got a bronchitis that went deep down into my lungs and it turned into a thick, difficult chest cold that I just couldn't shake. I had real high temperatures. I wish I could've stayed, but I didn't care for the coldness of China.

Q. What was the point of the trip?

A. The point of the trip was to share our beliefs on sports and learn what they're doing to maintain a physical culture, as they call it. The body, you know, is one third of man's existence. He has a body and he has to take care of it if he doesn't want to become a burden on society. A person who doesn't exercise is becoming a burden on society.

Q. Were you impressed with what the Chinese were doing?

A. Very impressed. I was impressed with the way the kids seemed to enjoy themselves all the time and loved to play and help each other out instead of belittling. I see a lot of belittling going on here when someone makes a mistake. Over there they take a kid aside and work with him. It's something we could learn in this country.

Q. Now, are the Chinese like that because of their politics or because of the philosophy they've had there for centuries?

A. I think Mao would've said it was because of the politics, but I think it's because of the essence of Chinese culture that they take care of each other. There are only three per cent that have over there, the other ninety-seven per cent have not. The have-nots are in power, it's government of the people at the lowest levels. So the old time life philosophies of Lao Tsu and others are now being practiced. It seems very constructive over there.

Q. You were raised as a Catholic, are you still Catholic?

A. I'm all religions now. I'm very religious, I think. All my friends say I am. I believe in what Paramahansa Yogananda said — "Believe in all religions because they're making an attempt." Roman Catholic? Yeah, but I was always fearful of that hell and brimstone they profess, that duality of the joys of heaven and the pains of hell. It tears at people — makes them dislike their bodies because they make the body sound like it's synonymous with hell. And me being left-handed they always said the Latin derivation *sinistra,* you know sinister, means left handed, therefore I am sinister. That's why they always wanted me to work with the right side of the body.

Q. You mean you had to repress your lefthandedness along with all those other guilts?

A. Yeah, I had to repress it. Now I believe in combining things. You can learn to be an Eastern man through knowledge. Your brain can then balance those Western urges to move, to leave, like the man in the covered wagon, there's always been that restlessness. We've got to learn to harness that restlessness and energy and become constructive on the planet. Like my grandfather who couldn't handle teaching and the fast pace of L.A. He had a breakdown, then went to the farm and found harmony with the land.

Q. As a native Californian was there much of an adjustment for you in settling in New England?

A. Oh, yeah. I was always kind of put down in Boston, they like to think of themselves as the greatest there. . . .

Q. You mean it's not the hub of the universe?

A. It is. By the way it's shaped, I mean, by the way of the traffic patterns it is a hub. It's remarkable. It looks like a wheel with spokes and hub caps. But it's a nice place. It's made the mistakes, but it's maintained its old frame and is working within it to be better; whereas in California it's expanded out, made a lot of mistakes and eventually, when fossil fuels run out, it's going to be tough to survive there. You waste all your time getting places instead of doing things there. You're always in transit. It's like in the James Taylor song "Traffic Jam," you know — I looked in my rearview mirror and saw myself in the car behind me looking in my rearview mirror. It's like an Escher print — you see yourself sitting there in life, watching yourself slipping, slipping.

Q. I hear echoes of Jerry Brown in your speech.

A. I'm an advocate of Jerry Brown. I kind of like his philosophy. It sounds like he's winged out and crossed over, you know, trying to combine East and West.

Q. And he's always talking about how we've got to stop going places all the time and start thinking about where we want to go.

A. Yeah. You see, people who consider him a liberal don't realize that his beliefs are ultra-conservative, and people who are ultra-conservative don't realize that their beliefs aren't conservative at all. They don't see that the earth is turning, always moving, always changing, and they don't adapt to that. They don't have organic beliefs. Their beliefs are pinnacle beliefs — you have to dominate things — get on top. It's the Western male philosophy, the superiority thing.

Q. Have you ever actively campaigned for a candidate?

A. I made a mistake in Boston once. A guy at the Eliot Lounge wanted me to meet him and his girlfriend, wanted to buy me a few beers. He was running for office and was telling me how he believed in everything I believed in dut . . . da . . . dut. But the guy had so much duality in his life, I had to come out later and retract the statements I made for him. He got elected anyway, and I felt guilty.

Q. Was that a lesson learned?

A. It was a lesson learned.

Q. So now you don't support politicians or issues?

A. Issues, yes; not politicians.

Q. What issues?

A. ERA, Clamshell Alliance, Fair Share, Bottle Bill — I worked actively for recycling all forms of bottles, trash, everything. I believe in recycling everything. Issues that pertain to harmony with the earth. Issues are the things, not the people who are running them.

Q. If the ERA passes, are we going to have women in the major leagues?

A. If they're physically capable of performing, yeah.

Q. What would be the biggest obstacle women would face coming into the majors?

A. I would say that their biggest obstacle would be their lower center of gravity, their fatty tissue, their inability to get from first to third quick enough — basic biological things. It would have nothing to do with periods, though, because that has nothing to do with slowing people down. It's just the fact that they have this lower center of gravity. They're built that way to protect their female organs for childbirth and then they spread out. You know, she was great till she was 23, then she started spreading out and couldn't turn the double-play anymore.

Q. What about the pressure on a major league ball player? It almost seems overwhelming when one considers that the best hitters in the game fail seven out of every ten times they go to the plate.

A. You can't think that way. Ball players die at a relatively young age after their game is over. There must be something wrong there. The game is really insignificant in the scheme of things. All you have to do is take a player who's going bad over to the Sidney Farber Cancer Research Institute and have him watch all those kids with needles in their arms and no hair on their heads and . . . hey, what are your problems? They're insignificant. People dwell on themselves too much. You can't do that.

Q. Writer Mike Sheeter has described ball games as the human equivalent to chasing cars and barking. Any response to that?

A. I can see what he says. It's like Bukowski, this guy I'm reading now, who says that gambling is a form of sublimate or masturbatory reflex. That's gambling. But sport? I believe sport is how we keep the body in shape and in harmony with the earth. Games were created a long time ago as respites between wars. It's a creative way to use all that energy we have. An art form such as baseball is good, I think, but people get too caught up in the winning and losing because of the economics involved. There's a contradiction there. People come to the park and see a good game, but their team loses and they leave with an empty feeling. They shouldn't. They should enjoy the game for the game's sake. Root . . . root . . . root for the home team is fine, but not all this negative booing that goes on. That's what's really wrong with American sports.

Q. How would you characterize the Red Sox as a group of men?

A. As a group of men? I've got a lot of respect for them on the field. Off the field, I feel like they should be trying to change certain points in their lives. They shouldn't always be making such negative remarks and should try to treat other people a little nicer. But they're OK, they're good guys. They've just resigned themselves to the fact that things are the way they are and you can't change them. They say to me, "Why do you always want to go out there and be Don Quixote, running into all those windmills all the time?"

Q. How about the Red Sox in regards to major leaguers in general?

A. Ball players are ball players. They go out there and live their lives for the moment. That's the nature of sport. You never know what way the ball's going to hop. You can't anticipate. You have to go out there and play the game as it lies.

Q. There seems to be a general stereotype about athletes, and ball players in particular, that they're not very imaginative individuals.

A. It's because they only think about baseball, nothing else. I don't know exactly how to say this, but what they should do when they take a kid out of high school and bring him into an organization as a commodity is give him tests to find out what he wants to do when he gets out of baseball, so he can follow a trade or go to school and become an integral part of society. We're all pawns in this game. It builds up your ego and then, all of a sudden, it's over and you're out. That's a problem with our sports. We have to make it easier for the athlete when he gets out of the game, for his transition back into society.

Q. Sounds like prison rehabilitation.

A. A guy can make his own prison. Everyone should be a virtuoso on two levels, that way you have something to fall back on.

Q. You mean like Joe Don Loony, the footballer who went off to become a mahout in India?

A. I like Joe Don Loony. Going up into the Himalayas looking for the answers is about where it's at. He can find peace and tranquility through yoga. I believe in it.

Q. You've been player representative for the Red Sox for a number of years, how's that worked out, given the personality conflicts you've had with various teammates?

A. No one else has wanted it. It's a job, and you have to put time and work into it and most ball players can't be bothered with that.

Q. Earlier in the season you retired from baseball after the Red Sox sold your friend Bernie Carbo to the Cleveland Indians. Given the emotionalism of your retirement, was coming back to the team much of a compromise for you?

A. It was the biggest compromise of my life. I've always said "friendship first, competition second." That's a motto I learned, and that's why I walked out. Bernie asked me to come back. He was really the only one and he did it in an honest way. He said he didn't want what happened to him happening to new kids coming up, and he said, "You're in a position of authority in baseball where you might be able to effect change within the system." I said I didn't think I really could because of the economics of baseball. I'd like to think I could. I'd like to think I could change professional sports in America towards the betterment of treating people like people instead of treating them like expendable components.

Q. Do you expect to be with the Red Sox next season?

A. That's the $64,000 question. I didn't expect to be with Boston in '70. I was just going to be up for a while in '69. When '70 came, they said "Don't make any long-range plans."

In '72 I was supposed to be going to New York. I don't know. All I've ever done for Boston was give 100% and constructively criticize them when I thought they needed it. That's the way I am. I'm their conscience. I'm Jiminy Cricket.

Q. One of the things you've criticized over the years has been the dealing management has done, in particular the deals that sent Sparky Lyle, Tim McCarver and Bernie Carbo away to other teams. . . .

A. Tim McCarver was released. They didn't even bother to trade him. He liked to play, you know, he created an air of enthusiasm and confidence throughout the club. Everyone wanted to play for the right reasons — went out and enjoyed themselves. It took a lot of pressure off.

Q. All those guys were spirited, outspoken types. Is there something about the Boston organization that makes it impossible for such players to fit in?

A. I don't know. All those guys were great players and enjoyed to play. I don't know the answer to that question. I wish I did.

Q. This year the Sox went into a terrible slump and blew what seemed like an insurmountable lead to the Yankees. What causes a good team to slump like that? Physical fatigue? Mental fatigue?

A. That, plus hitting a hot club at the wrong time and getting really lambasted like we did. That set in and we never really recovered until after that Saturday in New York. It was a good sign and it showed that the nucleus of the club was made up of a lot of gamers and guys that really liked to play. We could sink no lower. We were three and a half games out and fading fast, about to go down in infamy with the '64 Phillies and the '67 Egyptians.

Q. Aside from the team slump, you experienced quite a bad personal slump after getting off to a tremendous start.

A. All I was doing was paying the fiddler because I had been pitching a lot of games and winning when I shouldn't have been out there. My arm was killing me. I had developed tendonitis after throwing a ball game on bad feet. When you have a bad foundation, something in your house is going to go wrong. I had this inflammation in my big toe of my pitching foot and we didn't know what it was. I went to a foot doctor and found out that I had three sesamoid bones in my left foot where I should only have had two.

Q. What about your teammates' errors? You were victimized by ten unearned runs in one three game stretch.

A. Yeah, I got hit with a tremendous streak of unearned runs. In fact, I looked at the stats and saw that I'd had twice as many unearned runs scored against me as anyone else during that period. I was just getting the bad luck of pitching on days when the team just wasn't putting it together. It was a shame, but I kind of enjoyed it. I said to myself, if any ball player on the team can accept defeat based on my belief of friendship first, competition second, it was good that I was getting the losses and letting the other guys maintain that edge and keep on going because I knew I would come out of it. I always had. I always had a good two-thirds of a season and a lousy third.

Q. Is a slump inevitable then?

A. Oh, it's inevitable. Everyone goes through a slump. The trouble was that they were looking to bury me and that's what happened.

Q. Is the press in Boston hard to deal with?

A. Oh, very difficult. It's the height of duality. Ted Williams said the only thing he disliked about his stay in Boston was dealing with the press. Jimmy Rice is having trouble handling it and I can understand why. He's a nice easy-going guy. He'll come to you when he has something to say. Don't be standing around his locker with these same questions all the time. It gets so repetitive. Leave him alone; he's going to be fine.

Q. What about the remarks attributed to him in *Sport* magazine about the Red Sox being a racist team?

A. Oh that. Jimmy was kind of like a detective back with Charles Lindbergh, coming up with the theory five years later that the kidnapper used a ladder. It was that kind of thing — thanks, Jim, but it's a little late. Jimmy's heart was there, but it's like I've said, ball players are perceptive, it just takes them a long time.

Q. Well, is racism still a problem with the Red Sox?

A. Oh, yeah. It always has been. Always has been.

Q. More so than the rest of the major leagues?

A. Always.

Q. Is that because of the ownership or because of the city?

A. Ownership. It's ownership catering to the demands of the city. But this city's got potential because people haven't been fleeing from it like in other big cities. Fans always come to the ball park because it's in close proximity to the working people. It's structured so you can get off work, get a pizza and a beer and watch a good ball game. And before it got so media dominated, the games would start at 7:30 and be over at 9:00 You'd be home with your wife by 10 o'clock. Now it's gotten so media oriented, it's changing the lifestyles of the fans.

Q. Speaking of the fans, once you were "buried" in the bullpen, they started chanting — "We want Lee! We want Lee!" How'd that make you feel?

A. I'll tell you, the greatest day for me, after being buried and being so depressed, I came out to the bullpen before the game and all my loyal fans out in the right-field corner gave me a standing ovation. Then when I got called into the game, I got a standing ovation from all over. It felt great to be appreciated like that, but they also gave poor Don Zimmer corresponding standing boos. He was just a victim of short-sightedness by higher management. It's a basic problem in baseball. You have to give managers security with long-term contracts. Managers, in turn, have to communicate with their players — all 25 of them — make everyone feel like part of the team. But back to the standing ovation, that was nice. That was a nice day.

Q. Was that an expression that the fans had forgiven you for your statement that Judge Garrity was the only man in Boston with any guts after he ordered busing to integrate Boston schools?

A. The fans have realized what I was saying about Judge

Garrity. Whether he was right or wrong, he was enforcing the U.S. Government. He wanted us all to start liking each other. He didn't want anymore of this hate. I hate change being forced on me too, but at least that was an attempt to make things better.

Q. You told *Sports Illustrated* that you used to get embarrassed for your friends when you went to ballgames as a kid and they'd go running up to players asking for autographs. Now you have the reputation for being the most accommodating autograph signer in the league.

A. Yeah, well that's because I look at the people and say "hi" to them. That's part of it for me, getting out and meeting people — not signing for signing's sake. That's the worst reason to receive an autograph — just to collect it. That's not the point. It's the moment that's important, not the fact that you have all this memorabilia. Hey, I've got 45,000 baseball cards and when we get in the energy crisis, I'll be able to burn Ted Kluszewskis for a week!

Q. In this same regard, after one crucial loss earlier this season, the rest of the team walked off the field with heads hung low. But you stayed out in the bullpen for some 20 minutes after the last out signing autographs. Defeat hit 24 guys one way, but you react to it so differently, how's that?

A. It has to do with my belief about winning and losing. It's going out and playing the game and once it's over — BOOM — it's over. You don't carry it home with you. You just try to get away from it, and the next day when you come out you won't be moping around.

Q. Is that why you got the reputation with some of the press and fans that you don't take the game seriously?

A. Oh, yeah. Exactly.

Q. They want you to wear your losses on your sleeve?

A. They want you bleeding.

Q. How do your teammates react?

A. They say, that's Bill Lee.

Q. This is somewhat parenthetical. . . .

*   *   *

At this point on what had been a heavily overcast day in Boston the sun came out, and Bill Lee became transfixed — not by the sun, but by the tall man who'd just appeared on the field in street clothes. It was, wondrously enough, the first hero of New England boyhood, making a rare appearance at the sight of his most heroic deeds. Bill Lee, the quintessence of the iconoclastic, modern-day athlete, sat in totally muted awe for the two or three minutes it took Ted Williams to walk across the outfield grass.

A. He's an idol, I tell you. Boy, he could hit, he could play. He's an amazing guy. I disagree with him. We're on opposite sides of the spectrum, but when the world is round like it is, we're actually standing back to back. We're yelling at each other politically, like on the back of his car he has all these stickers, you know, if guns are banned only outlaws will have them, or something like that, but he's a character.

Q. Ever talked politics with him?

A. No. We talk dominant eye theory — the fact that he was such a great hitter because he had such strong right eye domination. He could really see the low ball. He had great hand-eye coordination that allowed him to keep his head in there. He didn't know what I was talking about. He got into me about how a curve ball spins, and I said "Yes, it's physics. It breaks from a high pressure to a low pressure, and it's caused by the spin on the ball and the humidity and resistance. And he said, "Hey, you know that! How about that?"

Q. Did you ever read his autobiography?

A. Never.

Q. There's an amazing character there — rough and raw — an American original.

A. Oh, John Wayne. Ted Williams and John Wayne are synonymous. Someone down in spring training once said that John Wayne has spent his whole life playing Ted Williams.

Q. Are there any major leaguers you hold in especially high esteem?

A. Yeah. Tony Oliva — probably the toughest left-handed hitter I ever faced. I always liked Gates Brown.

Q. How about off the field?

A. Frank Howard. I like Frank Howard. Gary Peters, too. He's in the mold of Yastrzemski and Ted Williams — they're the kind of guys that'd jump in the lake with a knife between their teeth and swim through the crocodiles to save the damsel in distress.

Q. That's your view of Carl Yastrzemski?

A. Not so much Yaz. Yaz would do the same thing, but he'd get in a boat and row over there. He's more practical. You see, Yaz is basically right-handed, he just happens to swing from the left. Peters is left-handed like me and we do things off the cuff. We don't really think about it. We're not the kind of guys that are going to discover light.

Q. How about heroes outside of the game?

A. Heroes? Buckminster Fuller, Frank Lloyd Wright. Gurdjieff Paramahansa Yogananda, who tried to bring Eastern mysticism into the West. Religious figures — St. Francis of Assisi, Martin Luther King Jr. A guy I really like is Tom Robbins. He wrote *Another Roadside Attraction* and *Even Cowgirls Get the Blues.* He tries to point out the duality that exists in the world.

Q. How about in music? You're a rock fan. Who are your favorites?

A. Jackson Browne. Bob Seger. Zevon. I like Zevon, but I feel he's going to self-destruct eventually. Drinks too much, he's really unhappy. I like Bowie's creativity — his blending of sounds. Bob Marley is another one I like.

Q. Do you know any good rock songs about baseball?

A. A guy sent me a song called "Blasted in the Bleachers." It was about Fenway Park.

Q. How about Dylan? Do you like Bob Dylan?

A. Yeah, I listen to Bob Dylan all the time. My roommate at USC used to pick a guitar and sing all these weird songs that I never knew and after a while I really started to like them. He was an engineering student and I was a jock. He taught me great things. The first time I ever passed out was with him. It was great. His girlfriend came down from Denver and we went out drinking. I drank something like 17 beers and passed out, and she drank a whole case and walked away. She said it was the altitude.

Q. Have you ever seen yourself in terms of being a rock star?

A. Only when I'm pitching. It's more like a painter, like an artist out there painting the corners — fast ball, slow ball, slow curve, fast motion change-up, slow motion change, differing tempos all the time. It's an artistic thing like a guy up on stage performing.

Q. How about your relationship with the crowd? There's probably no other sports figure who can dominate the play of the game as much as a pitcher can.

A. I think I'm more of a starter. I start things — the catcher gives the sign and then I start things in motion. I've got a man on first — I want a ground ball to short or second — I wind up and throw — the batter swings — the ball is hit to short — he flips the ball to second — the second baseman throws it to first — suddenly all of these people are involved in the action. See, baseball's a religion. It's the essence of perfection. If you do everything perfect, you're going to get positive results all the time — except for the randomness of the law of averages. You break a guy's back and he still manages to dump a single over the shortstop's head. There's nothing you can do about it. The law of averages says that that's eventually going to happen. It's like a Cartesian coordinate — you're working on a plus-minus axis. Sometimes in your life you're going to do everything right and get negative results and sometimes you're going to do everything wrong and get positive results.

Q. How does all this fit in with the statement you once made that your ideal was to give up 27 hits in a game and pitch a shutout?

A. Oh, right. That is perfection. That's taxing everything to the maximum — having the maximum number of people on base — getting the maximum number of double-plays — and still achieving perfection — the shutout. It's got sort of a Zen quality to it. I've always said that everything between the lines is perfect. When you get outside of the lines — the personality conflicts, management problems — that's when the game breaks down. People always come back to baseball because it's relatively pure — between the lines — and it's slow-paced where you can think a thought while you're watching it, and carry on a conversation, and eat a meal. It moves at a nice, easy-flowing pace. That's contradictory to our fast-paced, football-like life of rushing to get to the other side to beat the other guy down and climb up on top.

Q. Relevant to your statement about baseball being a game that allows you time to think, you once said you liked it because you had time to think an entire thought during a pop-up. What's a thought you've had during a pop-up?

A. The ball's up there. You think, what if the ball's dropped, and then you look over at the scoreboard and then back at the ball and it's caught and the game's over.

Q. So, they're just baseball thoughts then?

A. Not always baseball. The ball's up there — you kind of judge it — has it got enough oomph to go against the wind? To hit the wall? And then you say, I wonder why they changed the wall. The thing looked so much better with the old panels. And then they sold it as paperweights. They cut it all up and sold it as paperweights.

Q. How about during long lay-offs? What do you do to occupy your mind?

A. I read a lot.

Q. During the games?

A. When I got buried. I read *Another Roadside Attraction,* started working on *Dune.*

Q. Will Bill Lee ever write a book?

A. Yeah. I'm going to read a few more authors first. I just can't sit down and write. I can't type, can't sit and talk into a microphone. I just can't sit down. I'm too antsy. All these publishers write and tell me "We've got this great angle," or

"Let's do it this way." Nothing ever really appeals to me, but it'll come. I realize there's a time and a place.*

Q. What's after baseball for you?

A. After baseball? I'll probably be playing baseball with one of my grandchildren or great-grandchildren the day before I die. I ain't worried about it. Death is after baseball.

*Bill Lee's book *The Wrong Stuff* was published by Viking Press in 1984.

Ray Fitzgerald

Lee Will Be Missed

Boston Globe, December 10, 1978

Miss him? You bet I'll miss him. I write about sports and the people in sports, for a living. I write about the way they play, certainly, but also about the things they say, and Bill Lee said plenty of writeable things.

I'd miss anybody who said of Bowie Kuhn: "Bowie's all right, but I know he put eight of us to sleep the last time he spoke to the team."

Who wouldn't miss somebody who fielded ground balls behind his back, who ran to Fenway Park from his home in Belmont on nights he was to pitch, who rehabilitated a torn shoulder by hanging from MBTA train straps, who called Billy Martin a neo-Nazi, who stood in parking lots and handed out leaflets, who suggested the powerless California Angels could take batting practice in the lobby of the Sheraton-Boston?

In the hot summer of '79 I'll long for the man who, when asked what he was thinking about during a 27-minute rain delay in the '75 World Series, replied: "I was thinking about asking Kissinger where all our wheat was going," and who described the Reds bench as "a drill team of Marines from Parris Island. Jack Webb should be their manager."

Oh, yeah, I'll miss him all right. But he went too far, didn't he? Bill Lee got so far out on the limb he reached the point of no return. He burned all his bridges.

For a long time, Lee got away with murder in a business that takes itself more seriously than General Motors, but in the end he committed athletic suicide, at least as far as staying around here was concerned.

The freedom of speech that made him delightfully different was his undoing. His utter disregard for the rules of the game shot him down.

He had always criticized management, which was his prerogative. For a long time management said: "Hey, you know Bill Lee. Don't get too worked up over what he says." But, finally, management talked back. And what management said was: "Here's a ticket to Montreal and be careful going through customs."

Eddie Kasko didn't like him, Darrell Johnson didn't like him, and Don Zimmer . . . Zimmer . . . well . . . we know about Don Zimmer.

Lee said what he thought, but often, especially in later years, was intolerant of the opinions of those at variance with him.

And if a man says what he believes, he also must be ready to pay the price for his principles, especially if the remarks concern those who pay his salary or control the way he makes a living.

He called Haywood Sullivan "a gutless sonofabitch." He called Don Zimmer a gerbil, which the dictionary defines as "any of numerous old world burrowing desert rodents that have long hind legs well adapted for leaping."

Okay. If I walked into the sports editor's office and called him a gerbil, chances are he would not laugh and say: "Hey, that's just good old Ray Fitz's way." Un-uh, especially if my sports editor was as old school as Don Zimmer.

And if I walked into the publisher's den and suggested he was a gutless s.o.b., he might laugh, but it would be as he handed me a broom and a pink slip, not necessarily in that order.

Perhaps if I were Ernest Hemingway or Red Smith, other arrangements could be made, a compromise could be found. And if Bill Lee had been Sandy Koufax or Warren Spahn in their prime, a way out might have been discovered.

But I'm not and he's not.

For several seasons, Bill Lee had his cake and ate it, too. He refused to play the game off the field but still was able to play on the diamond.

He came out of the doghouse and into the guest room more often than my pet Schnauzer. He walked the tightrope of athletic irreverence like a champion.

Yet all the time he was operating on a death wish, and this week the guillotine fell.

Nobody should have been surprised, though to judge from the phone calls to *The Globe* and to the talk shows his fans never thought it would happen. Or if it did the Red Sox should have received the entire Expos outfield and a couple of starting pitchers for him, instead of a lifetime .230-hitting utility infielder.

But the Red Sox had said in September that Lee would not be with them next season. They had dug a "we'll-have-to-take-what-you-want-to-give-us" hole.

Neither Lee nor Zimmer could backtrack. Lee had walked out on the team in the Bernie Carbo stickiness. Zimmer had buried him in the bullpen. Too much had been done. Too much had been said.

Asking either the pitcher or the manager to change would have been asking for the sun to rise each morning out of Park Street station.

Nobody wins this argument. The pitcher-hungry Red Sox are without a lefty who might still have helped them. Lee is gone from a baseball-mad area that cared deeply about him, one way or the other.

Saying the Red Sox could or should have held onto Bill Lee is like saying you could stop the 20th Century Limited with a toothpick.

His departure for a nonentity was a sure thing, and perhaps the best thing for both sides.

But, yeah, I'll miss him. Miss him a lot.

Peter Gammons

Yaz: To the End,
True to Himself

Boston Globe, October 3, 1983

There were hundreds, maybe thousands still out on Yawkey Way when Yaz came out of his final press conference in the dining room atop Fenway Park. He was signing autographs for some security guards and ballpark workers who were waiting for him on the roof when he heard the "We Want Yaz" roar from the street and looked down.

He stepped to the edge of the roof and waved out to them with another Papal gesture in his uniform pants, team under-shirt and shower clogs, then turned to Red Sox public rela-tions director George Sullivan and suggested that he'd like to go down into the street, and 10 minutes later, there were women and children and red-eyed truck drivers in a line that stretched down around the corner of Van Ness Street.

The people came in through an entrance, two-by-two, and he signed one program and poster after another for 40 minutes until there was no more line. When he had finished that, he came back into the park and signed autographs for people who get paid by the hour to work in the ballpark. It was 6:22 P.M. and dusk when he'd finished signing whatever they had for him to sign, then he stood atop the Red Sox dugout, pulled the cork out of a bottle of champagne, raised it, turned to survey Fenway and toasted them.

An hour later, as he came out to the parking lot to go to a party that Bob Woolf had for him at the Marriott, the hundreds still out on Van Ness Street chanted "Yaz, Yaz, Yaz," and he signed a few more programs, shook a few more hands, climbed into the car and pulled out around the corner.

As the car turned onto Ipswich Street, he was former Red Sox player Carl Yastrzemski. He was history — .285 average, 3,419 hits, Hall of Fame history. He had driven into that parking lot for the first time with a sixth-place team, being asked to replace Ted Williams, and he left with a sixth-place team under a cloud of the Updike good-bye of Williams.

And he had outdone Ted, he had outdone anyone who ever wore the uniform or possibly ever played in any sport in this city. No one really cared that, in his last at-bat, he threw himself at a Dan Spillner pitch in his eyes and popped up to someone named Jack Perconte, or that in his good-bye he had grounded to second, singled to left, walked and popped up that final 3-and-0 pitch, or that his last home run in a Red Sox uniform came Sept. 12 off Jim Palmer and was erased when rain wiped out the game in the third inning. Yaz didn't have to do something worthy of the ABC Network News. He was never Ted, only Yaz, never celluloid, only calloused flesh. On the day Hub Fans Bid Yaz Adieu, he didn't have to hit a Jack Fisher or Dan Spillner pitch into the bleachers. Playing left field and holding Toby Harrah to a single on a ball off The Wall — His Wall — was exactly what he should have done.

He had outdone Ted or anyone else because in the last two days of a 23-year career Yaz had thrown his arms and his emotion to the people. He passionately explained that he understood what makes the Olde Towne Team what it is as if he'd worked at the mill on the Nashua River and paid his way in. He said that it isn't the stars — only two baseball teams have gone longer without a championship — or the General or Limited Partners or titled executives that made the Red Sox the Red Sox.

New Englanders. "As I stepped out of the box that last time at-bat," he explained, "I tried to look around at every sign and every face to say 'thank you' to the people of New England who make this the greatest place to play baseball in the world."

He didn't ride around the park in a limousine. He ran around the park to touch the fans "who made this all possible" on Saturday, and long after he'd been replaced by Chico Walker in left field in the eighth inning yesterday as Ted had been replaced by Carroll Hardy 23 years before, he came out after the game in his jacket and did it again. "The people at the park today weren't the same people that were here yesterday," he said. Because so many things he couldn't control happened — Tony Conigliaro, Jim Lonborg and Jose Santiago being lost within 10 months around The Impossible Dream, then the Messersmith Decision coming one game after The Sixth Game of the 1975 World Series — he could never give New England what he wanted to give them, so he did the next-best thing.

He touched and signed and repeatedly broke down and cried, explaining to every kid in Bellows Falls and Otisfield and Jewett City that what made all those records so great was to have done them for the team that they have made what it is. To the media, for whom he brought in bottles of champagne and toasted them for their fairness, and in penultimate taste remembered those who'd passed away like Harold Kaese and Ray Fitzgerald and Fred Ciampa and Bill Liston and George Bankert and Larry Claflin. He remembered the times he could have left and made the big money. Like in October 1976. As a 10/5 man, he could refuse to go in the expansion draft, but both Toronto and Seattle called him and told him he could sign for "any contract I wanted," and that they could deal him to the two New York teams; the Blue Jays had a deal worked out that would have gotten them a kid pitcher named Ron Guidry.

"I called Woolf and told him to go to Toronto to talk," Yaz recalled, "but I thought about it, remembered that I'd given Mr. Yawkey my word that I wouldn't leave and told Woolf to forget it." In 1979, he could have made big bucks from

George Steinbrenner, and in 1981 both Steinbrenner and Ted Turner had let it be known to him that they'd pay him "three times what I could make here. But I didn't want to leave. I liked it here. I liked the Red Sox. And what they are."

The pregame ceremony was emotional, and simple. He walked out to the mike between the first-base coaching box and the dugout, then had to circle away to fight the tears. When he came back he said "I saw the sign that read 'Say It Ain't So, Yaz,' and I wish it weren't. This is the last day of my career as a player, and I want to thank all of you for being here with me today. It has been a great privilege to wear the Red Sox uniform the past 23 years, and to have played in Fenway in front of you great fans. I'll miss you, and I'll never forget you."

He lifted his cap and turned, waving to the fans, as he would do each at-bat. The park swelled when he reached out and tapped a Bud Anderson fastball into left in the third inning, and when it came to the bottom of the seventh and two out and Wade Boggs on first and everyone from Eastport to Block Island knew it was Yaz' adieu, they'd have loved a home run. They stood again. Yaz stepped out again, and he swallowed hard to fight back the tears.

Spillner and all the Indians pitchers understood the moment and the ground rules. "We were in the bar with the umpires Friday night and Rich Garcia told us, 'Look fellows, if he doesn't swing, it's a ball,'" said Indians pitcher Lary Sorensen. "I could see Spillner was trying to aim the ball, it was coming in at 80 miles an hour," said Yaz, but home plate umpire Vic Voltaggio called them balls until it was 3-and-0 and Spillner "aimed" a pitch over the plate but up around the bill of Yaz' cap.

"I was trying to jerk it out," Yaz admitted and he popped up to end the inning. He returned to left field, then, as Yastrzemski and Ralph Houk had planned earlier, Walker ran out to take his place, and Yaz came in, shaking hands with his teammates, the umpires and the Indians as he came across the infield. He stopped at the dugout, turned back to the first-base coach's box, turned 360 degrees as he waved again, then started his dash to the dugout unbuttoning his uniform ("I wanted to let them know that was really it"). He stopped to hand his cap to 8-year-old Brian Roberts of Needham, "because I wanted to give it to a kid and if I threw it into the stands it would have been havoc."

He'd done what he had to do. Carl Yastrzemski won't be remembered for a specific hit; the closest would be the ninth-inning homer off Mike Marshall in Detroit in September 1967, and that game was won on an eventual Dalton Jones homer. Even he listed his greatest memories as his diving stop off Reggie Jackson in the third game of the '75 playoffs, the throw that cut down Bob Allison on Oct. 1, 1967, and the catch off Tom Tresh that kept alive Billy Rohr's no-hit bid that was lost in the ninth, but symbolized New England's leap out of the Dark Ages. "I wanted to make a diving catch out there," he said. "And I wish the ground had been more solid. . . ."

In the second inning, in his first time in left field since he cracked his ribs on Aug. 30, 1980, hitting The Wall catching a Jim Essian line drive, he charged an Essian single with Alan Bannister rounding third. "I really wanted to throw him out," said Yaz, "but my foot gave out. I wanted to hold onto the ball, pump fake and get Essian going for second, but the ball slipped out of my hand." And rolled in.

He got no fly balls, per se, but in the seventh inning Harrah, who'd reached third in the previous inning, lined a ball off The Wall. Yaz didn't play it quite the way he used to, but he stretched for the carom, whirled and fired in toward second. Harrah stopped 30 feet past the first-base bag, turned, and went back.

The 33,491 people in Fenway stood and roared. They once might have booed him so badly that he had to wear cotton in his ears to left field, but after 23 years they understood what made Yaz Yaz, and Yaz turned back to them and, fighting back the tears, told them that he understood what makes The Townies The Townies. He, who so long played stoically, was in the end as emotional as the emotional fans he once saw give Garry Hancock a standing ovation as he approached the plate for his first major league at-bat. "You know what was great?" he beamed afterward. "The standing ovation for Jim Rice. Give Red Sox fans something, and they'll give it back to you many times over."

Hours afterward, he admitted that he felt "super, the best I've felt in a long, long while. I feel 10 years younger than I did 15 minutes ago."

For the two-day Easter celebration was over, and Yaz was a former Red Sox player. He knew he had expressed what he wanted to express, and because he'd even cared enough to try to do so, he turned off Van Ness Street onto Ipswich out of the sight of the hundreds that stood in the dark chanting "Yaz, Yaz, Yaz," the most popular man who ever wore the uniform of The Olde Towne Team.

George F. Will

The Pursuit of Excellence

Boston Globe, October 6, 1986

Recently, in the Speaker's Dining Room in the US Capitol, a balding, hawk-nosed Oklahoma cattleman rose from the luncheon table and addressed his host, Tip O'Neill. The man who rose was Warren Spahn, the winningest lefthander in the history of baseball. Spahn was one of a group of former All-Stars who were to play in an old-timers' game in Washington. Spahn said, "Mr. Speaker, baseball is a game of failure. Even the best batters fail about 65 percent of the time. The two Hall of Fame pitchers here today (Spahn, 363 wins, 245 losses; Bob Gibson, 251 wins, 174 losses) lost more games than a team plays in a full season. I just hope you fellows in Congress have more success than baseball players have."

The fellows in Congress don't, and they know it. There are no .400 hitters in Washington. But there always have been lots of fans. (In October 1973, Potter Stewart, associate justice of the Supreme Court and avid Cincinnati Reds fan, was scheduled to hear oral arguments at the time of the Reds–Mets playoff game. So he asked his clerks to pass him batter-to-batter bulletins. One read, "Kranepool flies to right. Agnew resigns.") I am not a Red Sox fan, but I am a WBO — A Wade Boggs Obsessive.

The first — the very first — thing I look at in the morning newspaper is the Red Sox box score. I well remember the moment when my obsession was born. It was a sparkling

Sunday dawn last summer. I was on the back veranda putting off the evil moment when I would have to turn my mind to the task of ginning up questions with which to torment the victims who would be appearing that morning on "This Week With David Brinkley." I was attending to weightier matters — the survey of baseball arcana compiled each Sunday by Richard Justice (then of the *Baltimore Sun,* now of the *Washington Post*). One item was labeled, enchantingly: "The Latest Incredible Wade Boggs Statistic."

I do not remember that particular incredibilium. It was some progress report on the 1985 season, in which Boggs popped up only three times in 653 at-bats, only once in fair territory; a season in which 125 of his 240 hits came with two strikes; a season in which he swung and missed at just one first pitch. Since that Sunday morning I have known the constant pleasure of savoring his craftsmanship.

It has been said that the problem with many modern athletes is that they take themselves seriously and their sport lightly. Not Boggs. He is not a conspicuously gifted natural athlete, but by dint of painstaking discipline, he has made himself baseball's best hitter. Baseball is indeed a game of inches, and the most important 17 inches are the width of the five-sided slab of rubber that is home plate. In that product, Boggs is The Boss.

For the fan, baseball is the game that most rewards attention to detail. For the player, attention to detail is the difference between mere adequacy and excellence. Boggs is unexcelled at the analytic approach to hitting, breaking the problem down into small component parts and mastering them, one at a time.

Ours is an age preoccupied, sometimes in melancholy or pathetic ways, with "self-improvement" schemes and nostrums. There is a glut of books that presume to teach readers how to become better executives (or lovers, or whatever) in a minute or so, or how to achieve thin thighs in 30 days. If you want to study the art of self-improvement, you can load up with a shelf full of such books. Or you can study Boggs.

America has been called the only nation consciously founded on a good idea. The idea has been given many and elaborate explanations, but the most concise and familiar formulation is: the pursuit of happiness. For a fortunate few people, happiness is the pursuit of excellence in vocation. The vocation can be a profession of a craft, elite or common, poetry or carpentry. The important thing is an ideal of excellence against which to measure achievement.

Boggs' career is a case study of the pursuit of happiness through excellence in a vocation. Fortunate people have a talent for happiness. Possession of a talent can help a person toward happiness. As Aristotle said, happiness is not a condition that is produced or stands on its own; rather, it is a frame of mind that accompanies an activity. Boggs is a man happy in his work.

The connection between character and achievement is one of the fundamental fascinations of sport. Some say that sport builds character. Others say that sport reveals character by defeating those who lack it. Boggs reveals his character in the everyday of baseball, by failing fewer times than anyone now playing.

THE PLAY

Think of it: any objective list of the five greatest baseball games played in the television era would probably include three games featuring the Red Sox (the sixth game of the '75 Series, the '78 playoff game, and the fifth game of the '86 league championship series). A hundred years from now when the results of the 1978 World Series will be reduced to a mere line item in a baseball annual, there'll be more than a few utterly timeless pieces on the Sox–Yanks playoff — two of the best to be found in the pages that follow, authored by Thomas Boswell and Roger Angell respectively. The estimable Mr. Angell also weighs in with his artful recollections of the '75 series, and there's a reprise of Mr. Boswell's joyful style in his recounting the parade of ironies in the Red Sox–Angels game of '86. Ward Just enlists the aid of Capt. Carl Maria von Clausewitz in assessing the '86 campaign. And yours truly adds a fictional look at the '75 Series (although given the incredible twists and turns of that October epic, fiction may seem a bit redundant). We begin, however, with a look back at the pretelevision era when the Sox were just beginning to fashion their now legendary close but no cigar image. Dan Shaughnessy and David Halberstam remind us that the '40s were no less excruciating for Sox fans than the '70s or the '80s. Mr. Shaughnessy reopens wounds with a glimpse back at the 1946 World Series, and Mr. Halberstam rubs in a little salt with his report from the summer of '49.

Dan Shaughnessy

The 1946 World Series

The Curse of the Bambino, 1990

Even to this day, some people look at me like I'm a piece
of shit.
— Johnny Pesky

John M. Paveskovich was born in Portland, Oregon, on
September 27, 1919, the same day Babe Ruth played his last
game in a Red Sox uniform. He married Ruth Hickey on
January 10, 1945. *Ruth Pesky.* Is it any surprise that John
Paveskovich was the first vivid victim of the Curse of the
Bambino?

The 1946 Red Sox were unstoppable. For once, the April
optimists in the press box were right. Williams, Pesky, Bobby
Doerr, Dominic DiMaggio, Tex Hughson, Mickey Harris, Joe
Dobson, and Hal Waner came back from the war, and first
baseman Rudy York was acquired in a winter trade with the
Tigers. Cronin had four top starters in Harris, Boo Ferriss
(twenty-five-game winner), Dobson, and Hughson . . . and
the Red Sox won their first pennant since 1918, and their last
until 1967.

This was a wire-to-wire job. The 1946 Sox were in first
place for all but two days of the season, ripped off fifteen
straight (still a franchise best) in April and May, broke to a
21–4 start, won forty of their first fifty, and went 60–17 at
Fenway. They shredded the competition. President Harry

Truman threw out the first ball when Boston opened at
Washington in April, and Williams's homer led the Sox to a 6–
3 victory. The All-Star game was at Fenway, and Williams hit
two homers (including one off Rip Sewell's famous eephus
pitch) and two singles in a 12–0 rout of the National League.
The mighty Red Sox had eight players on the American
League All-Star team. York hit eighteen home runs in August,
while Williams was on his way to the MVP (.342, 38, 123)
despite the introduction of a daring defensive alignment by
Cleveland player/manager Lou Boudreau. Pesky slapped 208
hits, Dominic DiMaggio hit .316, and Williams and Doerr
combined to drive home 239 runs. Yawkey's millions were
finally paying off (it's estimated that he poured $4 million into
the team between 1933 and 1946), and there was little doubt
that Boston had the best baseball team on the planet. It had
been twenty-eight years since Boston's AL entry won its last
pennant, and Sox fans already were answering to the sur-
name "long-suffering." The Red Sox won the flag by twelve
games, clinching in Cleveland September 13, a few hours
after Hughson beat the Indians, 1–0, on an inside-the-park
homer by Williams. The Yankees defeated Detroit later in the
day and the Sox were champions of the American League for
the first time since Frazee sold Ruth to the Yankees. New
York finished third, seventeen games behind Boston.

Thomas A. Yawkey was with his boys at the Statler Hotel
in Cleveland when the Sox learned of their official pennant-
clinching. Yawkey heaped all the credit on Cronin's shoulders.
Cronin got into a swearing contest with Huck Finnegan of the
Boston American, and Yawkey almost came to blows with
Duke Lake of the same paper. Everything was in place.

Sox fans, revived by the end of the drought, pushed the
turnstile count to a record 1,416,944, and the Townies drew
1,250,000 on the road. World Series tickets were almost
impossible to get.

How could any of these people have known that this would
be it? With Williams and DiMaggio and Doerr and Pesky and
young Boo Ferriss and Tex Hughson, all bankrolled by

Yawkey's millions, Sox fans figured this would be the first of many World Series delivered by the Splendid Splinter and friends. There was no hint, no signal that the 1946 Series would one day represent nothing more than a disappointing aberration in a fifty-year, post-Ruth period of frustration.

In 1946, there were still plenty of breathing, working New Englanders who remembered the 1918 World Champs. The Red Sox had never lost a World Series, and these 1946 fence-busters were 20–7 favorites over the St. Louis Cardinals.

After waiting twenty-eight years to get back into the Fall Classic, the Sox had to wait a few extra days to find out who they'd be playing. The Cardinals and Dodgers tied for first and had a best-of-three playoff for the right to face Boston. Cronin worried about this delay. His stardust club had grown stale in September, losing six straight before clinching in Cleveland. Now the start of the Series was delayed four days while the Cardinals and Dodgers dueled. Cronin decided that the only way his group could regain its sharpness was to play some more hardball, so a team of American League All-Stars was assembled for a three-game series with the Red Sox. In the fifth inning of the first superfluous game, diminutive Senator lefty Mickey Haefner threw a pitch that hit Williams on the right elbow.

Williams came out of the game and skipped the rest of the senseless series. There are those who believe the bruise contributed to his subsequent silent World Series. The Kid's morale was further dented when a big-splash trade rumor claimed he would be shipped to Detroit after the Fall Classic.

The Cardinals beat the Dodgers, then went to work on a plan to stop Boston's MVP. St. Louis manager Eddie Dyer devised his own Williams shift and moved his third baseman to the first-base side of second while shifting shortstop Marty Marion slightly to the right of his normal position.

The first two games were in St. Louis, and the Red Sox won the opener, 3–2, then dropped Game 2, 3–0, when 160-pound lefty Harry Brecheen blanked them on four hits. Williams had only one single in the two games.

The Series finally came to Boston on October 9, and the inimitable Ferriss shut out St. Louis, 4–0, allowing only six hits. Williams was 1–3 and his hit came when he grudgingly foiled Dyer's strategy with a bunt single to the third-base side. Fans cheered as if Williams had homered, and at least one Boston paper ran a headline that screamed "Williams Bunts."

The Cardinals routed Hughson in Game 4 and evened the Series with a twenty-hit, 12–3, victory. A catcher named Joe Garagiola had four hits for the Cardinals while Williams went 1–3 again, managing nothing more than a single. The favored Red Sox began to question themselves slightly, but felt much better when Dobson beat the Cardinals, 6–3, in Game 5. The Red Sox were going back to St. Louis and planned on bringing the World Championship home for the first time since 1918. Cardinals players took the train home while the Sox went out in style, flying west so they could get an extra night's sleep at the Chase Hotel.

Brecheen beat the Red Sox again in Game 6, 4–1, forcing a seventh and deciding game. One day before Game 7, the *Boston Globe* ran a page-one cartoon by Gene Mack. The sketch showed a Red Sox player bouncing out of the dugout to do battle — while the ghosts of past Sox series entries (1903, 1912, 1915, 1916, and 1918) exhorted him to victory with this war cry: "Don't forget, Boy, we've never lost one." The headline read: "Don't Let Us Down," right below "Sox favored 10 to 7."

This cartoon no doubt today would cause gales of laughter among Boston baby boomers and their progeny, but in 1946 the Red Sox still were expected to win the Big One. These Red Sox were the heirs of that first generation of world champions and there was no reason to expect anything would be different this time around. The public perception was that the Sox were unbeatable. Fortified by Messrs. Williams, Doerr, Pesky, DiMaggio, and a raft of young arms, the Yawkey Red Sox appeared to be on the threshold of a decade of dominance. Game 7 of the 1946 Series was to be the first of many triumphs as the Red Sox returned to their rightful place atop the American League.

All of the above was shattered by the ghastly events of Game 7, and since this day the legacy of the Red Sox has been that of the underachieving loser. The Red Sox are usually competitive, sometimes good enough to make it to the postseason, but in the end they will always let you down. Tuesday, October 15, 1946, was the turning point. This was the first time the Red Sox took their fans to the edge, then failed.

Cronin had his ace, Ferriss, ready for the finale and was applauded for manipulating his rotation so adroitly. Meanwhile, Dyer had to go with Murray Dickson, who'd been beaten by Rudy York's homer in Game 3.

Williams went out on a couple of long blasts in the first and fourth. Meanwhile, the Cardinals rocked Ferriss and took a 3–1 lead in the fifth. The Red Sox stayed silent until the eighth, when DiMaggio doubled two runs home against Brecheen, who was pitching in relief. In the excitement of watching the Red Sox tie the game on DiMaggio's clutch hit, few noticed the Little Professor limping into second base. He'd suffered a charley horse and could not continue. Backup Leon Culberson went in to run for DiMaggio and would play center in the bottom of the eighth. Take note.

"Evidently when he turned the base, he hurt it," said Pesky. "It was very noticeable. In those days they didn't drag the infield in the middle innings, which had an effect. When that happened, Dom had to come out of the game. Culberson replaced him. He could play a little infield, a little outfield. He was a pretty good player. A good hitter. I think that year he hit .310. He was all right."

With Culberson on second and two out, Williams had one last chance to do something, but hit a weak pop-up to second baseman Red Schoendienst. Bob Klinger came in to pitch the bottom of the eighth.

Enos Slaughter led off with a single and was still standing on first after outs by Whitey Kurowski and Del Rice. Harry

"The Hat" Walker came up and hit a sinking shot to left center, and Culberson gave chase. Shortstop Pesky went out for the relay, but did not notice that Slaughter hadn't stopped running. Third-base coach Mike Gonzalez gave Slaughter no sign. Pesky took the relay throw, turned to his left and hesitated, ever so slightly (grainy film footage is fairly conclusive on this), before making a desperate heave home to get the streaking Slaughter. It's been said and written that Pesky turned toward second when he got Culberson's throw, but the footage doesn't show this and Pesky denies it.

It is interesting to note that in official box scores and newspaper accounts of this play, Walker was credited with a double. Oral history has been more convenient and less kind, and for forty-four years Pesky and the Red Sox have heard that Slaughter scored from first on a single. He didn't. He scored from first on a double. It's a little like "Play it again, Sam," a phrase that Humphrey Bogart certainly did not utter in *Casablanca*. Bogey might as well have said it because that's the way it's been passed down, just as Slaughter might as well have scored from first on a single because Walker's hit has shrunk by one base in millions of retellings.

Forty-two years after the fact, Pesky remembered it this way.

> Slaughter was on first. He was stealing. Harry Walker was the hitter. Bobby [Doerr] gave all the signs and I was covering. Klinger was pitching and he didn't really hold him. He got a helluva jump. Slaughter could run. He was a good runner. I went to the bag, and when I got to the bag the ball was hit. Now I got to get out into left field. I wasn't really, really deep. There's a film of it and I've watched that a hundred times and I thought I was out deeper than I actually was after watching it. But the throw I got was a lob. No one dreamed that Slaughter would try to score. I'm out in short left center field. It was late in the afternoon and Christ, when I picked him up he was about twenty feet from home plate. I'd have needed a rifle to get him. You look over your left shoulder. You're not going to turn this way [turns right]. A lot of people thought I went this way and said that I dropped my hands and went "Oh, gosh." I was

just getting ready to throw the ball. I've got the ball like this and I'm looking. I was just going to flip the ball into the infield so the ball wouldn't be mishandled. And he just kept on going. I couldn't hear anything. Everybody was screaming and hollering.

The funny thing about that. I got accused that I hesitated and I watched the movies and I didn't think that I did. That Arch McDonald, who was announcing, said that I held on to the ball too long. I felt terrible about it because really and truly I should have got the ball quicker and he'd have never have scored. But he just kept on going and he got a helluva jump and Culberson had to go for the ball in left center and I'm sure he felt the same way I did.

Clif Keane, of the *Globe,* said, "They blame Pesky. I don't blame Pesky. I saw the play. The guy threw the ball and Pesky got the ball up here and brought it down. And then he went back up. Some people claimed that Doerr never yelled 'home.' You had to sense, I think, that Slaughter was gonna run. Johnny brought the ball down and he brought it back up and didn't have anything on it."

There was one final frustration for the Red Sox. York and Doerr led off the ninth with singles, and with one out the Sox had runners on first and third. Catcher Roy Partee went out on a foul pop to Stan Musial. Pinch hitter Tom McBride hit a tough-play grounder to Schoendienst, who flipped to short-stop Marty Marion at second. The throw beat a sliding Pinky Higgins by the narrowest of margins, and the Red Sox had lost a World Series for the first time in franchise history.

In the loser's clubhouse, Williams was as silent as his bat had been. In the heat of the moment Pesky chose to shoulder all the blame. "I'm the goat. It's my fault. I'm to blame. I had the ball in my hand. I hesitated and gave Slaughter six steps. . . . I couldn't hear anybody. There was too much yelling. It looked like an ordinary single."

Teammates put a stop to the self-flagellation. Someone said, "Sit down, Johnny."

Legally, he was still John M. Paveskovich. His father immigrated from Yugoslavia after the turn of the century, and young Johnny was one of six children. His parents could neither read, nor write, but his father found work in an Oregon sawmill. Oregon kids, not accustomed to Yugoslavian names, didn't bother saying Paveskovich, and John M. Paveskovich became Johnny Pesky on all but the most official documents. Even his teachers called him Pesky.

His father discouraged baseball and told him, "If you play ball, you'll be a bum. All your life, you'll be a bum." The Tigers, Indians, Yankees, Browns, and Cardinals were interested in young Johnny, but Mr. and Mrs. Paveskovich liked the Red Sox scout Ernie Johnson, and Johnny signed up with Boston. He signed in 1939, just as Williams was making a big splash in the majors. Pesky was in the big leagues three years later and cracked 205 hits at the age of twenty-one when he replaced Cronin at short. After his rookie season, he went off to war with Williams, DiMaggio, and the rest. He broke the 200-hit barrier again in 1946 and was a table-setter for Williams throughout the golden days of the late forties.

Pesky was just another Series role player struggling to contribute when the Curse of the Bambino tapped him on the throwing shoulder. In subsequent years he moved to third base to accommodate slugging shortstop Vern Stephen and became more than adequate at the hot corner. He was the first Red Sox player to have three straight 200-hit seasons (Williams never did it, he walked too often) and hit .307 in ten seasons with the Sox. Since retiring as a player he's served the BoSox in every department except concessions and ground crew. He's been a coach, a radio and television broadcaster, an advertising salesman, and managed the team in 1963. He was named assistant general manager after the 1984 season but continued to help on the field, swatting fungoes and offering advice to young players seeking help. Pesky has served the Red Sox faithfully and loyally for well over forty years and is one of the great gentlemen of the game. Perhaps he was chosen to carry the weight because he was one of the few strong enough to survive.

Generations of fans have blamed Pesky for hestitating, for holding the ball.

"I don't think I did," Pesky said a lifetime [forty-three years] later. "I was just turning to see it all in one motion because anytime you're a cutoff man you've got to get rid of the ball.

"At first I was a little sensitive to it. I didn't like the insinuations. People made me feel like I was insignificant and that I did it on purpose, which is far from the truth because, Christ, no one ever wanted to win a ball game more than I did, or any of us for that matter. After a few years, you know, you get used to the idea. And I said well, if people wanna blame ya they're gonna blame ya. And those that are sympathetic say, 'Gee, John, it's just one of those things that happened,' and I say, 'Yeah, but it happened in the World Series.'

"I used to get mad when I was asked about it. Now I just take it in stride. Time heals a lot of wounds. If a guy is honest about it and says, 'Well, Johnny, I think you did,' what am I gonna say? I can't change it. I respect opinion. If he wants to blame me, that's his right. I don't think I held on to the ball that long."

Doerr remembered it this way: "Higgins was at third and he might have a play and he can't leave his position. I might have a play at second base and I can't leave my position. There were thirty-three thousand people yelling. Everybody said, 'Well, why didn't you call out the play?' Well, I could have yelled my lungs out and he never would have heard me. It was just one of those split-second things. I say that if the ball had been right center and I had the play, the same thing probably would have happened to me. It was just one of those unfortunate things and Johnny got more blame in that than he should have. He didn't hesitate all that much. It was just one of those daring things that Slaughter got away with. He would have been a bum if he got thrown out. . . . We just didn't play the kind of ball we were capable of playing."

Pesky said he never had nightmares about the play but continued to replay it in his head. He was forced to think about it when asked, but admitted there were times when he thought about it even when he was alone. "But not so much in the last fifteen years," he added.

That's a comfort. A guy *maybe* makes a tiny mistake in 1946 and by the time 1975 rolls around, he's just about stopped dwelling on it.

"That happened forty-three years ago. I'm an old bastard," the little big man said between cigar puffs. "There are so many guys that throw cold water on everything. It's a terrible way to be remembered and I wish I could have done something of importance that was involved in winning the ball game, like a base hit or a good play or whatever. Stealing a base. It just didn't happen in my case and I thought sure we'd be in four or five World Series."

There were no more World Series for Pesky, Doerr, Dominic DiMaggio, and the great Ted Williams.

Pesky still wears the horns, but the true goat of the 1946 World Series was the Splendid Splinter, Ted Williams. After the final out in 1946, Williams wept in the showers, gave his World Series check ($2,077.06) to clubhouse man Johnny Orlando, then got on a train from St. Louis and cried some more.

"He felt very bad," Pesky remembered. "He actually cried. He had his head down. They had a picture [an Associated Press photo that ran worldwide] that didn't show the tears, but I know he cried. He wanted to win so badly for Mr. Yawkey. He had a great love for that man."

It was an awful couple of weeks for Williams, starting with the bruise on the elbow in the senseless exhibition game. Against the Cardinals, he went 5–25, all singles, one bunt. He walked five times, struck out three times, and fouled out or flied out eleven times. He scored only two runs and knocked in one. In Game 7 he was twice stung by sensational catches — one by broken down Terry Moore and one by Walker.

Babe Ruth sounded like a man who knew something. When Ruth was asked about the 1946 Sox, the first Red Sox World Series team since his 1918 edition, the Bambino said, "Bobby Doerr and not Ted Williams is the number-one man of the

Red Sox in my book." Doerr had at least one hit in every Series game and batted .409, more than double Williams's .200.

"We had quite a spell between the time we clinched the pennant and the World Series," Doerr remembered in 1989. "I really wasn't hitting good going into the World Series and I was quite concerned about it. But just a day or two before I just felt real good. It just happened to be a lucky deal. I can't really explain it other than it was just one of those cycles or periods of time that I felt good. Brecheen wasn't tough to look at. We should have tried to take him more to the opposite field or through the middle. He had great command of mixing his speeds, a little scroogie, and I think that if we could have just gone the other way with him we would have done much better with Brecheen. He wasn't really that tough. He had good command of everything, but he was nice to walk up and hit at.

"We were flat for that Series. I have to say you have a letdown after you clinch the pennant, and we had too much time. And of course Ted, a lot of people didn't realize he'd get that virus once or twice a year and he had that little virus where he wasn't that sharp and then he got hit in the elbow. They said they knew how to pitch him and that they scouted him and all that. Well, you could scout him forever, but if you throw the ball over the plate, there was no way you were going to get him out. He didn't have that real good Series, but he wasn't up to par really and I never heard him say he had the virus. He never did alibi on that and of course I admire him for it."

"We just didn't hit that Series," remembered Ferriss, the Game 7 starter. "We had to wait for St. Louis and Brooklyn to play it off, and Williams got hit in the elbow. We didn't think he swung as good after that. He was in the whirlpool every morning with that thing. He never made anything to do with it, never used it as an excuse, but you know, he didn't hit in that Series. The really great ones can have a bad series in a short series and the Cardinals had a good ball club."

"I'll be damned if I know how they stopped Ted," Pesky said. "And the thing of it is, those Cardinals had a couple of rabble-rousers over there and Eddie Dyer told them, 'Don't say anything to Williams. Just leave him alone. Don't get him mad.'"

Clif Keane remembered, "Brecheen, of course, stopped Williams cold. I always felt, ever since that Series, that umpires would become pitcher's umpires during the World Series. Brecheen would throw inside and Williams would back away and during the season those were balls, but during the World Series they became strikes. Umpires work better with pitchers during the World Series."

Williams still wouldn't use the elbow alibi in 1989 when he spoke of the Series. "I can't really say," he said. "I've never made that excuse and I'm not really sure whether it hurt me that much or it didn't. I'm not sure at all that that was the reason I didn't hit. Hell, they didn't pitch me any different. I got 1–9 against Brecheen in the World Series and the next year in Chicago I got up against him twice and hit two bullets to right field — doubles. Just hot and cold."

The train ride home was a twenty-five-hour funeral procession. Williams sat alone in his roomette and glanced at books on saltwater, trout, and fly fishing. Teammates tried to cheer up Pesky in the dining car and friendly scribes flashed stats that showed past Series flops by Joe Gordon, Billy Herman, Bill Dickey, and Red Rolfe. General Manager Eddie Collins, a veteran of nine World Series, said this was the toughest of them all.

There was a little action on the quiet procession. According to Keane, the Sox manager went after one of the writers.

"Maybe three hundred writers had voted on who would win the Series and two hundred ninety-eight voted for the Red Sox," said Keane. "Roger Birtwell and Huck Finnegan voted for the Cardinals in seven games and the Cardinals won in seven. We got on the train coming home after losing and Joe Cronin went after Finnegan with a bread knife at the table. Went after him with a knife. Believe me."

As the train got closer to Boston, there were some Red Sox fans gathered on platforms in western Massachusetts factory towns. There were three hundred loyalists waiting at the Huntington Avenue stop and another fifty at South Station. Bobby Doerr got off the train and packed his car for the long drive to Oregon. Ruth Pesky came in from Lynn to greet her husband, John. Williams was whisked away by a policeman friend. Mayor James Michael Curley had planned a win-or-lose reception for Boston's team, but it was called off. Losers didn't ride in floats in the forties.

"It was a great letdown," said Doerr. "Every time I see the Super Bowl or a World Series now I always have a feeling of what the losing part of the thing is, and I always felt that was the one thing I look back on. You can't do anything about it. Looking back, that's the one thing that you miss."

"It was a good ball club, but I thought our '48, '49, and '50 clubs were better," said Pesky. "You can't win without pitching. We had great power, and the guys who didn't hit for power were good players. That was a series that we should have won, but it didn't work out. Brecheen was a guy like [Mike] Boddicker, but he was left-handed. The only left-handed hitters in our lineup in those years were Ted and myself."

In one final, telling bit of housekeeping, Thomas A. Yawkey scheduled appointments with his fallen heroes, and a parade of players filed through the owner's chambers where they were presented with salary raises for 1947. "I did not give the boys bonuses," said Yawkey. "It was just a salary increase. Judge Landis made a rule against giving bonuses for winning the pennant. I didn't give them all the same sized check. After all, a fellow who sat on the bench all year hardly deserved as much as one who won twenty-five games. But they all got something."

Ernest Lawrence Thayer's "Casey at the Bat" was quoted on the front page of the *Globe* the day after the stunning loss. It would not be the first time Boston would take on the joyless characteristics of Mudville, USA.

In 1947, John M. Paveskovich walked into a Massachusetts probate court, plunked down $75, and officially changed his name to Pesky. He might just as well have changed his name to Denny Galehouse, Joe McCarthy, Luis Aparicio, Jim Burton, Mike Torrez, or Bill Buckner. He was immortal, a man with no need for a name. Fair or unfair, he was, is, and forever will be the man who held the ball. He still stands in shallow left-center, holding the ball and waiting . . . waiting for the Game 7 World Series victory that never comes.

David Halberstam

From *Summer of '49*

While the Red Sox played with the Senators, the Yankees took on the Athletics, winning two of three. The Red Sox came into the Stadium with a one-game lead, with two games left to play. All they had to do was to win one of two against the Yankees. Had the Red Sox won the Scarborough game, they would have had a virtual lock on the pennant, a two-game lead. The Yankees would have been forced to win both games, and then there would have been a one-game play-off — meaning the Yankees would have had to win three in a row. Most of the Yankee players had waited in the Yankee locker room to listen to Mel Allen's re-creation of that key Boston–Washington game, and the tension had been enormous. Jerry Coleman was too nervous to listen with the others, so he had gone to his apartment a few blocks away on Gerard Avenue. The moment the game was over, his friend Charlie Silvera called him. "Did you hear?" Silvera asked. "Yes," Coleman said. "We're still alive, Jerry," Silvera said.

Now the door was open just a little again. The Yankee veterans were confident that they would win. Fred Sanford, new to the team, new to the idea of winning, asked a few of his teammates whether, if the Yankees won the pennant, they got any money even if they lost in the World Series. The moment the words were out of his mouth, he realized he had made a terrible mistake. No one said anything to him, but the looks he got were very cold. These were the Yankees, he realized, and if you were a Yankee you never thought about losing, and you certainly did not talk about it. You expected to win and you won.

The Boston writers coming to the Stadium early before the next-to-last game found out the same thing. Joe Cashman of the *Record* stopped to talk to Tommy Henrich. "Tommy, how do you feel — it must be hard to be behind after leading for most of the season?" What struck Cashman was how confident Henrich was. "Well, Joe," he said, "we would have liked to have wrapped it up earlier, and maybe we should have, but we're glad to be in this situation," Henrich said. "We don't have to depend on anyone winning it for us — we can do it ourselves. All we have to do is win two games. That's fair enough." These guys, Cashman thought, have played in so many games like this that they really do have an advantage.

Tom Yawkey was equally confident. Wives had not accompanied the Boston players to New York, but Yawkey sent out word that every wife was to have her things packed. The moment the Red Sox clinched the pennant, a special train would leave for New York for the great celebration.

Ted Williams, though, thought the Yankees had the advantage. It was their ball park, and it tilted away from most of the Red Sox lineup. The Yankee pitchers were not going to give him, the one left-handed power hitter, anything good to hit. He was right. The Yankees were convinced that they could handle Junior Stephens in the Stadium. His Fenway homers would become easy outs. But not so with Williams. Years later Allie Reynolds was at an All-Star Game when he suddenly felt a pair of immensely powerful arms wrap around him. He thought he was in a vise. "When are you going to give me a decent pitch to hit, you Indian SOB?" the voice belonging to the arms of Ted Williams asked. "Not as long as Junior's hitting behind you," laughed Reynolds. Williams normally liked to hit in the Stadium, but he hated it near the end of the season when the shadows were long. That made hitting much tougher. He thought the Yankee management should turn the lights on during the day games at this time of the year, but he knew why they didn't — it was an advantage to the Yankee pitchers, and New York's strength was its pitchers, not its hitters. The Yankee hitters were accustomed to the shadows. But Williams, purist that he was, thought that anything that diminished a hitter's ability subtracted from the game.

It was a sports promoter's dream: the two great rivals playing two games at the very end of the season with the pennant in the balance. The pitching matchups were perfect — Reynolds against Parnell, and Raschi against Kinder. The great question was: Would DiMaggio be able to get back into the lineup? He had been sick with viral pneumonia for almost two weeks, during which time he had lost eighteen pounds. But he was determined to play. The first of those two games in the Stadium was, by chance, Joe DiMaggio Day. The Yankee star, drawn and emaciated, husbanding his energy, had been forced to stand in front of the huge crowd of 69,551 while receiving endless gifts. His mother had come east for the games (his father had died earlier in the year), and she was introduced to the crowd. She came on the field and, much to the amusement of the huge crowd, raced past Joe to greet Dominic in the Red Sox dugout — she had seen Joe the day before but had not yet seen Dom. Dominic came out of the Red Sox dugout to be a part of the ceremonies, and he could feel his brother leaning heavily on him. Dominic was wary of staying too long in Joe's spotlight, and he quietly asked his brother if he should leave. Joe quickly said, "No, don't go!" and Dominic understood that Joe needed him to lean on.

Parnell was sure it was going to be a great game; he thought Allie Reynolds a magnificent competitor. This was a great Yankee team, Parnell thought, far better than most people realized, with an exceptional blend of the old and the new: DiMaggio, Henrich, Berra, Bauer, and Woodling, and that great pitching staff; also a late-season pickup — Johnny Mize. No one should underrate a team that had Johnny Lindell and Johnny Mize on its bench. Maybe the 1927 Yankees had been as good, but Parnell was by no means sure.

When he got up that morning Allie Reynolds felt strong and ready; it was one of those glorious days when he felt he could throw a ball through a battleship. Then he went out to the mound and his control simply evaporated. It was, he later decided, probably a case of overpitching, of trying too hard. The game started as a disaster for the Yankees. The Red Sox scored one run in the first — Dom DiMaggio singled, Williams singled, Reynolds threw a wild pitch that moved DiMaggio to third. Then Junior Stephens lined to left and Dom DiMaggio scored.

In the Boston third Reynolds did himself in. It was clear to his infielders that he was unable to find his true rhythm. He got Dom DiMaggio out on a well-hit ball to right. But then he walked Pesky, Williams, and Stephens. Doerr sliced a ball just past Coleman, and Pesky scored. The Red Sox led 2–0 with the bases filled and only one out. Stengel immediately brought in Joe Page. It might be only the third inning, but there was no time to waste. If Stengel needed a relief pitcher the next day, he could always use Reynolds. But Page started disastrously. He walked Zarilla, forcing in a run. Then he walked Billy Goodman on four pitches. That made it 4–0. The Yankee bench was completely silent. Two runs walked in, and Birdie Tebbetts was at bat. On the bench, Gus Niarhos kept thinking to himself, The one hope we have with Page is his rising fastball. Probably no pitcher in the league, he thought, forced hitters to chase as many bad balls as Page. The ball left Page's hand looking like it was going to be in the zone, but it kept rising, and the hitter could not control himself. Now, with one out and the bases loaded, Niarhos sensed that Page, wild though he was, might work himself out of it. Tebbetts seemed to want to end the game right then and there. Birdie swung away, trying to kill the ball; he jumped on three pitches, all of them, Niarhos thought, well out of the strike zone. Then Page struck out Parnell, a good hitter, again with pitches outside the strike zone. Maybe now Joe will settle down, Niarhos thought. But Boston had a 4–0 lead.

That looked like a very big lead for a team as good as Boston. Some of the Yankees thought a critical moment had taken place in the third inning. In the bottom of the third, when Rizzuto came up, Tebbetts began to needle him. With Rizzuto, Tebbetts usually concentrated on his Italian origins, his size, and his hitting ability: "You goddamn little Dago, you know you can't hit the ball out of the infield. You know you should be out behind the Stadium playing in some kids' game," he would say. This time he went further. With Boston's big lead, he couldn't resist. Rizzuto fouled off a pitch, and while they were waiting to get a new ball, Tebbetts started in. "Hey Rizzuto," he said, "tomorrow at this time we'll be drinking champagne, and we'll pitch the Yale kid against you guys. Think you can hit a kid from Yale, Rizzuto?" He was referring to Frank Quinn, the bonus-baby pitcher out of Yale who had pitched a total of twenty-two innings and had never started a game. (Tebbetts denies saying this, but the memory of it and Rizzuto's reaction remain fresh with almost all the Yankees.)

Rizzuto was stunned and then angered. He grounded out, and on the way back to the dugout he hurled his bat. Then he kicked the water cooler. "Do you know what that goddamn Tebbetts just said," he shouted. "They're going to pitch the kid from Yale against us tomorrow!" Rizzuto was normally mild-mannered and slow to anger. No one on the team had ever seen him like this before. The Yankee dugout, which had been silenced by Reynolds's failure and the four-run Boston lead, began to come alive. Henrich remembered it as if the entire team had been slapped in the face. But Vic Raschi had a terrible feeling that the season was slipping away from them. He sat in the dugout squeezing a baseball with his right hand to control his nervous tension.

By the fourth it was obvious to everyone in the Yankee dugout that Page was overpowering on this day. His ball was fast, and he had great movement on it. Vic Raschi, watching from the bench, decided that the Red Sox were not going to add to their lead, that now it was a matter of trying to chip away at it. On the Red Sox bench, Johnny Pesky, watching

Page, was awed. This was a great pitcher at his best. This was pure power. Page was pitching without deception on this day. There were no curves, no change-ups. Every pitch was a challenge. It was as if he were taunting the Red Sox hitters: Hit me if you can. God, what a pitcher, Pesky thought. This game was not over.

In the fourth Joe DiMaggio came up. He had told Stengel earlier that he would try and play three innings, but at the end of the third he held up five fingers, meaning he would go at least five innings. He had struck out in the first inning, but now in the fourth he lined a double to right field. Billy Johnson struck out, but Bauer singled DiMaggio home with a hard shot to left. Lindell hit another hard single to left, sending Bauer to third. Then Coleman hit a fly to Dom DiMaggio and Bauer scored. It was 4–2.

As the Yankees began to come back, Raschi squeezed the ball harder and harder. In the fifth, Rizzuto singled. Henrich hit a ball past first base, sending Rizzuto to third. Then Berra singled and Rizzuto scored, with Henrich stopping at second. With DiMaggio up, McCarthy pulled Parnell and brought in Joe Dobson. DiMaggio hit a vicious line drive low and to the right of the pitcher. With perfect fielding it might have been a double play. But Dobson did not get around on it quickly; the ball bounced off his glove and rolled fifteen feet behind the mound. By the time Dobson recovered it the bases were loaded. Billy Johnson hit into a double play, but Henrich scored. It was 4–4 now.

The game continued 4–4 through the sixth and seventh innings. On the Yankee bench there was a sense of growing confidence. Page seemed untouchable. In the bottom of the eighth Stengel sent up both Bobby Brown and Cliff Mapes, left-handed pinch hitters, to face the right-handed Dobson. But Dobson handled them. The next man up was Lindell, a right-handed hitter. Stengel had the left-handed Charlie Keller on the bench. But Lindell already had two hits, and he had driven Williams back to the fence his first time up against Dobson. Stengel decided to stick with Lindell. Lindell was the team rogue. He was exuberant, generous, and crude, and his humor seemed to dominate the locker room. In order to avoid being snared by one of his gags, the others always checked to see where he was before they entered. Even the trainer's table was not safe. A player lying down for treatment would often get whacked on the forehead by Lindell's phallus, which was considered one of the wonders of the Yankee locker room. His favorite victims were Page and Rizzuto, but no one was spared. Coleman was christened "Sweets" because he was so good-looking and because once at a restaurant he had ordered crabmeat in an avocado instead of steak, which was preferred by the other ballplayers. "Isn't that sweet," said Lindell, and the nickname stuck.

Even DiMaggio was vulnerable. Once DiMaggio walked into the locker room in a beautiful and obviously expensive new Hawaiian sports shirt. Lindell immediately shouted out, "Hey, beautiful, where'd you get that sports shirt? You look pretty in it." DiMaggio froze, his face reddened, and he never wore the shirt again. "We've got to keep the Dago honest," said Lindell when the others looked at him quizzically.

His teasing was generally good-natured, however, and he was generous with the younger players. When the team arrived in New York, he would take them to his favorite hangouts near the Stadium, including one where the specialty of the house was something called "The Lindell Bomber." "Try one, you're going to love it," he told the young Charlie Silvera earlier that season. It turned out to be the biggest martini anyone had ever seen — as big as a birdbath. He was the bane of management because his off-field activities were so outrageous. He liked to boast about how much money George Weiss had spent putting private detectives on him.

Lindell was a low-ball hitter, so Dobson and Tebbetts decided to feed him high fastballs. The first pitch was a ball. Again Dobson came in with a fastball. The ball was both high and inside. Lindell knew he was not going to see anything low. But he got ready, and he crushed the next ball. The moment he hit it, everyone knew it was a home run. We went to the well once too often, Dobson thought to himself. I had probably lost just enough off my fastball, and he was ready for it.

Vic Raschi was thrilled; it meant that he was going to get a chance the next day at the biggest game of his life. The celebration in the clubhouse was almost out of control. Finally Joe DiMaggio decided to calm his teammates down. "Hey, we've got to win tomorrow," he kept saying, "just don't forget that. It's not done yet." But they had escaped a bullet, and it seemed inconceivable to them that they could come that close to defeat and not win the pennant. DiMaggio, they thought, was amazing. They knew he was desperately ill, but he had played the entire game and gotten two hits.

John Lindell III was ten years old that summer and he did not like living in New York. As far as he was concerned, home was Arcadia, California. Arcadia was where his friends were. In New York there were thousands and thousands of little boys who would have given anything to have a father playing for the Yankees, but young John Lindell was not one of them. He had no interest in baseball, and when on occasion he went with his father to the locker room, he did so grudgingly.

Near the end of the season his parents had explained the immediate future to him: If the Yankees did not win the pennant, the family would return to Arcadia immediately, but if they did, then the family would stay on in New York for two more weeks. So it was on October 1 that when Johnny Lindell hit his dramatic home run, everyone in their Bronx neighborhood was happy and excited but little John Lindell. Hearing the news, he burst into tears because he was sure it meant staying in New York for an additional two weeks.

On October 2 the Yankees and Red Sox faced each other in the last game of the season with identical records. On that morning John Morley, a student at Manhattan College, rose at the unbearably early hour of five-thirty and dressed quickly for work. Morley, then eighteen, considered himself exceptionally lucky. He worked for Harry Stevens, the company that did the catering at Yankee Stadium. In the eyes of his neighborhood buddies and college friends, he was a privileged insider in the magic world. If he did not actually know Joe DiMaggio, he often saw him beautifully dressed in civilian clothes, and to Morley's friends in the Bronx, the ability to spot a player in civilian clothes was the same as intimacy. Morley was able to report on how he treated the fans who waited after the game, and in the minds of Morley's friends this also was something like true intimacy. Morley sometimes worked serving such prominent sportswriters as Joe Trimble, Bob Considine, and Dan Parker. They were spiffy, well dressed, and wore straw hats (though they were not necessarily great tippers).

Morley had worked for Stevens for three years and had slowly advanced to a privileged position: He was a gateman/ beerman, first working at the outside gates before the game selling scorecards, and then, the moment the game started, switching to roving beer salesman. On a normal day during the season, he made, with his 10 percent commission, about $50 or $60 a game. On a big game like this, with every seat in the Stadium sold, he might make as much as $150. It was a long day of hard, backbreaking work, because refrigeration within the Stadium was primitive in those days. Therefore, almost all preparation had to be done on the day of the game. Because it was the weekend, someone had already gone to the Corn Exchange Bank at 170th and Jerome Avenue for the thousands of dollars in coins that would be needed for change during the weekend.

An old-timer named Tom Carmody ran the Stevens operation at the Stadium. He had been there for twenty-six years, since the day the Stadium first opened, and he ruled with an iron hand. He was always the first one there, and the first thing he did was make a large vat of coffee, the strongest and most vile Morley had ever tasted, then or since. Then Carmody would turn into a nineteenth-century drill sergeant. The rules for the boys were exactly the same as they had

been in 1923, when Carmody first came. They were simple:
You were to show up exactly on time, never a minute late,
never be flip, and always, *always* say "sir." To Carmody the
failure of even the lowliest Stevens worker was his own
failure.

The hardest part of the day was the morning delivery of ice
to the big cooler tubs throughout the Stadium. The young
men had to cart three-hundred-pound blocks of ice. Then
they would break up these giant slabs and place them over
beds of beer bottles, which were lying on the bottom of the
giant tubs. After the game they would run hoses from the
tubs so that the water from the melted ice could run out
through the drainage system. The only thing that cheered
Morley while doing such exhausting work was the knowledge
that for every bottle of beer sold (at 35 cents), 3.5 cents
would go toward his college education.

Like the other Stevens workers he hoped for a long game,
because that meant more hot dogs, soda, and beer sold, and
more money earned. But he was also a Yankee fan, and on
this day he was as nervous as anyone else. This was the big
game. They expected crowds so large that Stevens had sent
over extra help from Ebbets Field. The regulars viewed them
not as colleagues but as intruders. Obviously, the Dodgers
were not as good a team as the Yankees, nor was their ball
park as elegant.

That morning as he worked, Morley stole glances at the
players coming out of the dugout for their early workouts. He
was struck by how casual they seemed, as if this were just
another day. Then, suddenly, the long slow morning was
over. It was time to go out and sell programs.

It was a huge crowd, and it was arriving early. Many people
had come the night before and camped out in their cars in the
parking lot in order to buy bleacher tickets, which went on
sale early in the morning. It was as large as a World Series
crowd, but not as fancy, Morley immediately decided. The
World Series drew a reserved-ticket crowd, the kind of
people who were called swells in those days; the men wore

sport jackets, and often came with women instead of other men. But today it was a baseball crowd, knowing and hard-edged; these people would be quick to complain if a vendor blocked their view, even momentarily. As the crowd crushed forward to get into the Stadium, Morley was struck most of all by the noise, and then by the excitement in the air.

Vic Raschi was confident that he was ready to pitch. His last few starts had been good, and he felt as if he had worked through his dry spot. He had won for the Yankees in the 152nd game, a game they absolutely had to win against the Athletics.

After the Yankees came from behind to beat Boston, Raschi was determined to stay calm. He never had trouble sleeping before a big game, and this one was no exception. He was up at eight, and he, Reynolds, and Lopat drove to the ball park early together. Their wives would come later. He was not nervous. The previous day he had been nervous because events were beyond his control. Now he was not bothered by the crowd and the thunderous noise. Even as the players were dressing in the locker room before noon, they could hear the crowd's excitement. The key to pitching in this game, Raschi thought, was to concentrate, to cut out the crowd and noise, to think of only one thing: what to do on each pitch. Jim Turner, now his pitching coach, a few years earlier his manager in Portland, had taught him that at a critical juncture of his professional life.

Turner was a marvelous teacher, Raschi thought. He knew when to teach and when not to. If a pitcher threw the wrong pitch and lost a game, Turner did not intrude at the height of the pitcher's pain and anguish. Rather, he waited a day or two. Then he would make the pitcher himself talk his way through the situation — what had happened and why. Every game, Turner said, could be broken down, hitter by hitter, pitch by pitch. Each pitch was connected to the next pitch, Turner thought, for the strength of a pitcher lay partly in his ability to set up a batter for the next pitch.

Raschi had come to him desperate to learn — he was proud of his skills, deeply wounded by the failure of Yankee management in the spring of 1947 to see his career as he did. Turner immediately saw Raschi's talent. But there were too many lapses — moments when he was pitching but not thinking. In an early Portland game, Raschi had a lead in the third inning. With two outs, two men on base, and the pitcher up, Raschi had allowed the pitcher to get a hit, and that had cost him the game. Turner waited a day and then took Raschi aside. "When you have a situation like a weak hitter up, you crucify him. You never let a pitcher beat you, Vic. Never!" Raschi's ability to concentrate improved immediately.

Turner taught him not just to study the hitters but also to prevail over them. "Vic — those hitters are your enemy. If they get their way, you're out of baseball," he would say. "I've seen pitchers with talent who might have made the major leagues, but they didn't hate hitters enough." Raschi proceeded to do well with Portland, winning 9 and losing 2, and in mid-season the Yankees brought him back to New York. He won two games during their extraordinary 19-game winning streak.

Raschi had a good fastball to start with, though perhaps not quite as good as Reynolds's, but he lacked a curve, or Aunt Susie, as the other pitchers called it. He worked on it with Turner, and in 1948 it began to work — a change more than a curve, actually. He had great stamina, far more than Reynolds, the other power pitcher. It was an article of faith among the Yankee players that if you were going to beat Vic Raschi, you had to do it early because he got stronger as the game wore on. If given a lead, he simply refused to lose. In the last innings he wanted to throw nothing but fastballs. "From now on just give me one sign," he would say to his catcher as they entered the seventh inning. Once, during a game with the Red Sox, Raschi had the lead but seemed to be struggling in the seventh inning. With Walt Dropo up, Stengel sent Jim Turner out to talk to Raschi. The resentment in Raschi's face was visible from the dugout. Turner quickly returned to the bench. "What did you say?" asked Stengel. "I asked him how he was going to pitch to Dropo," answered Turner. "And what did he answer?" Stengel asked. "Hard," said Turner.

Now nothing was to interfere with Raschi's concentration. He sat in front of his locker, cutting out all else around him, thinking only of what he wanted to do. If his teammates tried to come near him to exchange a pleasantry, he waved them away. He did not like photographers to take his picture on game days, and that was more than mere superstition. Photographers in those days still used flash attachments, and Raschi hated the fact that for five or six minutes after each pop he could not see properly. He tried to warn them off, but if they did not listen he would spray their shoes with tobacco juice. He had a reputation among the writers as the hardest man on the team to interview.

With Ellis Kinder, the knowledge that the Sunday game might be the biggest in his life did not deter him in the least. He started partying hard on Saturday night. Joe Dobson, who was rooming with Kinder that year, was awakened at about four A.M. by a knock on the door. There was Kinder, quite drunk, with a lady friend whom Dobson had never seen before. Dobson went back to sleep and then got up and left the room around nine A.M. As he departed he heard Kinder's whiskey-roughened voice speaking into the phone: "Room service, get some coffee up here."

Charlie Silvera, the backup catcher, lived on Gerard Avenue, about a block from the Stadium. To his amazement, the noise from the crowd started late Saturday afternoon and grew through the evening as fans gathered in the parking lot and formed a line waiting for bleacher seats. Throughout the night, as game time approached, the noise grew steadily louder. Curt Gowdy was equally impressed by the noise of the crowd. He thought of it as a war of fans — the Yankee fans cheering wildly, then their noise answered by deafening volleys from the many Red Sox fans who had driven down from New England. Gowdy's job was to help Mel Allen, for this was Mel's game. Gowdy was impressed at how calm Allen was, as if he had been broadcasting games like this all his life. "We've been so full of tension all year long, that honest-to-goodness today I'm just forgetting about everything," Allen told his audience at the beginning of the game. "Whatever happens, happens. Something's gotta happen today. That's just the way it's going to be. The Yankees have done an out-of-this-world job this year, and the Red Sox have just been magnificent."

Vic Raschi heard none of it. He thought only about the Red Sox. Keep Dominic DiMaggio off the bases. That was important because Pesky was a much better hitter when Dominic was on base. Pitch carefully to Williams and walk him if necessary. Williams could kill a right-handed fastball pitcher in the Stadium. No curveballs to Junior Stephens, who murdered Raschi's curve. Nothing but high fastballs slightly outside. Let Stevie do battle with Death Valley in left center. To Bobby Doerr, as good a hitter as they had, with no real weakness, just pitch carefully and around the edges.

Raschi saw Joe DiMaggio in the locker room. DiMaggio looked gray and wan and was moving poorly. Raschi knew he was sick and exhausted. He wondered if DiMaggio was really well enough to play that day. Probably not, he decided, but nobody on this team was going to tell Joe DiMaggio that he should not be playing.

At last Raschi went out to the mound, and started to pitch. Within minutes he was pleased. Everything was working that day; he had speed, placement, and his little curve. This was not the day to go out and find that one of his pitches was missing, or that he could not put the ball where he wanted. And he was pleased to be pitching against Ellis Kinder. Kinder was tough too, a man who, in the phrase that Raschi liked to apply to himself and his friend Allie Reynolds, liked to make hitters smell the leather. Kinder would almost surely pitch well and make the game close. Raschi wanted that; he wanted a close game where the pressure was on the pitcher.

Dom DiMaggio and Pesky went out quickly. After he got a man out Raschi would always observe a certain ritual: He would straighten his cap, pull his sweatshirt down toward his wrist, and fix the mound. Then he would plant his right foot on the rubber. All the while the infielders would throw the ball around. Then Raschi was ready to receive the ball from the third baseman, either Bobby Brown or Billy Johnson. He wanted the ball thrown right at his glove so that he wouldn't have to move. Sometimes, when the Yankees had a big lead, Johnson or Brown would throw the ball slightly behind him, forcing him to leave the rubber. He hated it. There would be none of that today. With two out, Ted Williams came to the plate. Raschi kept everything close to the plate, but he also walked Williams on four pitches. Then he got Junior Stephens out.

Rizzuto was the lead-off man in the bottom of the first. By then he had come to share the Yankees' admiration for Kinder, who had so completely mastered them that season. Four victories. If there was one advantage Rizzuto had over his teammates when it came to hitting against Kinder, it was that he was not a power hitter. Instead he went with the ball. With a pitcher as smart as Kinder, Rizzuto never tried to guess. The pitch came in, somewhat on the inside, and Rizzuto swung. It was a slider, not a fastball, he realized immediately, because a fastball that much inside would have broken his bat. Because it was slightly off-speed, Rizzuto got out ahead of it. He slapped it down the line, past Pesky at third base, and he knew immediately it was extra bases. The ball hugged the left-field line and went into the corner, and as Rizzuto raced for second, he watched Ted Williams go into the corner. Williams played back slightly, waiting for the ball to come back to him the way it would at Fenway. Rizzuto knew the fence better, and he raced for third. The ball stayed along the contours of the park, more like a hockey puck than a baseball, and went past Williams. Rizzuto had an easy triple. He watched with relief as McCarthy played the infield back.

Henrich was up now, the perfect batter for this situation. Kinder pitched and Henrich choked up on the bat. With the softest swing imaginable, he hit a grounder toward Bobby Doerr. Classic Henrich, Rizzuto thought, giving himself up and getting the run. No ego in the way. The Yankees had a one-run lead.

Inning after inning passed. The lead held up. Raschi was on top of his game, and the Yankees could do nothing with Kinder. If anything, he was even more in control than Raschi. His placement was almost perfect. When he missed the corner with a pitch, it was because he wanted to miss the corner. He was varying his speed nicely. And he showed no signs of getting tired.

In the eighth, the first batter was Tebbetts, and he went out; then it was Kinder's turn up. Kinder badly wanted to bat; he was sure he was as good a hitter as anyone on the bench, but McCarthy played the percentages. He sent up Tom Wright, a player just called up from the minors, to bat for Kinder. On the Yankee bench the players had been watching McCarthy closely. When he made his signal, there was among the Yankee players a collective sigh of relief and gratitude. Kinder was out and the Red Sox had a notoriously weak bullpen. On the Red Sox bench, Matt Batts, the catcher, who liked McCarthy more than most of the bench players (McCarthy had given him his chance at the majors), thought, God, don't do it; that's a mistake. We're down only one run, they can't touch Ellis, and we are weak, I mean weak in the bullpen. Kinder was furious. Wright walked, but Dominic DiMaggio grounded to Rizzuto, who turned it into a double play. The inning was over and Kinder, to the relief of the Yankees, was out of the game.

The first two Yankee batters in the eighth, Henrich and Berra, were both left-handed, so McCarthy again played the percentages and went to Parnell, his pitcher from yesterday. Sitting by himself in his attic in South Hadley, eleven-year-old Bart Giamatti heard Jim Britt say that Parnell was coming in to relieve Kinder. Giamatti was young, but he knew that Parnell had pitched too often in recent weeks, and that he had pitched the day before and must be exhausted. He had an immediate sense that this was a gallant but futile gesture. Giamatti was filled with sadness. Something in Jim Britt's voice over the radio made it clear that he was equally pessimistic.

Giamatti was right to be pessimistic. Parnell's was to be a short appearance. He was tired, and he had lost his edge. Henrich had hit him hard in the past ("My nemesis," Parnell later called him), and now was eager to bat against someone other than Ellis Kinder. Lefty or no, he saw the ball better with Parnell than with Kinder. This time Parnell threw him a fastball. Henrich hit it about ten rows back into the right-field seats and the Yankees got their cushion, 2–0. Then Berra singled and McCarthy called to the bullpen for Tex Hughson. Hughson turned to Joe Dobson and said, "Well, Joe, they've finally gone to the bottom of the barrel." It was odd, Hughson thought, that McCarthy had shown nothing but contempt for him all season, and now at this most important moment he had decided to use him.

DiMaggio hit into a double play, and there were two outs and no one on. But Lindell singled and Hank Bauer was sent in as pinch runner. Then Billy Johnson singled, and when Williams juggled the ball, Bauer went to third. Then Hughson deliberately walked Mapes to get to the rookie, Jerry Coleman.

Coleman had thought in the early part of the season that he liked to hit against Kinder, and then gradually as the season progressed he decided he was wrong. Kinder had seemed to improve as a pitcher in every outing. You just never got a good pitch. There was the change, the sudden fastball, and then, of course, the last-second slider. Like his teammates, he had been relieved when McCarthy had played by the book and pulled Kinder for a pinch-hitter. Now, in the eighth, he was up with the bases loaded. The Yankees were ahead, but even so Coleman did not want to look foolish at this moment. The season might be nearly over, he might have done everything the Yankees wanted of him and more, but he had never felt more on trial.

Hughson was absolutely sure he could handle the rookie. Tex could still throw hard, and the ball came in letter-high and inside. Hughson was delighted. He had placed it almost perfectly, an impossible pitch for a hitter to do anything with, he thought, and he was right; Coleman did very little with it. He hit it right on the trademark of the bat and sliced the ball, a pop-up, just past second base; Coleman was disgusted with himself.

In right field Al Zarilla was not playing Coleman particularly deep. Bases loaded, he thought, two out, short right-field fence, two runs behind. We cannot let them have any more runs. Coleman was not a power hitter. For Zarilla, the ability to come in on a pop fly or a soft liner was more important than going back on the ball, particularly with two out. Zarilla watched Hughson's pitch and he thought, That is a lovely pitch. Then he saw the ball leave the bat and he knew at once that it was trouble — too far back for Bobby Doerr, the ball spinning away toward the line, a dying swan if there ever was one. It had to be Zarilla's ball. He charged it, and kept charging, but the ball kept slicing away from him. At the last second Zarilla was sure he had a play. He dove for it, his fingers and glove outstretched. He was diving at the expense of his body, for he was not positioned to break a fall. He missed it by perhaps two inches. By the time the ball came down, Zarilla realized later, it was almost on the foul line.

When Coleman saw it was too deep for Doerr and that Zarilla was desperately charging, he knew the ball was going to drop. He turned past second and raced for third. He was out at third, but three runs had scored. The lead was 5–0. When he came into the dugout, everyone patted Coleman on the back as if he were an old veteran and an RBI leader. But he thought of it as a cheap hit, and was more than a little ashamed of himself. A three-run double in the box score, he thought, was a cheap pop-up on the field.

He was ashamed of it for a long time afterward. Then three years later he ran into Joe McCarthy at a banquet. He started to mumble something about it being a bloop hit, but McCarthy interrupted him. "You swung at it, didn't you?" he asked, and Coleman nodded. Coleman understood McCarthy's meaning immediately — you didn't strike out and they didn't put anything past you. So don't apologize, you did your job.

The Red Sox gave it one more shot. In the top of the ninth, they rallied for three runs. Pesky fouled out, and then Williams walked. Stephens singled to center. Then Bobby Doerr hit a long drive to center field. It was a well-hit ball, but the kind that Joe DiMaggio normally handled readily. This time, his legs cramping up, it went over his head and Doerr had a triple. DiMaggio signaled for time and took himself out of the game. His long regular season was over. Two runs were in. Zarilla flied out to Mapes. Two outs. But Goodman singled through center, and Doerr scored. The score was 5–3.

The next batter was Birdie Tebbetts. Since they had fattened their lead, the Yankee bench jockeys had been needling the needler mercilessly: "Hey, Birdie, get the kid [Quinn] to lend you some of his money for your World Series share." "Hey, Birdie, we'll send you over a bottle of our champagne." Tommy Henrich was playing first, and he walked over to Raschi to give him a small pep talk, to remind him that he needed only one more out. "Give me the goddamn ball and get the hell out of here!" Raschi snarled. Henrich turned, and grinned to himself. We've got it, it's a lock, he thought, there is no way Birdie Tebbetts is going to get a hit off this man right now. Tebbetts popped up in foul territory. "It's my ball," he shouted, and he thought to himself, It's the one I've been looking for all year. The regular season was over.

The Red Sox locker room was silent. No one was able to talk. This ending had been even worse than 1948's. For two years in a row they had come so close, and had ended up with nothing. They had played 309 regular-season games over the two seasons, and had ended up a total of one game behind the two pennant winners in that period.

But at least 1948 had ended with a sense of optimism. This season was ending with the taste of ashes. They had come into the Stadium needing to win only one game, they had a four-run lead in the first game, and they had blown it and the two-game series. They had no one to blame except themselves. Boo Ferriss, looking at his teammates Pesky and Williams, thought they looked like men who had died in some way. Williams sat immobilized in front of his locker, his head down. He was unreachable. If any reporters approached him, he just waved them away. He later said it was the worst moment in his baseball career, worse than the 1946 World Series defeat, worse than the 1948 playoff defeat.

Clif Keane thought there was only one exception to the gloom and that was predictable: Junior Stephens. "Tough game, wasn't it, Clif?" Junior said. There was, Keane understood, still fun ahead for someone like Stephens.

Dominic DiMaggio immediately went to the Commodore Hotel, where his young wife, Emily, was waiting. Grossinger's, the Catskills resort, had offered them a free vacation when the season was over. Emily DiMaggio, who had not the slightest interest in baseball, was thrilled because now they could go to Grossinger's right away and not have to wait the extra week or ten days that the World Series would take. "Isn't it wonderful, Dominic," she said, "now we can go on vacation right away." Dominic DiMaggio's eyes were filled with tears. "Emily," said her husband, "don't you realize what's just happened?"

For the team members, the train ride back to Boston was like a funeral procession. It seemed endless. There was almost no desire, as there sometimes was on occasions like this, to replay the game. No one wanted to talk about the next season. No one wanted to take solace in the clichés about how close they had come, and how they had made up eleven games on the Yankees. No one wanted to talk about what if — what if they had beaten Ray Scarborough; what if Hughson's arm had been a little better. In 1948 there had been some consolation that they had been cheated by Charlie Berry's bad call on the Boudreau foul/home run.

No one was more bitter than Ellis Kinder, who, as the evening passed and more alcohol flowed, became angrier and angrier about being pulled for a pinch hitter. In his mind, it became ever more clear that had McCarthy left him in, he would have held the Yankees, the Red Sox would have scored the same number of runs, and he would have won. Near the end of the ride he finally accosted McCarthy and exploded. As far as he was concerned, McCarthy had blown it. He was a screw-up, a drunk, and a manager who treated his star players one way and his other ballplayers another. Ellis Kinder got it all off his chest, and he never forgave Joe McCarthy.

Roger Angell

Excerpted from Agincourt and After

October, 1975

The New Yorker, 1975

Tarry, delight, so seldom met. . . . The games have ended, the heroes are dispersed, and another summer has died late in Boston, but still one yearns for them and wishes them back, so great was their pleasure. The adventures and discoveries and reversals of last month's World Series, which was ultimately won by the Cincinnati Reds in the final inning of the seventh and final game, were of such brilliance and unlikelihood that, even as they happened, those of us who were there in the stands and those who were there on the field were driven again and again not just to cries of excitement but to exclamations of wonder about what we were watching and sharing. Pete Rose, coming up to bat for the Reds in the tenth inning of the tied and retied sixth game, turned to Carlton Fisk, the Red Sox catcher, and said, "Say, this is some kind of game, isn't it?" And when that evening ended at last, after further abrupt and remarkable events, everyone — winners and losers and watchers — left the Fens in exaltation and disarray. "I went home," the Reds' manager Sparky Anderson said later, "and I was stunned."

The next day, during the last batting practice of the year, there was extended debate among the writers and players on the Fenway sidelines as to whether game six had been the greatest in Series history and whether we were not, in fact, in on the best Series of them all. Grizzled coaches and senior scribes recalled other famous Octobers — 1929, when the Athletics, trailing the Cubs by eight runs in the fourth game, scored ten runs in the seventh inning and won; 1947, when Cookie Lavagetto's double with two out in the ninth ended Yankee pitcher Bill Bevens' bid for a no-hitter and won the fourth game for the Dodgers; 1960, when Bill Mazeroski's ninth-inning homer for the Pirates threw down the lordly Yankees. There is no answer to these barroom syllogisms, of course, but any recapitulation and reexamination of the 1975 Series suggests that at the very least we may conclude that there has never been a better one. Much is expected of the World Series, and in recent years much has been received. In the past decade, we have had the memorable and abrading seven-game struggles between the Red Sox and the Cardinals in 1967, the Cardinals and the Tigers in 1968, and the Orioles and the Pirates in 1971, and the astounding five-game upset of the Orioles by the Mets in 1969. Until this year, my own solid favorite — because of the Pirates' comeback and the effulgent play of Roberto Clemente — was the 1971 classic, but now I am no longer certain. Comebacks and late rallies are actually extremely scarce in baseball, and an excellent guaranteed cash-producing long-term investment is to wager that the winning team in any game will score more runs in a single inning than the losing team scores in nine. In this Series, however, the line scores alone reveal the rarity of what we saw:

In six of the seven games, the winning team came from behind.

In one of the games, the winning team came from behind twice.

In five games, the winning margin was one run.

There were two extra-inning games, and two games were settled in the ninth inning.

Overall, the games were retied or saw the lead reversed thirteen times.

No other Series — not even the celebrated Giants–Red Sox thriller of 1912 — can match these figures.

It is best, however, not to press this search for the greatest Series any farther. There is something sterile and diminishing about our need for these superlatives, and the game of baseball, of course, is so rich and various that it cannot begin to be encompassed in any set of seven games. This Series, for example, produced not one low-hit, low-score pitching duel — the classic and agonizing parade of double zeros that strains teams and managers and true fans to their limits as the inevitable crack in the porcelain is searched out and the game at last broken open. This year, too, the Reds batted poorly through most of the early play and offered indifferent front-line pitching, while the Red Sox made too many mistakes on the base paths, were unable to defend against Cincinnati's team speed, and committed some significant (and in the end fatal) errors in the infield. One of the games was seriously marred by a highly debatable umpire's decision, which may have altered its outcome. It was not a perfect Series. Let us conclude then — before we take a swift look at the season and the playoffs; before we return to Morgan leading away and stealing, to Yaz catching and whirling and throwing, to Eastwick blazing a fastball and Tiant turning his back and offering up a fluttering outside curve, to Evans' catch and Lynn's leap and fall, to Perez's bombs and Pete Rose's defiant, exuberant glare — and say only that this year the splendid autumn affair rose to our utmost expectations and then surpassed them, attaining at last such a level of excellence and emotional reward that it seems likely that the participants — the members of the deservedly winning, champion Reds and of the sorely disappointed, almost-champion Red Sox — will in time remember this Series not for its outcome but for the honor of having played in it, for having made it happen. . . .

By September 16, the Pirates and the A's were enjoying comfortable leads in their divisions, the Reds had long since won their demi-pennant (they clinched on September 7 — a new record), and the only serious baseball was to be found at Fenway Park, where the Orioles, down by four and a half games and running out of time, had at the Red Sox. The game was a pippin — a head-to-head encounter between Jim Palmer and Luis Tiant. Each of the great pitchers struck out eight batters, and the game was won by the Red Sox, 2–0, on two small mistakes by Palmer — fastballs to Rico Petrocelli and Carlton Fisk in successive innings, which were each lofted into the left-field screen. Tiant, who had suffered through almost a month of ineffectiveness brought on by a bad back, was in top form, wheeling and rotating on the mound like a figure in a Bavarian clock tower, and in the fourth he fanned Lee May with a super-curve that seemed to glance off some invisible obstruction in midflight. The hoarse, grateful late-inning cries of "Lu-is! Lu-is! Lu-is!" from 34,724 Beantowners suggested that the oppressive, Calvinist cloud of self-doubt that afflicts Red Sox fans in all weathers and seasons was beginning to lift at last. The fabulous Sox rookies, Jim Rice and Fred Lynn, did nothing much (in fact, they fanned five times between them), but Boston friends of mine encouraged my belief with some of the shiny new legends — the home run that Rice hammered past the Fenway Park center-field flagpole in July; the time Rice checked a full swing and snapped his bat in half just above his hands; Lynn's arm, Lynn's range, Lynn's game against the Tigers in June, when he hit three homers and batted in ten runs and the Sox began their pennant drive. The night before my visit, in fact, against the Brewers, Lynn and Rice had each accounted for his one hundredth run batted in *with the same ball* — a run-forcing walk to Lynn and then a sacrifice fly by Rice. I believed.

Baltimore came right back, winning the next game by 5–2, on some cool and useful hitting by Tommy Davis and Brooks Robinson, and the Sox' cushion was back to four and a half. The Orioles' move, we know now, came a little too late this year, but I think one should not forget what a loose and deadly and marvelously confident September team they have been over the last decade. Before this, their last game at Fenway Park this year, they were enjoying themselves in their dugout while the Sox took batting practice and while Clif Keane, the *Boston Globe*'s veteran baseball writer (who is also the league's senior and most admired insult artist), took them apart. Brooks Robinson hefted a bat, and Keane, sitting next to manager Earl Weaver, said, "Forget it, Brooksie. They pay you a hundred and twenty-four thousand for your glove, and a thousand for the bat. Put that back in your valise." He spotted Doug DeCinces, the rookie who will someday take over for Robinson in the Oriole infield, and said, "Hey, kid, I was just talkin' to Brooks, here. He says he'll be back again. You'll be a *hundred* before you get in there. Looks like 1981 for you." Tommy Davis picked out some bats and went slowly up the dugout steps; his Baltimore teammates sometimes call him "Uncle Tired." Keane leaned forward suddenly. "Look at that," he said. "Tom's wearin' *new shoes* — he's planning on being around another twenty years. Listen, with Brooks and Davis, Northrup, May, and Muser, you guys can play an Old Timers' Game every day." Davis wandered off, smiling, and Keane changed his tone for a moment. "Did you ever see him when he could play?" he said, nodding at Davis. "He got about two hundred and fifty hits that year with LA, and they were all line drives. He could *hit*." His eye fell on the first group of Oriole batters around the batting cage. "See them all lookin' over here?" he said to Weaver. "They're talking about you again. If you could only hear them — they're really fricas seein' you today, Earl. Now you know how Marie Antoinette • felt. . . ." The laughter in the dugout was nice and easy. The men sat back, with their legs crossed and their arms stretched along the back of the bench, and watched the players on the ball field. The summer was running out.

The Sox just about wrapped it up the next week, when they beat the Yankees, 6–4, at Shea, in a game that was played in a steadily deepening downpour — the beginning of the tropical storm that washed away most of the last week of the season. By the ninth inning, the mound and the batters' boxes looked like trenches on the Somme, and the stadium was filled with a wild gray light made by millions of illuminated falling raindrops. The Yankees got the tying runs aboard in the ninth, with two out, and then Dick Drago struck out Bobby Bonds, swinging, on three successive pitches, and the Boston outfielders came leaping and splashing in through the rain like kids home from a picnic. The winning Boston margin, a few days later, was still four and a half games.

The playoffs, it will be remembered, were brief. Over in the National League, the Reds embarrassed the Pittsburgh Pirates, winners of the Eastern Division title, by stealing ten bases in their first two games, which they won by 8–3 and 6–1. Young John Candelaria pitched stoutly for the Pirates when the teams moved on to Three Rivers Stadium, fanning fourteen Cincinnati batters, but Pete Rose broke his heart with a two-run homer in the eighth, and the Reds won the game, 5–3, and the pennant, 3–0, in the tenth inning. I had deliberated for perhaps seven seconds before choosing to follow the American League championship games — partly because the Red Sox were the only new faces available (the Reds, the Pirates, and the A's have among them qualified for the playoffs fourteen times in the past six years), but mostly because I know that the best place in the world to watch baseball is at Fenway Park. The unique dimensions and properties of the Palazzo Yawkey (the left-field wall is 37 feet high and begins a bare 315 feet down the foul line from home plate — or perhaps, according to a startling new computation made by the *Boston Globe* this fall, *304* feet) vivify ball games and excite the imagination. On the afternoon of the first A's–Sox set-to, the deep green of the grass and light green of the wall, the variously angled blocks and planes and triangles and wedges of the entirely occupied stands, and the multiple seams and nooks and corners of the outfield fences, which encompass eleven different angles off which a ball or a ballplayer can ricochet, suddenly showed me that I was inside the ultimate origami.

There were two significant absentees — Jim Rice, who

had suffered a fractured hand late in the campaign and would not play again this year, and Catfish Hunter, the erstwhile Oakland meal ticket, whose brisk work had been so useful to the A's in recent Octobers. Boston manager Darrell Johnson solved his problem brilliantly, moving Carl Yastrzemski from first base to Rice's spot under the left-field wall — a land grant that Yaz had occupied and prospected for many years. Oakland manager Alvin Dark found no comparable answer to his dilemma, but the startling comparative levels of baseball that were now demonstrated by the defending three-time champion A's and the untested Red Sox soon indicated that perhaps not even the Cat would have made much difference. In the bottom of the very first inning, Yastrzemski singled off Ken Holtzman, and then Carlton Fisk hit a hopper down the third-base line that was butchered by Sal Bando and further mutilated by Claudell Washington, in left. Lynn then hit an undemanding ground ball to second baseman Phil Garner, who muffed it. Two runs were in, and in the seventh the Sox added five more, with help from Oakland center fielder Bill North, who dropped a fly, and Washington, who somehow played Lynn's fly to the base of the wall into a double. Tiant, meanwhile, was enjoying himself. The Oakland scouting report on him warned he had six pitches — fastball, slider, curve, change-up curve, palm ball, and knuckler — all of which he could serve up from the sidearm, three-quarter, or overhand sectors, and points in between, but on this particular afternoon his fastball was so lively that he eschewed the upper ranges of virtuosity. He did not give up his first hit until the fifth inning or, incredibly, his first ground ball until the eighth. The Sox won, 7–1. "Tiant," Reggie Jackson declared in the clubhouse, "is the Fred Astaire of baseball."

The second game, which Alvin Dark had singled out as the crucial one in any three-of-five series, was much better. Oakland jumped away to a 3–0 lead, after a first-inning homer by Jackson, and Sal Bando whacked four successive hits — *bong! whang! bing! thwong!* — off the left-field wall during the afternoon. The second of these, a single, was converted into a killing out by Yastrzemski, who seized the carom off the wall and whirled and threw to Petrocelli to erase the eagerly advancing Campaneris at third — a play that Yaz and Rico first perfected during the Garfield Administration. The same two elders subsequently hit home runs — Yaz off Vida Blue, Rico off Rollie Fingers — and Lynn contributed a run-scoring single and a terrific diving cutoff of a Joe Rudi double to center field that saved at least one run. The Sox won by 6–3. The A's complained after the game that two of Bando's shots would have been home runs in any other park, and that both Yastrzemski's and Petrocelli's homers probably would have been outs in any other park. Absolutely true: the Wall giveth and the Wall taketh away.

Not quite believing what was happening, I followed the two teams to Oakland, where I watched the Bosox wrap up their easy pennant with a 5–3 victory. Yastrzemski, who is thirty-six years old and who had suffered through a long summer of injuries and ineffectuality, continued to play like the Yaz of 1967, when he almost single-handedly carried the Red Sox to their last pennant and down to the seventh game of that World Series. This time, he came up with two hits, and twice astonished Jackson in the field — first with a whirling throw from the deep left-field corner that cleanly excised Reggie at second base, and then, in the eighth, with a sprinting, diving, skidding, flat-on-the-belly stop of Jackson's low line shot to left that was headed for the wall and a sure triple. The play came in the midst of the old champions' courageous two-run rally in the eighth, and it destroyed them. Even though it fell short, I was glad about that rally, for I did not want to see the splendid old green-and-yallers go down meekly or sadly in the end. The Oakland fans, who have not always been known for the depths of their constancy or appreciation, also distinguished themselves, sustaining an earsplitting cacophony of hope and encouragement to the utter end. I sensed they were saying goodbye to their proud and vivid and infinitely entertaining old lineup — to Sal Bando and Campy Campaneris, to Joe Rudi and Reggie Jackson and Gene Tenace and

Rollie Fingers and the rest, who will almost surely be broken up now and traded away, as great teams must be when they come to the end of their time in the sun.

The finalists, coming together for the Series opener at Fenway Park, were heavily motivated. The Reds had not won a World Series since 1940, the Sox since 1918. Cincinnati's Big Red Machine had stalled badly in its recent October outings, having failed in the World Series of 1970 and '72 and in the playoffs of 1973. The Red Sox had a record of shocking late-season collapses, the latest coming in 1974, when they fizzled away a seven-game lead in the last six weeks of the season. Both teams, however, were much stronger than in recent years — the Reds because of their much improved pitching (most of it relief pitching) and the maturing of a second generation of outstanding players (Ken Griffey, Dave Concepcion, George Foster) to join with the celebrated Rose, Morgan, Perez, and Bench. The Red Sox infield had at last found itself, with Rick Burleson at short and Denny Doyle (a midseason acquisition from the Angels) at second, and there was a new depth in hitting and defense — Beniquez, Cooper, Carbo, and the remarkable Dwight Evans. This was a far better Boston team than the 1967 miracle workers. The advantage, however, seemed to belong to Cincinnati, because of the Reds' combination of speed and power (168 stolen bases, 124 homers) and their implacable habit of winning ball games. Their total of 108 games won had been fashioned, in part, out of an early-season streak of 41 wins in 50 games, and a nearly unbelievable record of 64–17 in their home park. The Red Sox, on the other hand, had Lynn and Tiant. . . .

Conjecture thickened through most of the opening game, which was absolutely close for most of the distance, and then suddenly not close at all. Don Gullett, a powerful left-hander, kept the Red Sox in check for six innings, but was slightly outpitched and vastly outacted over the same distance by Tiant. The venerable stopper (Tiant is listed as being thirty-four and rumored as being a little or a great deal older) did not have much of a fastball on this particular afternoon, so we were treated to the splendid full range of Tiantic mime. His repertoire begins with an exaggerated mid-windup pivot, during which he turns his back on the batter and seems to examine the infield directly behind the mound for signs of crabgrass. With men on bases, his stretch consists of a succession of minute downward waggles and pauses of the glove, and a menacing sidewise, slit-eyed, Valentino-like gaze over his shoulder at the base runner. The full flower of his art, however, comes during the actual delivery, which is executed with a perfect variety show of accompanying gestures and impersonations. I had begun to take notes during my recent observations of the Cuban Garrick, and now, as he set down the Reds with only minimal interruptions (including one balk call, in the fourth), I arrived at some tentative codifications. The basic Tiant repertoire seems to include:

(1) Call the Osteopath: In midpitch, the man suffers an agonizing seizure in the central cervical region, which he attempts to fight off with a sharp backward twist of the head.

(2) Out of the Woodshed: Just before releasing the ball, he steps over a raised sill and simultaneously ducks his head to avoid conking it on the low doorframe.

(3) The Runaway Taxi: Before the pivot, he sees a vehicle bearing down on him at top speed, and pulls back his entire upper body just in time to avoid a nasty accident.

(4) Falling Off the Fence: An attack of vertigo nearly causes him to topple over backward on the mound. Strongly suggests a careless dude on the top rung of the corral.

(5) The Slipper-Kick: In the midpitch, he surprisingly decides to get rid of his left shoe.

(6) The Low-Flying Plane (a subtle development and amalgam of 1, 3, and 4, above): While he is pivoting, an F-105 buzzes the ball park, passing over the infield from the third-base to the first-base side at a height of eighty feet. He follows it all the way with his eyes.

All this, of course, was vastly appreciated by the Back Bay multitudes, including a nonpaying claque perched like seagulls atop three adjacent rooftop billboards (WHDH Radio, Windsor Canadian Whiskey, Buck Printing), who banged on the tin hoardings in accompaniment to the park's deepening chorus of "Lu-is! Lu-is! Lu-is!" The Reds, of course, were unmoved, and only three superior defensive plays by the Sox (including another diving, rolling catch by Yastrzemski) kept them from scoring in the top of the seventh. Defensive sparks often light an offensive flareup in close games, and Tiant now started the Sox off with a single. Evans bunted, and Gullett pounced on the ball and steamed a peg to second a hair too late to nail Tiant — the day's first mistake. Doyle singled, to lead the bases, and then Petrocelli and Burleson singled, too. (Gullett had vanished.) Suddenly six runs were in, and the game — a five-hit shutout for Tiant — was safely put away very soon after.

The next afternoon, a gray and drizzly Sunday, began happily and ended agonizingly for the Sox, who put six men aboard in the first two innings and scored only one of them, thanks to some slovenly base running. In the fourth inning, the Reds finally registered their first run of the Series, but the Sox moved out ahead again, 2–1, and there the game stuck, a little too tight for anyone's comfort. There was a long delay for rain in the seventh. Matters inched along at last, with each club clinging to its best pitching: Boston with its starter, Bill Lee, and Cincinnati with its bullpen — Borbon and McEnaney and Eastwick, each one better, it seemed, than the last. Lee, a southpaw, had thrown a ragbag of pitches — slow curves, sliders, screwballs, and semi-fastballs — all to the very outside corners, and by the top of the ninth he had surrendered but four hits. Now, facing the heaviest part of the Reds' order, he started Bench off with a pretty good but perhaps predictable outside fastball, which Bench whacked on a low line to the right-field corner for a double. Right-hander Dick Drago came on and grimly retired Perez and then Foster. One more out was required, and the crowd cried for it on every pitch. Concepcion ran the count to one and one and then hit a high-bouncing, unplayable chop over second that tied things up. Now the steal was on, of course, and Concepcion flashed away to second and barely slipped under Fisk's waist-high peg; Griffey doubled to the wall, and the Reds, for the twenty-fifth time this year, had snatched back a victory in their last licks. Bench's leadoff double had been a parable of winning baseball. He has great power in every direction, but most of all, of course, to left, where the Fenway wall murmurs so alluringly to a right-handed slugger whose team is down a run. Hitting Lee's outside pitch to right — going with it — was the act of a disciplined man.

Bill Lee is a talkative and engaging fellow who will discourse in lively fashion on almost any subject, including zero population growth, Zen Buddhism, compulsory busing, urban planning, acupuncture, and baseball. During the formal post-game press interview, a reporter put up his hand and said, "Bill, how would you, uh, characterize the World Series so far?"

Two hundred pencils poised.

"Tied," Lee said.

The action now repaired to the cheerless, circular, Monsan-toed close of Riverfront stadium. The press box there is glassed-in and air-conditioned, utterly cut off from the sounds of baseball action and baseball cheering. After an inning or two of this, I began to feel as if I were suffering from the effects of a mild stroke, and so gave up my privileged niche and moved outdoors to a less favored spot in an auxiliary press section in the stands, where I was surrounded by the short-haired but vociferous multitudes of the Cincinnati. The game was a noisy one, for the Reds, back in their own yard, were sprinting around the AstroTurf and whanging out long hits. They stole three bases and hit three home runs (Bench, Concepcion, and Geronimo — the latter two back-to-back) in the course of moving to a 5–1 lead. Boston responded with a will. The second Red Sox homer of the evening (Fisk had hit the first) was a pinch-hit blow by Bernie Carbo, and the third, by Dwight Evans, came with one out and one on in the ninth and tied the score, astonishingly, at 5–5. The pattern of the game to this point, we can see in retrospect, bears a close resemblance to the classic sixth, and an extravagant dénouement now seemed certain. Instead, we were given the deadening business of the disputed, umpired play — the collision at home plate in the bottom of the tenth between Carlton Fisk and Cincinnati pinch-hitter Ed Armbrister, who, with a man on first, bounced a sacrifice bunt high in the air just in front of the plate and then somehow entangled himself with Fisk's left side as the catcher stepped forward to make his play. Fisk caught the ball, pushed free of Armbrister (without trying to tag him), and then, hurrying things, threw to second in an attempt to force the base runner, Geronimo, and, in all likelihood, begin a crucial double play. The throw, however, was a horrible sailer that glanced off Burleson's glove and went on into center field; Geronimo steamed down to third, from where he was scored, a few minutes later, by Joe Morgan for the winning run. Red Sox manager Darrell Johnson protested, but the complaint was swiftly dismissed by home-plate umpire Larry Barnett and, on an appeal, by first-base umpire Dick Stello.

The curious thing about the whole dismal tort is that there is no dispute whatever about the events (the play was perfectly visible, and was confirmed by a thousand subsequent replayings on television), just as there is no doubt but that the umpires, in disallowing an interference call, cited apparently nonexistent or inapplicable rules. Barnett said, "It was simply a collision," and he and Stello both ruled that only an intentional attempt by Armbrister to obstruct Fisk could have been called interference. There is no rule in baseball that exempts simple collisions, and no one on either team ever claimed that Armbrister's awkward brush-block on Fisk was anything but accidental. This leaves the rules, notably Rule 2.00 (a): "Offensive interference is an act . . . which interferes with, obstructs, impedes, hinders, or confuses any fielder attempting to make a play." Rule 6.06 (c) says much the same thing (the baseball rule book is almost as thick as Blackstone), and so does 7.09: "It is interference by a batter or a runner when (1) He fails to avoid a fielder who is attempting to field a batted ball. . . ." Armbrister failed to avoid. Fisk, it is true, did not make either of the crucial plays then open to him — the tag and the peg — although he seemed to have plenty of time and room for both, but this does not in any way alter the fact of the previous interference. Armbrister should have been called out, and Geronimo returned to first base — or, if a double play had in fact been turned, *both* runners could have been called out by the umps, according to a subclause of 6.06.*

There were curses and hot looks in the Red Sox clubhouse that night, along with an undercurrent of feeling that Manager Johnson had not complained with much vigor. "If it had been me out there," Bill Lee said, "I'd have bitten Barnett's ear off. I'd have van Goghed him!"

Untidiness continued the next night, in game four, but in more likely places. The Reds did themselves out of a run with some overambitious base running, and handed over a run to

---

* I have truncated this mind-calcifying detour into legal semantics, because time proved it both incomplete and misleading. Shortly after the publication of this account, the news filtered out of the league offices that the Series umpires had been operating under a prior "supplemental instruction" to the interference rules, which stated: "When a catcher and a batter-runner going to first have contact when the catcher is fielding the ball, there is generally no violation and nothing should be called." This clearly exonerates Larry Barnett and explains his mystifying "It was simply a collision." What has never been explained is why the existence of this codicil was not immediately divulged to the fans and to the writers covering the Series, thus relieving the umpires of a barrage of undeserved obloquy. We should also ask whether the blanket exculpation of the supplemental instructions really does fit the crucial details of Armbrister v. Fisk. Subsequent pondering of the landmark case and several viewings of the Series film have led me to conclude that fairness and good sense would have been best served if Armbrister had been called out and the base runner, Geronimo, returned to first. It is still plain, however, that Carlton Fisk had the best and quickest opportunity to clarify this passionate affair, with a good, everyday sort of peg down to second; irreversibly, he blew it.

the Sox on an error by Tony Perez; Sparky Anderson was fatally slow in calling on his great relief corps in the midst of a five-run Red Sox rally; the Boston outfield allowed a short fly ball to drop untouched, and two Cincinnati runs instantly followed. The Sox led, 5–4, after four innings, and they won it, 5–4, after some excruciating adventures and anxieties. Tiant was again at center stage, but on this night, working on short rest, he did not have full command of his breaking stuff and was forced to underplay. The Reds' pitcher over the last three innings was Rawlins J. Eastwick III, the tall, pale, and utterly expressionless rookie fireballer, who was blowing down the Red Sox hitters and seemed perfectly likely to pick up his third straight win in relief. Tiant worked slowly and painfully, running up long counts, giving up line-drive outs, surrendering bases on balls and singles, but somehow struggling free. He was still in there by the ninth, hanging on by his toenails, but he now gave up a leadoff single to Geronimo. Armbrister sacrificed (this time without litigation), and Pete Rose, who had previously hit two ropes for unlucky outs, walked. Johnson came to the mound and, to my surprise, left Tiant in. Ken Griffey ran the count to three and one, fouled off the next pitch, and bombed an enormous drive to the wall in deepest center field, four hundred feet away, where Fred Lynn pulled it down after a long run. Two outs. Joe Morgan, perhaps the most dangerous hitter in baseball in such circumstances, took a ball (I was holding my breath; everyone in the vast stadium was holding his breath) and then popped straight up to Yastrzemski, to end it. Geronimo had broken for third base on the pitch, undoubtedly distracting Morgan for a fraction of a second — an infinitesimal and perhaps telling mistake by the Reds.

Tiant, it turned out, had thrown a total of 163 pitches, and Sparky Anderson selected Pitch No. 160 as the key to the game. This was not the delivery that Griffey whacked and Lynn caught but its immediate predecessor — the three-and-one pitch that Griffey had fouled off. Tiant had thrown a curve there — "turned it over," in baseball talk — which required the kind of courage that baseball men most respect. "Never mind his age," Joe Morgan said. "Being smart, having an idea — that's what makes a pitcher."

Morgan himself has the conviction that he should affect the outcome of every game he plays in every time he comes up to bat and every time he gets on base. (He was bitterly self-critical for that game-ending out.) Like several of the other Cincinnati stars, he talks about his own capabilities with a dispassionate confidence that sounds immodest and almost arrogant — until one studies him in action and understands that this is only another form of the cold concentration he applies to ball games. This year, he batted .327, led the National League in bases on balls, and fielded his position in the manner that has won him a Gold Glove award in each of the past two years. In more than half of his trips to the plate, he ended up on first base, and once there he stole sixty-seven bases in seventy-seven attempts. A short (five foot seven), precise man, with strikingly carved features, he talks in quick, short bursts of words. "I think I can steal off any pitcher," he said to me. "A good base stealer should make the whole infield jumpy. Whether you steal or not, you're changing the rhythm of the game. If the pitcher is concerned about you, he isn't concentrating enough on the batter. You're doing something without doing anything. You're out there to make a difference."

With the Reds leading, 2–1, in the sixth inning of the fifth game, Morgan led off and drew a walk. (He had singled in the first inning and instantly stolen second.) The Boston pitcher, Reggie Cleveland, now threw over to first base seven times before delivering his first pitch to the next Cincinnati hitter, Johnny Bench — a strike. Apparently determining to fight it out along these lines if it took all winter, Cleveland went to first four more times, pitched a foul, threw to first five more times, and delivered a ball. Only one of the throws came close to picking off Morgan, who got up each time and quickly resumed his lead about eleven feet down the line. Each time

Cleveland made a pitch, Morgan made a flurrying little bluff toward second. Now Cleveland pitched again and Bench hit a grounder to right — a single, it turned out, because second baseman Denny Doyle was in motion toward the base and the ball skipped through, untouched, behind him. Morgan flew around to third, and an instant later Tony Perez hit a three-run homer — his second homer of the day — and the game was gone, 6–2. Doyle said later that he had somehow lost sight of Bench's hit for an instant, and the box score said later that Perez had won the game with his hitting and that Don Gullett, who allowed only two Boston batters to reach first base between the first and the ninth innings, had won it with his pitching, but I think we all knew better. Morgan had made the difference.

Game six. Game Six . . . what can we say of it without seeming to diminish it by recapitulation or dull it with detail? Those of us who were there will remember it, surely, as long as we have any baseball memory, and those who wanted to be there and were not will be sorry always. Crispin Crispian: for Red Sox fans, this was Agincourt. The game also went out to sixty-two million television viewers, a good many millions of whom missed their bedtime. Three days of heavy rains had postponed things; the outfield grass was a lush, Amazon green, but there was a clear sky at last and a welcoming moon — a giant autumn squash that rose above the right-field Fenway bleachers during batting practice.

In silhouette, the game suggests a well-packed but dangerously overloaded canoe — with the high bulge of the Red Sox' three first-inning runs in the bow, then the much bulkier hump of six Cincinnati runs amidships, then the counterbalancing three Boston runs astern, and then, way aft, one more shape. But this picture needs colors: Fred Lynn clapping his hands once, quickly and happily, as his three-run opening shot flies over the Boston bullpen and into the bleachers . . . Luis Tiant fanning Perez with a curve and the Low-Flying Plane, then dispatching Foster with a Fall Off the Fence. Luis does not have his fastball, however. . . .

Pete Rose singles in the third. Perez singles in the fourth — his first real contact off Tiant in three games. Rose, up again in the fifth, with a man on base, fights off Tiant for seven pitches, then singles hard to center. Ken Griffey triples off the wall, exactly at the seam of the left-field and center-field angles; Fred Lynn, leaping up for the ball and missing it, falls backward into the wall and comes down heavily. He lies there, inert, in a terrible, awkwardly twisted position, and for an instant all of us think that he has been killed. He is up at last, though, and even stays in the lineup, but the noise and joy are gone out of the crowd, and the game is turned around. Tiant, tired and old and, in the end, bereft even of mannerisms, is rocked again and again — eight hits in three innings — and Johnson removes him, far too late, after Geronimo's first-pitch home run in the eighth has run the score to 6–3 for the visitors.

By now, I had begun to think sadly of distant friends of mine — faithful lifelong Red Sox fans all over New England, all over the East, whom I could almost see sitting silently at home and slowly shaking their heads as winter began to fall on them out of their sets. I scarcely noticed when Lynn led off the eighth with a single and Petrocelli walked. Sparky Anderson, flicking levers like a master back-hoe operator, now called in Eastwick, his sixth pitcher of the night, who fanned Evans and retired Burleson on a fly. Bernie Carbo, pinch-hitting, looked wholly overmatched against Eastwick, flailing at one inside fastball like someone fighting off a wasp with a croquet mallet. One more fastball arrived, high and over the middle of the plate, and Carbo smashed it in a gigantic, flattened parabola into the center- field bleachers, tying the game. Everyone out there — and everyone in the stands, too, I suppose — leaped to his feet and waved both arms exultantly, and the bleachers looked like the dark surface of a lake lashed with a sudden night squall.

The Sox, it will be recalled, nearly won it right away, when they loaded the bases in the ninth with none out, but an ill-advised dash home by Denny Doyle after a fly, and a cool, perfect peg to the plate by George Foster, snipped the chance. The balance of the game now swung back, as it so often does when opportunities are wasted. Drago pitched out of a jam in the tenth, but he flicked Pete Rose's uniform with a pitch to start the eleventh. Griffey bunted, and Fisk snatched up the ball and, risking all, fired to second for the force on Rose. Morgan was next, and I had very little hope left. He struck a drive on a quick, deadly rising line — you could still hear the loud *whock!* in the stands as the white blur went out over the infield — and for a moment I thought the ball would land ten or fifteen rows back in the right-field bleachers. But it wasn't hit quite that hard — it was traveling too fast, and there was no sail to it — and Dwight Evans, sprinting backward and watching the flight of it over his shoulder, made a last-second, half-staggering turn to his left, almost facing away from the plate at the end, and pulled the ball in over his head at the fence. The great catch made for two outs in the end, for Griffey had never stopped running and was easily doubled off first.

And so the swing of things was won back again. Carlton Fisk, leading off the bottom of the twelfth against Pat Darcy, the eighth Reds pitcher of the night — it was well into morning now, in fact — socked the second pitch up and out, farther and farther into the darkness above the lights, and when it came down at last, reilluminated, it struck the topmost, innermost edge of the screen inside the yellow left-field foul pole and glanced sharply down and bounced on the grass: a fair ball, fair all the way. I was watching the ball, of course, so I missed what everyone on television saw — Fisk waving wildly, weaving and writhing and gyrating along the first-base line, as he wished the ball fair, *forced* it fair with his entire body. He circled the bases in triumph, in sudden company with several hundred fans, and jumped on home plate with both feet, and John Kiley, the Fenway Park organist, played Handel's "Hallelujah Chorus," *fortissimo,* and then followed with other appropriately exuberant classical selections, and for the second time that evening I suddenly remembered all my old absent and distant Sox-afflicted friends (and all the other Red Sox fans, all over New

England), and I thought of them — in Brookline, Mass., and Brooklin, Maine; in Beverly Farms and Mashpee and Presque Isle and North Conway and Damariscotta; in Pomfret, Connecticut, and Pomfret, Vermont; in Wayland and Providence and Revere and Nashua, and in both the Concords and all five Manchesters; and in Raymond, New Hampshire (where Carlton Fisk lives), and Bellows Falls, Vermont (where Carlton Fisk was *born*), and I saw all of them dancing and shouting and kissing and leaping about like the fans at Fenway — jumping up and down in their bedrooms and kitchens and living rooms, and in bars and trailers, and even in some boats here and there, I suppose, and on back-country roads (a lone driver getting the news over the radio and blowing his horn over and over, and finally pulling up and getting out and leaping up and down on the cold macadam, yelling into the night), and all of them, for once at least, utterly joyful and believing in that joy — alight with it.

It should be added, of course, that very much the same sort of celebration probably took place the following night in the midlands towns and vicinities of the Reds' supporters — in Otterbein and Scioto; in Frankfort, Sardinia, and Summer Shade; in Zanesville and Louisville and Akron and French Lick and Loveland. I am not enough of a social geographer to know if the faith of the Red Sox fan is deeper or hardier than that of a Reds rooter (although I secretly believe that it may be, because of his longer and more bitter disappointments down the years). What I do know is that this belonging and caring is what our games are all about; this is what we come for. It is foolish and childish, on the face of it, to affiliate ourselves with anything so insignificant and patently contrived and commercially exploitative as a professional sports team, and the amused superiority and icy scorn that the non-fan directs at the sports nut (I know this look — I know it by heart) is understandable and almost unanswerable. Almost. What is left out of this calculation, it seems to me, is the business of caring — caring deeply and passionately, really *caring* — which is a capacity or an emotion that has almost gone out of our lives. And so it seems possible that we have come to a time when it no longer matters so much what the caring is about, how frail or foolish is the object of that concern, as long as the feeling itself can be saved. Naiveté — the infantile and ignoble joy that sends a grown man or woman to dancing and shouting with joy in the middle of the night over the haphazardous flight of a distant ball — seems a small price to pay for such a gift.

The seventh game, which settled the championship in the very last inning and was watched by a television audience of seventy-five million people, probably would have been a famous thriller in some other Series, but in 1975 it was outclassed. It was a good play that opened on the night after the opening night of *King Lear*. The Red Sox sprang away to an easy 3–0 lead in the third inning — easy because Don Gullett was overthrowing and walked in two runs in the course of striking out the side. By the fifth inning, the Sox had also left nine runners aboard, and a gnawing conviction settled on me that this was not going to be their day after all. It occurred to me simultaneously that this lack of confidence probably meant that I had finally qualified as a Red Sox fan, a lifelong doubter (I am sort of a Red Sox fan, which barely counts at all in the great company of afflicted true believers), but subsequent study of the pattern of this Series shows that my doubts were perfectly realistic. The Red Sox had led in all seven games, but in every game after the opener the Reds either tied or reversed the lead by the ninth inning or (once) put the tying and winning runs aboard in the ninth. This is called pressure baseball, and it is the absolute distinguishing mark of a championship team.

Here, working against Bill Lee, the Reds nudged and shouldered at the lead, putting their first batter aboard in the third, fourth, and fifth innings but never quite bringing him around. Rose led off with a single in the sixth. (He got on base eleven times in his last fifteen appearances in the Series.) With one out, Bench hit a sure double-play ball to Burleson, but Rose, barreling down toward second, slid high and hard into Doyle just as he was firing on to first, and the

ball went wildly into the Boston dugout. Lee, now facing
Perez, essayed a looping, quarter-speed, spinning curve, and
Perez, timing his full swing exactly, hit the ball over the wall
and over the screen and perhaps over the Massachusetts
Turnpike. The Reds then tied the game in the seventh (when
Lee was permitted to start his winter vacation), with Rose
driving in the run.

The Cincinnati bullpen had matters in their charge by now,
and almost the only sounds still to be heard were the
continuous cries and clappings and shouts of hope from the
Reds' dugout. Fenway Park was like a waiting accident ward
early on a Saturday night. Ken Griffey led off the ninth and
walked, and was sacrificed to second. Willoughby, who had
pitched well in relief, had been lost for a pinch-hitter in the
bottom of the eighth, and the new Boston pitcher was a thin,
tall left-handed rookie named Jim Burton, who now retired a
pinch-hitter, Dan Driessen, and then (showing superb intelli-
gence, I thought) walked Pete Rose. Joe Morgan was the
next batter, and Burton — staring in intently for his sign,
checking the runners, burning with concentration — gave it
his best. He ran the count to one and two and then threw an
excellent pitch — a slider down and away, off the outer sliver
of the plate. Morgan, almost beaten by it, caught it with the
outer nub of his bat and lofted a little lob out to very short
center field that rose slightly and then lost its hold, dropping
in well in front of the onrushing, despairing Lynn, as the last
runner of the year came across the plate. That was all;
Boston went down in order.

I left soon, walking through the trash and old beer cans and
torn-up newspapers on Jersey Street in company with
hundreds of murmuring and tired Boston fans. They did not
look bitter, and perhaps they felt, as I did, that no team in our
time had more distinguished itself in the World Series than
the Red Sox — no team, that is, but the Cincinnati Reds.

This series, of course, was replayed everywhere in memory
and conversation through the ensuing winter, and even now
its colors still light up the sky. In the middle of November that

fall, a Boston friend of mine dropped into a tavern in Cambridge — in the workingman's, or non-Harvard, end of Cambridge — and found a place at the bar. "It was a Monday night," he told me later, "and everybody was watching the NFL game on the TV set up at the other end of the bar. There wasn't a sound in the place, and after I'd been there about ten minutes the old guy next to me put down his beer glass and sort of shook his head and whispered to himself, "We never should have taken out Willoughby.""

Dan Riley

How the Boston Red Sox Won the 1975 World Series

A Story, Alas

I've had THE POWER for some time now. Inherited it from my father, I guess, and got my first intimations of it when I was no more than a kid of 12–12½. It was then that I began to see direct correlations between the success of my team, the Boston Red Sox, and where and how I positioned myself during their games.

It was back in 1961 and the Sox were about to play the Detroit Tigers in an afternoon game at Fenway Park. From the pre-game show through the "Star-Spangled Banner" I was receiving strong vibrations from the area of the family coffee table and sofa. I wasn't at all sure what the vibrations were about at the time. Being on the brink of adolescence, vibrations were coming from everywhere, but I went with my instincts. I nestled into the corner of the sofa, kicked off my PF Flyers, and propped my feet up on the coffee table.

The event would change my life, because there in the corner of the sofa with my feet upon the table and crossed at the ankles and my head resting upon a satin pillow inscribed *Festival of Our Lady of Sorrow Aug. 9–12, 1955. Thompson-ville, Conn.*, I had my first real experience with THE POWER. Call it native intuition or call it divine revelation, but I just knew that if I held my position on the sofa and my attention on the TV, the Red Sox would win that game. I decided to call the space my body occupied the POWER CENTER (PC) and the state of my mind TOTAL CONCEN-TRATION (TC). And neither thirst for Coke nor hunger for chips was going to make me abandon either until the last out of the game had been made.

Bill Monbouquette, then ace of the Sox staff, was the starting pitcher against the Tigers that day. It was a Satur-day — cleaning day. My mother, ace of our house-cleaning staff, was starting her vacuum cleaner against me and our Motorola. Neil Chrisly, an outfielder, was the Tiger lead-off hitter. Chrisly batted left-handed with what they now call an inside-out swing, meaning that his swing drove the ball to the opposite field. In those days Curt Gowdy was calling him a wrong-field hitter. (In Little League, if we did it, our coaches reemed us out for swinging too late.)

My mother cleaned right-handed and approached the coffee table from the left. "Just a minute, Mom," I said. "Just this one batter." But she drove forward with the hose of her vacuum, forcing my feet off the coffee table and out of the POWER CENTER. And Chrisly drove a Monbouquette fastball off the left-field wall for a double.

I was rattled — hopping mad, as they say in the big leagues — and I told my mother so. "You just ruined the guy's no-hitter!" I hollered above the roar of her Hoover. But she played deaf to my outburst and simply vacuumed her way out of the POWER CENTER, into the dining room and tracts of household dirt beyond.

Fortunately I regained my composure and the POWER CENTER in time to get Monbouquette through the next three batters, but let history record that Bill Monbouquette missed a no-hitter that day by one pitch — and that pitch became Neil Chrisly's vacuum cleaner double off the wall.

There was no mistaking the lesson of that game: it is not whether the game is won or lost, nor even how the game is played that counts so much as what I, with my newfound, awesome POWER, did at home. Games, I realized, could be decided before they even began, depending upon my ability to find the PC and get into TC — both of which could be elusive as a glance at the Red Sox composite won–lost record since '61 will reveal.

I've been out in front of the TV before virtually every game, feeling for the vibrations in the room. The pre-game chatter between the old batting coach who's become an announcer and the old announcer who's become a batting coach has helped imbue my being with a sense of baseball-ness. Then the National Anthem comes on and helps soothe the stresses of the workaday world in my body. By the time the drum and bugle corps gets to "rockets' red glare and bombs bursting in air," body and soul are reaching out for the POWER CENTER in the room.

Sometimes the vibrations come from the worn, red arm-chair in the corner — sometimes from the straight-back rocker by the door — often they come from my couch — eight handsome feet long, stuffed with duck feathers and upholstered in a custom-made fabric that featured thousands of pairs of tiny red socks. (That couch is the winningest three-cushioned couch in the majors, and I have the stats to prove it.) Occasionally THE POWER will settle in a hard place — like an end table — or worse. I've never liked watching ball games from the top of an end table.

There've been times, however, when there've been no vibrations at all — no signs — no clues as to where the old PC is. I once stood in front of the TV through an entire doubleheader waiting for the room to signal me. It never did and the Sox lost both games. As I grew more mature and adept at using THE POWER, I'd actively seek out the PC if I didn't get a message by the time of the first beer break. I'd sit here. I'd sit there. I'd hang my legs over the arms and backs of chairs. I'd turn the rocker around and straddle it from behind. I'd take the couch in the supine position or the belly-down position — the upright position if necessary. I'd assume any angle in any place for a Red Sox victory. (Posture isn't everything: it's the only thing!)

My mastery over THE POWER — and its subsequent mastery over me became apparent during the 1975 Championship Series between the Sox and the Oakland A's. In my haste to locate PC and get into TC before the start of game one, I tripped over a treacherously placed hassock which had been given to me by my mother as a house-warming gift. Before I could come to my senses, the Señor, Luis Tiant was on the mound for the Sox, and he was dazzling. From his very first pitch it was clear that the PC was on the floor, and I had my work cut out for me.

Playing the POWER CENTER from the floor is one of the most exhausting positions imaginable, but I played it naturally that day — stretching out laterally in front of the TV and cradling my head in the palm of my right hand. I'd played THE POWER from the floor before and was well acquainted with the discomfort it caused the hip and the elbow, and by the seventh inning of game one all the blood from my wrist to my shoulder had drained into the joint between them. The players call it "a handful of bees" when their bats make bad contact on a cold day and it stings, and that's what I had too — a handful of bees, caused by all those innings of propping my head up with my hand. It was an overall torturous, but gutsy performance on my part — and in the end it paid off. The Sox beat the A's 5–3 to take the lead in their best of five series.

My excitement about game two of the playoffs was near a fever pitch when I discovered to my dismay that the PC was again located on the living room floor. Later reference to the record book and my own infallible memory for such things revealed that on no previous occasion had the POWER CENTER stayed on the floor for two consecutive games. It was unprecedented, and although I winced at the thought of putting my body through the rigors of the floor position again I knew there was a pennant on the line and in a pennant drive everybody gives 150%. And once again the agony paid off in ecstasy — the Stockings beat the A's 6–3.

Both teams traveled the 3,000 miles from Boston to the West Coast for the third game in Oakland. Incredibly, the

POWER CENTER didn't move an inch. For the third game in a row every vibration in the house was coming from the same spot in the middle of my living room floor. I was astounded and not a little concerned about my health. I had ice-packed my arm and given my hip a whirlpool bath after game two. At best, I figured, both would be ready again for spring training. The prospect of playing the floor once more was, in a word, stupefying. Not to play the couch during a big series like the playoffs was one thing, but at this point I would've settled for the armchair — or the straight-back rocker — the end table even. I would've played the end table without a word of protest. But to return to the floor and submit my body to its excruciating demands was more than should've been asked of any one fan.

I paced the room and pondered my options. I even tried RATIONALITY. "This is nonsense," I argued to myself. "This ball game being played a continent away cannot be affected one way or the other by me. I can watch it from the floor — or the couch — or spread-eagle off the ironing board and it will still come out the same." I wasn't some dumb flat-earther, ignorant of the advances in modern thought. I took adult education classes, read *Psychology Today,* studied the social theories of Charles Reich and Robert H. Rimmer. Truly I was capable of rational thought and action. So why this obedience to such a superstitious ritual?

Because the evidence was irrefutable, that's why. My mind flashed back to 1967, the Red Sox Impossible Dream year — a 100–1 shot driving for the pennant. They were getting obliterated by the lowly California Angels one day, 8–0, and for the life of me I couldn't find the PC anywhere. In exasperation I decided to go out for a drive and clear my head. I walked through the side entry of my garage and got into my car. I turned on the ignition — and the radio — but before I could reach for my automatic garage door opener, there was Ned Martin's voice on the radio breathlessly announcing the Sox' comeback. Mercy! I couldn't believe it — the POWER CENTER was there in my garage, and I was nearly breathless myself by the time the Sox tied the game up. And I was nearly overcome with carbon monoxide by the time Rico Petrocelli turned in a nifty play in front of the bag at second, giving the Sox a miraculous come-from-behind victory. The Red Sox won the pennant by one game that year — and it was won as much by my clutch gasps on poison gas as it was by all of Carl Yastrzemski's home runs.

The memory inspired me. I knew I'd been through worse, so I took my place on the floor. My hip ached. My arm throbbed. The bees in my hand turned to wasps by the bottom of the third and by the top of the sixth the wasps had turned to Jews — and Arabs — fighting it out over the Golan Heights. But the Sox were winning the pennant and I was coming to understand the pleasure in pain.

The World Series of 1975 stacked up as a classic match-up. On the one hand there were the good-fielding, hard-hitting Reds of Cincinnati; on the other hand were the good-fielding, hard-hitting Red Sox of Boston. The only difference between the two teams could be found in my living room. It's not that I have an exclusive monopoly on THE POWER, because I don't. It wouldn't surprise me if variations on my power could be found throughout the American and National Leagues — although not in every city. There are some places — Cincinnati, for instance — that just don't have that mystical quality about them. The nickname The Big Red Machine . . . like the Bronx Bombers of old . . . rings more metallic than magical. Karma simply doesn't mix with machines big, red, or otherwise.

If the series had matched the Sox with one of the more otherworldly teams in the National League, however, we really would've had our hands full. My PC could've been neutralized if the Sox had met, say, the Cubs or the Phillies. Every time I occupied my POWER CENTER, some guy in Chicago or Philadelphia could've checkmated me. *Mana a mana,* as it were. The entire series then would've been decided by the ephemeral talents of so many infielders and outfielders — naive youngsters and cynical veterans — with no deeper understanding of the transcendent aspects of their calling than the unwitting belief that they should not leave their bats crossed in the on deck circle.

Cincinnati was just arrogant and haughty enough a city, just Aryan enough, to preclude the possibility of any supernatural intervention in the Reds' favor. Therefore the Boston–Cincinnati series shaped up as a good one, with the intangibles clearly on the side of the Sox.

Or were they?

Defying every law of probability known to man, the PC for the first game of the 1975 World Series was, believe it or not, located on my living room floor again! At the moment of what should've been my greatest triumph as a Red Sox fan, I found myself mired in anguish and despair. I looked longingly at my couch. I'd expected to ride it to at least half the post-season victories needed for the World Championship, yet I hadn't watched a game from it in over a week. If my power had indeed come from the gods, I decided in those grim moments before the start of game one, then those gods must surely be Yankee fans. This was just the kind of sick, demented trick I'd come to expect from New Yorkers.

I was all the more determined to stick it out now. Hip in place — arm cocked — head in palm. The clean-up man in the Sox order hadn't even come to the plate when all the hurt from the previous week came driving through my body again, only more wrenching than before. I wanted to scream, to cry, to whimper at least. The slightest hint of a Reds' rally would've broken me. I would've abandoned the floor — PC — TC — the whole POWER trip. But El Tiante was pitching — brilliantly again — and it was evident from the start that to cinch victory in the first game of the 1975 World Series I had to do one simple, solitary thing: endure.

Endure I did, and the Sox humbled the vaunted Big Red Machine, 6–0.

Any jubilation I may have felt over winning game one was severely dampened by my deteriorating physical condition. My right arm had become limp and practically useless. My awkward attempts at shaving with my left hand had turned my already ghastly face into a pitiful visage of scar and stubble. Worse still was the wretched condition of my hip. It'd become black and swollen, and I feared that the infection was spreading down to the lower regions of my leg. I shuddered at the thought of gangrene.

Sleep was impossible. A nightmarish vision materialized before my bed. The world had become floor. I could see nothing but linoleum clear to the horizons — no mountains, valleys, or streams — just floor. And I stood on it, trembling and alone, except for a black and white portable Sony, its rabbit ears pointing off in the direction of the eternal ballgame.

Game two was scheduled for a Sunday. I stayed in bed through breakfast and church, the Sunday paper and *Meet the Press*. Hiding under my covers, I wanted nothing more than that the world would pass me by and take its debilitating series of champions with it. But as game time approached, I was seized by a paroxysm of greater terror. If I turned my back on the Sox now, if I gave up on THE POWER now, I'd be making a mockery of my entire life. All the effort, the endless manipulation of body and furniture, had been in pursuit of one goal, the World Championship for the Boston Red Sox.

I had faltered once before. In '67, after playing the PC flawlessly and guiding the Sox through a four team scramble for the pennant, I went astray as the Sox met the St. Louis Cardinals in the World Series. It was a woman, of course, filling my head up with so many crazy ideas that I couldn't achieve TOTAL CONCENTRATION and I stopped caring where I sat and how. By the seventh game of the series, the animal in me completely dominated the spiritual — and the Cards dominated the Sox, 7–2.

It took me seven penitent years to find my soul again. If those Yankee gods had designated the floor as the POWER CENTER, then the floor it would be. After all, it was their ballgame.

I dragged my bashed and beaten body out of the bed and down the stairs. I could barely do better than crawl across the room. Indeed, I didn't have to because there on the floor in front of me was the PC again, manifest now as a grinning, hollow-eyed, she-creature who raised a long, crooked finger and beckoned me to her side. Could this alluring lamia be Lady Luck, I asked myself.

She pulled greying, withered hairs from her chin and belched into my face. The lower part of my body from the hip down went numb. Sustained by a slight Red Sox lead, I maintained TOTAL CONCENTRATION as long as I could. Then, in the seventh inning, it started to rain. They held up the game, and I grimaced as I watched them roll the tarp over the diamond. It was the last I would see of any of it that day. I blacked out before the game resumed and the Red Sox lost.

I've seen the hit that beat the Sox a dozen times since then. It was an infield bouncer up the middle that Denny Doyle grabbed behind second but couldn't convert into an out. Doyle can be forgiven. There are limits to what the body can do. As for my own lapse, there can be no forgiveness. A man's spirit should be limitless. Two more innings from me is all they needed and they would've had the Reds on the run. But I cracked. My faith died in a little cloudburst.

But as in all matters of the soul, that which can die can always be reborn. And my faith was reborn for game three. With the loss in game two, the spell on the floor had been broken. Euphoria pulsated through my rejuvenated organs and limbs. I even managed a modified jig around the room when I felt the unmistakable pull of the PC drawing me toward the couch. POWER and couch were united again. Dismantlement to the Big Red Machine! *Gloria in Excelsis* to the Boston Red Sox!

It was going to be easy. The vibrations were indicating I could take the couch on my back — my very best all-time position. It seemed certain now that the Big Red Machine was doomed to stutter and stop right before its own deluded fans.

The Red Sox took an early lead, and I was ready to take a three-day romp through Cincinnati lying down when, in the fourth, with Rick Wise pitching to Tony Perez, a faint knock-

knocking intruded on my TC. At first I dismissed it as a local woodpecker or the failing engine of some distant plane. But it persisted, breaking my TC, and Perez walked. I knew I had to find the source of the noise before any more damage was done, so I moved quickly to the door. Perez stole second. I answered the door. Bench hit a two-run homer. The Reds were ahead, 2–1.

She was shorter than I remembered her, older too. A grey ambience hung about her face like a shroud, and the shock of seeing her there in my doorway was given added voltage by the sight of baggage she clutched in her hand. It was my mother.

"It's your father!" she cried. "He's thrown me out at home!"

My dad knew a thing or two about THE POWER himself and taught me everything he'd ever learned about it. He was on the road a great deal selling St. Christopher medals and rabbits' feet, but whenever he was home the two of us worked out together. After supper he would take me down into his den, and we would practice moving furniture around. It was Dad in fact who helped to make me a switch-sitter, teaching me how to shift my weight from one cheek to the other while holding the PC in a particularly uncomfortable chair. He's a clothes man himself and not much into furniture, but he's got good natural instincts for THE POWER. Many evenings after our furniture sessions together he would take me up to his closet and show me some of the clothes in which he found THE POWER during crucial moments in history. There was the tuxedo he wore throughout the Cuban Missile Crisis. "Your mom and I were at the Harvest Ball when JFK gave his speech," he told me, "and I just knew that if I took that outfit off the whole world was a-goner." There was the pork pie hat he wore during Ike's heart attack. "Back then," he'd say, "that hat's the only thing that stood between Nixon and the White House." Then there were the Bermuda shorts and the polo shirt he wore while Ted Williams was off fighting the Korean War. "Good thing it was a short war," he confessed, "the winters nearly killed me."

Dad is a true believer in THE POWER, so it didn't surprise me at all to hear that the falling out between him and Mom was over her meddling in his power. "He said I lost the second game of the World Series," she sobbed into my sweater, "but all I did was wash his underwear."

"His underwear!" I exclaimed, knowing now what had happened.

"His underwear," she repeated tearfully, "his unsightly tops and bottoms which he hadn't taken off in over a week. He called them his lucky undies, but they were making me gag. So I took them and washed them last Sunday while he showered and he went out of his mind. He called me a debunker and an iconoclast and told me to get out of the house. 'You did it!' he screamed for all the neighbors to hear. 'You lost the second game of the World Series and I won't have you in my bed another night!'" She choked back another flood of tears and raised her baleful eyes to mine. "How could he say that? How could he say I lost the second game of the World Series?"

How indeed.

I looked over at my TV screen and the how was clear. The Reds had gone ahead 5–1 since she had crossed my threshold with her tale of woe. I staggered against the wall, weakened by the score. My mother, meanwhile, unloaded herself and her sorrow right in the middle of my POWER CENTER.

"You can't sit there!" I blurted out. "That's my lucky spot."

At that she began rocking back and forth, bewailing and bemoaning as only she could. "Oh my, my. Oh my, my. This can't be. This can't be. First my husband and now my son — my only begotten son, flesh of my flesh, blood of my blood." She stopped shaking long enough to cast a cold, hard look in my direction. "I endured a C-section for you, ingrate."

She had me. She had the couch as well. You can't throw a mother off your couch after she's gone and done something like that for you.

"Wanna beer?" I asked, resigning myself to the fact that the Reds were about to be up in the series two games to one.

She blew her nose and nodded yes.

As I reached in the fridge for a couple of brews, however, the bracing chill of inspiration blew over me. It was a million-to-one shot, but the Sox were down by four runs anyway and I had nothing to lose. It seemed slightly crazy at the time, but if I could get into TOTAL CONCENTRATION and if the POWER CENTER would accept my mother's body in place of my own, I just might pull off a baseball first — a cross-body transference.

The beer was the vital element in my scheme. I had to mellow my mother out so that she wasn't disturbing the PC, dusting things with her forefinger and whatnot. When I got back to the living room, she was arranging my magazines in chronological order. "Here, Mom, drink this," I said, trying to conceal the sense of urgency, "it'll make you feel better."

Two swigs into her bottle and she started to calm down; halfway through the bottle and she stopped muttering about my father and kicked off her shoes; a couple of inches short of empty and her eyes were sagging to a close and her head was sinking to repose. She was out and the Sox were up!

Two walks, a wild pitch, and a fly to center got them one run. A pinch hit homer got them another. It wasn't the Miracle of Coogan's Bluff, but it was a rally just the same and the cross-body transference was working! The PC was operating at full capacity in the ninth when Dwight Evans rocketed a two-run homer over the left-field fence to tie the score. Delirium swept through my parlor. I shot out of my chair with a mighty, joyous whoop!

Mom stirred. I eased myself back down into my chair. Polyester to Herculon, I hardly made a sound. If she awoke, the whole psyche-sphere would be upset. The game would fall out of control again. We'd come too far for that.

I maintained TC through the ninth and into the tenth. I was milking her recumbent body for all it was worth while keeping the Sox even with the Reds. It was remarkable.

And then, as the Reds came to bat in the bottom of the tenth, she stirred again. "Where am I?" she mumbled.

"Sleep," I intoned softly. "Sleep. You are very, very sleepy."

A deep, violent burp broke the hypnotic spell of my voice and she sat up.

Geronimo of the Reds singled.

"I must relieve myself," she said, rising.

"Not now!" I begged.

"Yes, now," she said, as Armbrister turned to bunt.

"Get back!" I shouted.

"I must relieve myself," she said, as Fisk went for Armbrister's bunt.

I dove for the POWER CENTER.

Collision!

Kubek beat the rule book crying foul from the broadcast booth and NBC replayed the Fisk-Armbrister collision as America, land of the grassy knoll and home of the Zapruder film, looked in vain for the interference call from Umpire Barnett. Controversy swirled around Riverfront Stadium, but it was misplaced. The instant replay should've been of my living room, of my mother teetering toward the toilet, of my diving headlong across the room, belly-flopping down on the glass-topped table, bashing my jaw off the wrought-iron hassock legs, crashing my head against a collapsing Tiffany lamp, and mashing my nose beneath the tumbling weight of a 176-pound, hysterical mother.

When I regained consciousness, I was in a local hospital, wrapped in bandages from head to foot. Time had become a blur. Months may've passed since the third game of the World Series. Years, even. I didn't know.

I peeked through the eye-hole of my bandages and saw a lanky left-hander in aviator glasses approach. He shoved a cigarette through the slit that led to my mouth. I choked on it. "Don't smoke," I coughed.

"Sorry, sport," he said, "don't want to lose you now. You've made quite a comeback. When your mom brought you in, you weren't much more than a shaky combination of contusions and lacerations but you're doing just fine now. We'll have you out of here before you can say 'Pinky Higgins.' By the way," he added, reaching into his pocket, "got this postcard from your mother this morning. 'Say goodbye to the lunatic for me,' she says. It's postmarked Cincinnati." He turned to leave, but the sound of Cincinnati had jarred my memory.

"Doc," I implored in a low, raspy voice, "the World Series, Doc. Who won the '75 Series?"

"Who won it?" he beamed broadly. "Why no one's won it. The Reds lead three games to two. It's been raining in Boston for almost a week now. You'll be able to see the sixth game for yourself tonight. We'll roll a TV in here for you." And with that he turned on his heel and vanished.

I could hardly believe my ears. We were still in it. The Series wasn't over. The Sox still had a chance. Rain, he'd said. Rain in Boston. Rain from Providence, no doubt, had given me one more chance to muster THE POWER together and destroy the Big Red Machine.

Could it be done, though? That was the question. My range was limited to a hospital bed. The odds against finding the POWER CENTER there were prohibitive. And even if I found it, the cocoon of bandages wrapped around me strictly constrained lateral as well as anterior and posterior movements. I wouldn't have the agility needed for occupying any but the most orthodox positions. The obstacles were damn near overwhelming, but I knew that I'd practically pulled off a successful cross-body transference in game three. Who could tell what might happen in game six?

Who indeed.

Seventy million Americans could tell, that's who. Seventy million Americans watched Bernie Carbo clout a three-run homer to tie for the Sox in the eighth; seventy million Americans saw Dwight Evans make an unheard of catch to save it in the eleventh; seventy million Americans looked on as Pudge Fisk lofted one in the screen in left to win it in the twelfth. Seventy million Americans enjoyed the greatest game ever played — thanks to a semi-invalid in a hospital bed a hundred miles away.

It was a feat unparalleled in the annals of sports phenomenology, and I'd done it under the direst conditions. For hours I just lay there savoring it all, replaying the Fisk home run again and again off the ceiling. Until the doctor broke my revelry. "Pinky Higgins," he said, twinkling.

"Huh?" I said.

"Time to take those bandages off and go home," he announced.

I took it as a joke and muffled a chuckle or two beneath my wrappings. Then he produced a shining set of shears, and I realized how serious he was. My eyeballs dilated to painful proportions and I yelled, "Can't do it, Doc! The seventh game of the Series is on tonight. I gotta see it. . . ."

"Sure you do," he said with maddening calm, "and you shall see it — at home on your own TV." And he began snipping away. "No, here!" I squealed. "This is the POWER CEN-TER . . . this bed . . . these bandages . . . I need them . . . the Sox need them . . . Yaz and Rico . . . El Tiante . . . they're counting on me!"

He continued to cut. I struggled to get free. Two grim nurses arrived to hold me down. One looked like my mother. I howled. They stripped me bare, stripped the POWER off my body like it was so much useless adhesive and rolled me out of the bed. I leaped to my feet and, in one last, inspired moment, I hurled my body through the wire mesh and glass to the shrubs and pavement three stories below.

I knew on impact that the Reds were dead. As they gathered my shattered body onto the stretcher and carried it away, I knew I was on my way back to bed and bandages — back to the POWER CENTER and onto the Championship of the World for the Boston Red Sox.

And I made it happen — me — the best 26th man in baseball. I made it happen just by being the right man in the right place at the right time. It didn't matter that I couldn't see it or hear it. I felt it and that's enough.

But try telling that to some of these doctors around here. What do they know about baseball? All they care about are dreams and childhood traumas. Baseball — POWER CEN-TERS, TOTAL CONCENTRATION, the old cross-body transference — none of it means baked beans to these guys.

Dad still understands though. He drops by every once in a

while to show off a pair of lucky slippers or something. And sometimes when he wheels me around the room I can still pick up a good vibration or two. Dad says that when I get better and out of here, I ought to start thinking beyond baseball. He says that if I can win the World Series for the Boston Red Sox there's probably lots more good I can do for mankind. So I'm thinking about writing a letter to the President and telling him about my power. Who knows? Maybe rearranging the White House furniture is just what this country needs.

Thomas Boswell

The Greatest Game
Ever Played

How Life Imitates the World Series

I was trying to will the ball to stay up there and never come
down.
   — Carlton Fisk on watching the Yastrzemski pop-up that
      ended the Red Sox–Yankee playoff

A baseball game, at its best, can be like an elaborate and
breathlessly balanced house of cards. Tension and a sense of
crisis build with each inning. Each deed of the game, each
player, finds his supporting role. In 1978 that house of cards
was built not for one afternoon, but for an entire six-month
season. By closing day each player seemed to carry with him
a nimbus of symbols, an entire personal history like some
Athenian warrior whose exploits against Sparta were memo-
rized by an entire community.

   In fact, one game — the playoff game between the Yankees and the Red Sox that decided the Eastern Division of
the American League — served as an almost perfect micro-
cosm of seventy-five years of baseball warfare between the
Apple and the Hub — a distillation of the game's richest and
longest rivalry.

   In the history of baseball, only one other moment —
Bobby Thompson's home run to end the '51 playoff between

the New York Giants and the Brooklyn Dodgers — has provided such a monumental house of cards as the bottom of the ninth inning of this Yankee victory.

When that impossible distinction "best game ever" is being thrashed out in heaven, these games must be mentioned first. Perhaps they should each have a crown — best in the annals of their respective leagues.

The '51 playoff, marvelous for its fireworks and confetti, was the epitome of baseball's age of innocence, a game that any child could grasp.

The '78 playoff, however, pitted teams of darker and more complex personality in a far subtler game — a contest for the student of inside baseball. Is there any other kind?

The '51 classic ended in raw pandemonium; the '78 masterpiece in utter profound silence. Certainly, it is possible to prefer the latter in such a matter of taste.

It must not be held against this masterpiece that it merely ended a divisional race, that the Yanks still had to upend two more pretenders before they could keep their World Championship for a second consecutive year. New York needed just four games to eliminate Kansas City in the American League playoffs and only six to lick Los Angeles in the World Series. Neither joust reached a moment of primitive emotion.

To beat the Bosox, the Yankees bled for six months, only to find themselves tied after the 162nd and last game of the regular season. Their final margin of triumph — 5–4 in this one-day sudden-death showdown — was thin as smoke, a distinction almost without a difference between the two most powerful teams in the sport.

Even now, that concluding moment of delicious indeterminance remains as fresh as the crack of the first line drive of spring. Baseball returns. But the Yankee–Red Sox playoff of 1978 lasts.

The sun is warm in Winter Haven now, the Florida orange trees nod their full branches over the outfield fences of the Red Sox spring training retreat.

But for Carlton Fisk, and many another Sox and Yank, the

air still seems crisp, the sky a dazzling autumn azure and one solitary pop-up hangs high over Fenway Park.

The final split-seconds of that playoff afternoon are one of baseball's indelible frozen paintings. Let Fisk speak about the moment when the air burst from a balloon that had been blown ever larger for 163 games.

"I knew the season would be over as soon as Yastrzemski's pop-up came down," said the tall, patrician catcher with his hair parted in the middle like Henry Mencken. "It seemed like the ball stayed up forever, like everything was cranked down into slow motion. I was trying to will the ball to stay up there and never come down . . . what a dumb thing to have run through your mind. Even the crowd roar sounded like a movie projector at the wrong speed when everything gets gravelly and warped.

"After the last out, I looked around and the crowd was stunned. Nobody moved. They looked at each other like, "You mean it's over now?. . . It can't be over yet . . . oh, nuts. . . .

"It had only been going on for half a year, but it seemed like a crime for it to end."

The buildup to that final crescendo actually began more than twenty-four hours before. The great playoff of '78 was, in reality, two days of absolutely contrasting atmosphere and mood.

Boston's Fenway Park is normally best on the worst days, in raw, misty spring and foggy fall. The streets around the Fens are crowded, narrow, and damp. Taxis blow their horns at the herds of Soxers in Lansdowne Street. That's the way it was on the first day of October — the last day of the regular season. A healing rain caressed that ancient, indescribably delicious ballyard — a rain of balm and absolution. In that soft October drizzle the Sox of Boston were washed clean just as New England was ready to give up hope, the prayers of Red Sox fans were answered. On that final Sunday, Boston won and the New Yorkers, playing three hundred miles away in Yankee Stadium, lost.

The most spectacular and sustained pennant race in American League history had reached the only climax worthy of it — the two best teams in baseball each had 99 victories. One of them would have to win 100.

Just two weeks before, the Red Sox had finished one of the most ignominious collapses in history — losing 17½ games in the standings to the inexorable Yankees, blowing all of a 14-game lead, and falling 3½ games behind with only 14 to play.

If Cotton Mather had been alive, he would have been a Bosox fan. And he would have been mad.

In other towns, the incipient collapse of a beloved team might bring forth prayers and novenas, as Brooklyn once lit candles for the Dodgers. In fickle Fenway, however, the faithful reacted as though the Sox had deliberately knelt in the hallowed Fens and licked the Yankees' boots.

The Red Sox have long memories. It is their curse. They are an imaginative team — more's the pity — susceptible to hauntings and collective nervous breakdowns. They prove that those who cannot forget the past are also condemned to repeat it. The evil that the Bosox do lives after them. The good is oft interred with their moans. Somewhere it must be written that the Carmine Hose shall suffer. When the Sox are winning, every player is a minor deity. When the angels fall, they are consigned to the nether regions.

So, that final-day victory, Boston's eighth in a row and twelfth in 14 games over the last two weeks, was like an emotional reprieve from the gallows. The entire final week of the season was summarized in that final chilling Sunday. Each day Boston would throw an early lead on the scoreboard, hoping to shake the New Yorkers' faith in their tiny 1-game lead. And each day the Yankee dreadnought would send its message back via the radio waves with an answering victory. A new punishment had been found to fit the Sox felony of squandering a huge lead — torture by victory. A sense of fatality, or inexorable and well-deserved punishment, seemed to hang over the Sox. The Prayer to St. Jude, patron saint of lost causes, was tacked to their bulletin board.

Finally, the ghost was all but given up. Brave talk ceased. Predictions of a playoff were swallowed. During that Sunday morning batting practice, the Sox were grim. Then the spirit of mischief seemed to enter Fenway. Toronto's flaky outfielder Sam Ewing snuck through the open door in the scoreboard and posted a fictitious "8" next to the name of the Yankees' opponent — Cleveland. The early-arriving crowd went into a tizzy that did not stop for three hours. Bizarre echoing eruptions rumbled through the stands whenever word of the Yankee demise arrived by radio. All afternoon, Sox relief pitcher Bob ("Big Foot") Stanley kept a transistor radio to his ear in the bullpen, leaping to his feet to lead hundreds of fans in ovations for Cleveland's runs. Slowly, a ripple, and finally a roar would erupt from 32,000 people as, one-by-one, the blessed message was passed like a fire bucket. Before the game even ended — with Boston ahead, 5–0, and New York behind, 9–2 — the scoreboard exulted: "Next Red Sox Home Game Tomorrow."

This was the afternoon that made '78 unique in baseball's century.

Two other teams had suffered breakdowns comparable to Boston. The New York Giants of 1914 got the rubber bone for blowing a 15-game, Fourth of July lead to the Miracle Braves of Boston, and eventually losing by a craven 10½ games. And the '51 Dodgers had a 13-game lead on August 11, only to be tied on the last day of the season, then beaten. But no team had ever looked into the abyss of absolute self-betrayal and recovered from it, come back to finish the season — despite injuries — like a furious hurricane.

At their nadir, the Sox had lost 6 straight September meetings with the Yankees by a total score of 46–9. They were outhit, 84–29. "It was so lopsided," said Boston pitcher Mike Torrez, "that you wouldn't have believed it if it had happened to the original Mets."

The real victims of the Boston collapse were, in part, the Yankees. The Horrid Hose were so disgraceful that they drained the glory from the Yanks' great comeback. "Never sell the Yankees short," said Boston coach Johnny Pesky, who has hated pinstripes for forty years. "They played great the last three months [52–22]. They'll never play that well again as long as they have assholes."

While other teams are too tight to breathe in a crisis, the Yankees spit their tobacco and smooth the dirt with their spikes. The Yanks, with their almost unsinkable raw talent, their polished passion for the game once the contest begins, and their partial immunity to the pandemonium that swathes them, have gradually come to resemble a sort of Leviathan with hiccups.

In midseason the champions were hemorrhaging in Boston. There are other New England sharks than the mythical Jaws of Amity. The pearly white teeth snapping around them on those moon-bathed nights at Fenway were the healthy and rapacious Sox. "If Boston keeps playing like this," said New York's Reggie Jackson, "even Affirmed couldn't catch them. We'll need motorcycles. . . ."

Every day and every night in those final hours of troubled manager Billy Martin the scene around the Yankees was the same. The crowds in the hotel lobbies, at the ticket windows and outside the players' entrances were huge, pummeling the players with kisses and curses.

Meanwhile, the Sox read their press clippings. Everyone from Ted Williams to the cop in Yawkey Way said these Sox were the best edition since '01. What blighter would point out that the Fenway Chronicles show an almost inexorable base-ball law: A Red Sox ship with a single leak will always find a way to sink. For documentation, see the Harvard Library. Doctoral theses are on file there.

In other seasons, the Sox self-immolation was a final act consonant with the team's public image for generations — a green wall at their backs, green bucks in their wallets, green apples in their throats. Red Sox fans had come to view their heroes with deep skepticism, searching for the tragic flaw. No team is worshipped with such a perverse sense of fatality. "Human, all too human," that's the Red Sox logo.

Ever since the day sixty years before when dastardly Harry Frazee sold Babe Ruth to the Yankees, fortune had forsaken the Sox. The axis of baseball power swung south with Ruth. Since Boston last raised a Series banner in 1918, the Yankees have been champions 22 times.

This grim heritage, however, was an unfair burden to the '78 Sox who were the antithesis of their predecessors. If the Sox had a critical flaw, an Achilles' heel, it was their excess of courage, their unquestioning obedience to the god of guts. This, they swore to a man, was the year for that eternally receding World Series Triumph. Let the '80s be damned.

The Sox scapegoat was easy to find — doughty little Manager Don Zimmer, the man with the metal plate in his head whom Bill Lee contemptuously called "the gerbil." Zimmer was publicly seen as a hard guy who was given a high-strung, high-octane Indy race car and kept the pedal to the metal as though he were driving an old dirt-track stocker. Naturally, the engine blew and the Sox coasted to a dead stop.

However, the Yankees also had catastrophic pitching problems, constant injuries for the first 100 games, and a manager who had to be fired for his own health's sake.

Why were the Yankees so good at cutting their losses, while the Red Sox were so poor at minimizing theirs? Why did the Yankees have the restraint to let their injured heal in June, when the Sox were pummeling them, while the Sox exacerbated their miseries by going full throttle?

It's all tied up with history and that old Yankee fear. It's axiomatic in the Northeast that no Red Sox lead is safe. And it is cradle lore that no Boston team ever has faced up to a Yankee challenge in September. Therefore, Zimmer had little choice but to push his delicately balanced power plant until the black smoke poured from the exhaust. Mythology forced his hand. Only a 20-game lead would suffice.

The Sox pushed that lead to 14, but then the black flag waved the Sox into the pits, while the Yanks kept circling the track.

The hordes of invading Yankee fans even took to taunting the Sox in their own lair. In the tunnel under the Fenway stands, Yankee fans set up a cheer each night as they passed the doors of the Boston locker room. "Three, three, three . . . two, two, two . . . one, one, one . . . ZERO, ZERO, ZERO," they counted down the dwindling Boston margin each night as the Yankees swept the famous 4-game series that will live in lore as The Boston Massacre.

As soon as the massacred Bostonians, the despair of eight states, threw in the towel, gave up the ghost, and tossed in the sponge, they pinned the Yankees' ears back in their seventh-and-last September meeting. That, of course, is the visceral clubhouse definition of choking. If you can't tie your shoelaces under pressure but play like a world-beater as soon as it's too late, that's worse in the dugout world than being a no-talent klutz. That is called taking the apple.

Even if Boston's sweet fruit of victory had a bitter pit of self-knowledge at its center, the hard swallow was medicinal. One day the Sox were pathetically cornering reporters, asking, "Tell me, what's wrong with us?" Soon, it seemed, they would be asking that sorrowful question of lampposts and parked cars. But a small thing like one victory over New York, even one that seemed meaningless, broke the grip of the curse.

So, when the Yankees arrived at Fenway on Playoff Day, they no longer came either as June victims or September conquerors. They came as October equals — very worried equals.

The house of cards was finally built. And it was monstrous. Which way it would fall no player claimed to know.

At baseball's showcase World Series games, the batting cage is as congenial as a Kiwanians convention. Teams arrive for fame and fun; no grudges fester. Before the playoff, the Yankees and Red Sox circled each other like lions and leopards around the same African watering hole. Their only words were taunting barbs disguised as light humor.

Some celestial handicapper must have written out the lineup cards. They were too symbolic to have been penned by mortals named Don Zimmer and Bob Lemon, the Yankees' caretaker manager.

Each team spotted the other a Golden Glover as both Dwight Evans and New York's Willie Randolph were side-lined. But far better for symmetry were the starting pitchers: Torrez against Ron Guidry, the man called "Lou'siana Light-nin'."

Just a year before, Torrez had been the Yankees' World Series pitching hero, winning 2 games. Then the Sox signed him at free agent auction for $2.7 million — their loud pronouncement that they would match the Yankee pocket-book. Just four days before, Torrez had emerged from the emotional low point of his career. If one player's failure epitomized the charge of gutlessness made against all the Sox, it was Torrez. For forty days down the stretch when he was desperately needed, he had not won a single game, while losing 6.

The Sox feelings about the great Guidry were simply summed up. "We have the home field. We have the momen-tum. They . . ." said shortstop Rick Burleson, pausing, "have Guidry."

Guidry's feelings were even more elemental. Asked if a mere 1-game playoff were fair, the left-handed executioner answered, "One's enough. I can only pitch one."

Discovering Guidry in the Yankee locker room is like stumbling over a dog in a cathouse. His story is the hidden moral kernel in the vain bluster of the Yankee saga. Imagine, if it can be done, a player amid these New Yorkers who has the innate confidence of an only child, the proud self-contain-ment of a Lou'siana Cajun, and the strong silences of a small-town boy raised on hawk hunting and walking the railroad tracks.

No star player is so invisible on his own team, whether loping across the outfield or lounging in the dugout. But for this playoff, no player approached Guidry for being conspicu-ous. The reason was cogent — Guidry entered the game with the best record of any 20-game winner in the history of baseball: 24–3.

Every game needs a call to arms, but this one started with trumpet blasts.

A brilliant fall light — a painter's vivid stark light — bathed Fenway as Torrez began the day by throwing his first four pitches to Mickey Rivers low, high inside, and outside. The Yankee speedster waited only one pitch to steal second base.

"So that's it," the throng seemed to say by its sigh. It was going to be just like last time, when New York jumped to leads of 12–0, 13–0, 7–0, and 6–0 in four Fenway days. When the long history of the Sox sorrows is written, those horrific first innings in September would rank infernally high. Each game came complete with the same chilling footnote: "Ibid . . . for full details, see previous night's game."

Would it be so again? Always, it was Rivers beginning the psychic unraveling, stealing second as though it had been left to him in old Tom Yawkey's will. That sad lopsided spectacle seemed underway again when Torrez made an egregious error — throwing Reggie Jackson a fastball strike on an 0–2 pitch with 2 outs. The ball climbed to the level of the left-field light towers, climbed until it seemed to look in the faces of the teenagers, who had scrambled atop the Gilbey's Gin sign beyond the wall. The Yankees would lead, 2–0, Guidry would breeze. The great day would be a dud. But the groaning crowd had forgotten the Fenway winds.

Whenever the Sox and Yanks meet in Boston, the first order of business is to inspect the flags. The Yankees, a predominantly left-handed hitting team, desperately want an inward breeze to enlarge the confines of the cozy Fens. The Sox, designed along Brobdingnagian lines, with seven home-run hitters, would settle for dead calm. Only when the flag points toward the plate do they droop. When the Yanks arrived in early September, for four straight days the Sox grumbled as the wind blew, sometimes thirty miles an hour, straight in from left. Betrayed again, even by Fenway Park.

So, when Jackson's blast was suddenly stymied by the wind and fell almost straight down, nearly scraping the wall as it fell into Carl Yastrzemski's glove, a marvelous sense of irony swept over the Boston dugout. The Yankees had been robbed by the same fates that had bedeviled Boston.

"That was no wind," said Lee later. "That was Mr. Yaw-key's breath."

It is a unique quality of baseball that the season ticket holders who see all of a club's crucial games believe they can also read the minds of the players. Each team's season is like a traditional nineteenth-century novel, a heaping up of detail and incident about one large family. After 162 chapters of that tome, chapter 163 is riddled with the memories, implications, and foreshadowings of the thousands of previous pages. Any play that rises above the trivial sends a wave of emotion into that ocean-size novel of what has gone before. Since everyone is reading the same vast book, the sense of a collective baseball consciousness can become enormous. With each at bat, each pitch, there is an almost audible shuffling of mental pages as the pitcher, hitter, and catcher all sort through the mass of past information they have on one another. Just this sort of extended personal history existed between the Yankee star Guidry and the Boston captain Yastrzemski to begin the second inning. In a word, Yaz was harmless against Guidry when the left-hander was at, or even near, his best. So, when Yastrzemski rocked back on his heels on the second pitch of the second inning to thrash at a fastball in his wheelhouse (up-and-in), it should have been a feeble mistake. Instead, it was a home run — a hooking liner that curled around the right-field foul pole by less than a bat length. Yaz had turned the Lightnin' around.

Suddenly, the afternoon bristled with potential.

Guidry was at his weakest. Torrez, who was to strike out Yankee captain Thurman Munson three times with nibbling, teasing sliders, was at his best. In other words, they were even.

"When these teams play," Fisk had said two weeks before, "it is like a gigantic will controls the whole game. And it's either all behind one team, or all behind the other."

But this day the forces of the game could not make up their minds. It was a beautiful ambivalence.

The crowd seemed to be in the grip of angina, the cheers

caught in their nervous throats. The Keep Your Sox On faithful sat silent in their fireman caps decorated with the nicknames of their undependable deities: Boomer and Butch, Soup and Scooter, Rooster and Pudge, Eck and Louie, Big Foot and Spaceman, Dewey and Yaz. By the end of the fifth, the day's work more than half done, the ball park was so silent that those in the rooftop seats could hear Blair pleading to his Yankees, "Let's go, man. Let's go."

For this single afternoon to achieve permanence, it had to be a miniature of the entire season, a duplication of the same emotional roller coaster. So, in the sixth, the Sox scored again, Burleson lining a double over third and Jim Rice clipping an RBI single to center. As Rice's hit, his 406th total base of the season, bit into the turf, it seemed that the game, the year, and a Most Valuable Player duel between Rice and Guidry had all been decided on a single pitch.

More folly. Any historian knows that a 2–0 lead after the sixth is the quintessential Red Sox lead — just enough to merit euphoria; just enough to squander. After all, in the seventh game of the 1975 World Series Boston could taste its incipient upset over Cincinnati, leading 3–0. And that turned to dust.

Every seesaw needs a fulcrum, and Lou Piniella quickly provided one for this game.

A ground out and an intentional walk put men on first and second, 2 outs, and Fred Lynn at bat. When fragile Freddy yanked a Guidry slider into the right-field corner, every dugout mind had the same thought: "Two runs." Piniella, however, materialized directly in the path of the ball. He was so far out of normal Lynn position that he ought to have had a puff of magical smoke curling up behind him.

"It was a ridiculous place for him to be . . . about twenty yards from where he normally plays me," said Lynn.

"I talked to Munson between innings," said Piniella afterward. "We agreed that Guidry's slider was more the speed of a curveball and that somebody could pull him." Even so, Piniella was stationed in a sort of private twilight zone.

"It was a hundred-to-one shot any way you look at it," said Lynn. "He plays hunches out there. The man's just a gambler."

At bat, Piniella says, "I've guessed on every pitch that was ever thrown to me . . . don't do too bad, do I?"

To those in the stands, the play looked routine, like so many in baseball: a blistering line drive directly at an outfielder standing a few feet in front of the fence. It was the hallmark of this game that its central plays reflected the true daily life of the inner sport. They were not flamboyant and egalitarian, but exclusive and subtle. Baseball's well-kept secret is that it has never been solely a democratic national pastime, but an elitist passion as well.

The Babe and the Iron Horse will never understand what happened next. Big Ed Barrow and Colonel Jacob Ruppert will take a lot of kidding in baseball heaven when tales are told of the tiny home-run hero of the Playoff. Since the roaring '20s, the diamond nine from New York that wore gray pinstripes has meant heartless hegemony, monolithic muscle. Bucky Dent, though he bats last in the Yank order, nonetheless is a symbol of power himself — the power of cash. For two seasons George Steinbrenner was obsessed with getting Dent away from the Chicago White Sox. Finally, a trade was made.

When Dent dragged his bat to home plate with 2 out and 2 men on base in the Yankee seventh, then fouled the second pitch off his foot, hopping out of the batter's box in pain, he looked as ineffectual and inconspicuous as a CIA agent with a bomb in his briefcase. Normally, the worrywart Fisk uses such delays to visit his pitcher with admonitions, or to demand warm-up pitches. "Fisk is out at the mound so much," needles Lynn, "that I've threatened to change the number of Carlton's position from '2' to '1½.'"

But for Dent, what's the worry?

As Dent was administered a pain-killing spray, on-deck hitter Rivers, who had forgotten his sunglasses and butchered a flyball earlier, suddenly became uncharacteristically observant. He saw a crack in Dent's bat and fetched him another one of the same style. Of such minutiae is history made. That and fastballs down the middle.

"After Dent hit it," said Fisk, "I let out a sigh of relief. I thought, 'We got away with that mistake pitch.' I almost screamed at Mike.

"Then I saw Yaz looking up and I said, 'Oh, God.'"

Several innings before, the wind had reversed and was blowing toward the left-field corner. Yastrzemski watched that boosting wind loft the ball barely over the wall, fair by thirty feet. As the 3-run homer nestled in the net, Yastrzemski's knees buckled as though he had been hammered over the head with a bat.

The Yankees erupted from the dugout like souls released from Hades. What followed seemed as inexorable as a shark eating the leg after it tastes the foot.

Quicker than you could say, "Rivers walks and steals second again," Torrez was leaving the game. Though he had fanned the next hitter — Munson — three times, Zimmer waved in Stanley. Naturally, Munson doubled to the wall for the inning's fourth run.

When Reggie Jackson, the Hester Prynne of sluggers who walks through the baseball world with a scarlet dollar sign on his chest, knocked a home run into the center-field bleachers in the eighth, it seemed like mere hot doggery. And when Jackson slapped hands with Steinbrenner in the box seats before greeting any of his mates to celebrate the 5–2 lead, it was just another of Reggie's compulsive theatrical gestures.

Little did the crowd suspect what all the players knew — that the war had not ceased.

Beyond the Fenway fences, the trees of New England were tinged with reds and oranges. They might as well have been tears.

This game, like the entire season, was about to be salvaged by the sort of Red Sox rally against fate that had no historical precedent.

If Torrez and Guidry went down as the pitchers of record — the official loser and winner, then Stanley and that ornery Goose Gossage were the pitchers of memory.

In the eighth, Jerry Remy grounded a double over the first-base bag off Gossage and scored on Yastrzemski's crisp single to center. Yaz followed Remy home when Fisk and Lynn cracked singles, using their quick strokes to combat Gossage's numbing speed.

The bear trap was set for the Yanks — men on first and second with only 1 out, and the lead down to 5–4.

The great book of the season had, however, been turned to the wrong page to suit Boston.

Gossage mowed down Butch Hobson and George Scott — low-average sluggers with long, looping swings. Neither could get untangled quickly enough to handle his rising fastballs.

Never mind. The stage had been set for the bottom of the ninth with Gossage protecting his 5–4 lead.

From the press box, baseball is geometry and statistics. From the box seats, it is velocity, volume, and virtuousity. From above, Gossage is a relief pitcher. From ground level, eye-to-eye in his own world, he is a dragon.

Nevertheless, the brave Bosox started beating on Gossage's ninth-inning door. The feisty Burleson drew a 1-out walk.

Winning is an ancient Yankee story, a heritage of talent, mixed with an audacious self-confidence and an unnerving good fortune. Losing is an old sadness for the Sox, a lineage of self-doubt and misfortune. All those threads of history and baseball myths were about to come together in one play.

The 5-foot-6 Remy slashed a liner to right when the Goose's 0–2 fastball laid an egg. The assembled parishioners sang "Hallelujah," then groaned their eternal "Amen" as they saw the ball fly directly toward Piniella. Little did they, or Burleson on first, know that only one person in the park had no idea where Remy's liner was — Piniella.

"I never saw it," he said. "I just thought, 'Don't panic. Don't wave your damn arms and let the runner know you've lost it.'"

So Piniella the Gambler stood frozen, trusting, as he has so often, to luck. While Piniella waited for the streaking ball to hit at his feet or in his face, Burleson waited between bases, assuming Piniella had an easy play.

These Yankees, who seem to abolish chance with their poise, let luck fall about their shoulders like a seignoral cloak. "I never saw it until the ball hit about eight feet in front of me," said Piniella later, drenched with champagne. "It was just pure luck that I could get my glove on the ball and catch it before it went past me. If it had gone to the wall, those two scooters would still be running around the bases."

Had Burleson, after stopping in his tracks, tried to go first-to-third, he would have been a dead Rooster. Piniella's throw was a one-hop strike to the bag. Had Piniella not had the presence of mind to fake a catch, Burleson would have reached third easily. From there, he could have scored to tie the game on Rice's subsequent fly to Piniella. From second, he could only tag and go to third.

If Dent's homer has been discussed throughout America, then Piniella's two gambles — his out-of-position catch on Lynn and his blinded grab on Remy — are still being dissected in every major league dugout. "It's the play I'll always remember," said Graig Nettles.

Steinbrenner will never forget either. "I have a tape cassette of the whole game in my office," said the owner. "I don't know how many times I've watched that game. And I always stop at the Piniella play and run it over and over. What if Jackson had been out there? He's left-handed, so the glove's on his other hand, the ball gets by him, Remy has an inside-the-park homer, and we lose.

"It's annoyed me that our playoff game seems to have been overshadowed by us beating the Dodgers in the Series for the second year in a row," said Steinbrenner. "Don't people understand? Somebody wins the Series every year. There's only one game like that in a lifetime. I'd call it the greatest game in the history of American sports, because baseball is the best and oldest game, and that's sure as hell the best baseball game I ever saw."

If any game ever brought seventy-five years of animosity to a climax, this was it.

"When they had two on in the ninth with Rice and Yaz coming up," said New York's Roy White, "I was just holding my breath. You wanted to close your eyes and not see 'em swing. The wind was blowing out and I could feel that Green Monster creeping in closer."

"All I could think of was Bobby Thomson and that '51 playoff," said Nettles. "I figured if anybody was going to beat us, those were the guys."

This playoff lacked only one thing: a time machine. When Captain Carl, Boston cleanup man, stood at the plate facing Gossage with the tying run dancing off third and the winning run on first, that moment should have been frozen. The 32,925 standing fans, the poised runners, Yaz's high-held bat, Gossage's baleful glare: For once baseball had achieved a moment of genuine dramatic art — a situation that needed no resolution to be perfect. A game, a season, and an entire athletic heritage for two cities had been brought to razor's edge.

"I was in the on-deck circle, just like I was when Yaz flew out to end the '75 Series," said Fisk. "You know, they should have stopped the game right then and said, 'Okay, that's it. The season is over. You're both world champions. We can't decide between you, and neither of you should have to lose.'"

Sports' moments of epiphany are written on water. The spell of timelessness must be shattered, the house of cards collapse. Yaz cannot stand poised forever, waiting for the Goose. Art may aspire to fairness, but games cannot aim that high. They must settle for a final score.

"I was thinking, 'Pop him up,'" said Nettles. "Then, Yaz did pop it up and I said, 'Jeez, but not to me.'"

When the white speck had fallen into Nettles' glove, the Fenway fans stood in their places. For long minutes no one moved, as the baseball congregation drank in the cathartic sweetness of the silence. Proud police horses pranced on the infield, waiting to hold back a crowd that never charged.

"They should have given both teams a standing ovation," said Nettles. But he was wrong. This was better.

Finally, the whir of a public address recording began. Gently, softly, the music of an old-fashioned melancholy carousel drifted through Fenway Park. The sun was going down, so we all went home, bearing with us canvases for a lifetime.

Roger Angell

Excerpted from
City Lights: Heartthrobs,
Prodigies, Winners,
Lost Children

The New Yorker, October 1978

A deadly smugness descended on me at this point in the baseball summer. After that night game in Milwaukee, the record of the Red Sox — my Red Sox — stood at sixty-two wins and twenty-eight losses, and the pennant race in the American League East looked almost over. The Boston batting was awesome. Fred Lynn was hitting .327, Rice was at .322 (with twenty-three homers), Yastrzemski was at .311, and Dwight Evans had eighteen homers. Only nine pinch-hitters had come up to bat for the team all season. On the mound, Dennis Eckersley — the young power pitcher acquired from Cleveland just before the season started — was eleven and two, Bill Lee was ten and three, Mike Torrez was twelve and five, and Luis Tiant was seven and two: forty wins and twelve losses for the four starters. The defense — with Lynn's range and Evans's incomparable arm and glove in the outfield, and with the harelike new second baseman, Jerry Remy, meshing impeccably with shortstop Rick Burleson in the infield — looked impregnable. Carl Yastrzemski said that this club had the best pitching and the best defense of any Boston team he had played on. In the previous month, I had watched the Bosox overwhelm the Yankees, winning four out of six clamorous games in Boston and New York. Eckersley, who had never beaten the Yankees before, whipped them three times in twelve days. The defending champions seemed broken by injuries and dissension. Mickey Rivers, Bucky Dent, Willie Randolph, and Thurman Munson had been side-lined or had gone on the disabled list for various periods; Reggie Jackson was having trouble with his eyes and his psyche. The champions' pitchers, once overabundant in depth and skill, were in the worst shape of all. Don Gullett, Andy Messersmith, Catfish Hunter, and Ken Clay had all been shelved with arm miseries; young Jim Beattie had been shipped back to Tacoma; Ed Figueroa was struggling. Up in Boston, Catfish Hunter was tried again in late-inning relief and instantly gave up four hits, two of them homers, before Yastrzemski struck out — perhaps intentionally, in order to save the Cat further humiliation. Young and utterly anony-mous pitchers — Dave Rajsich, Bob Kammeyer — were hastily called up from the minors and thrown into combat, like Eton boys at Passchendaele. The famous rivals looked so ill-matched that when their July 4th game at Fenway was rained out, after a one-sided Boston win the night before, I had a commiserating, condescending feeling of relief. It would be fairer and more fun for the two teams to play later on, when the odds were better. The Yankees went off to Texas and then to Milwaukee, where they were swept by the Brewers in three straight. By the time of my visit there, the Yankees were fourteen games behind, and, by their own admission, out of it.

In baseball, Yogi Berra once said, you don't know nothing. One thing I didn't know was that the Red Sox would lose the next night in Milwaukee, and would continue that road trip by dropping six of their next seven games. Rick Burleson's absence with a damaged ankle for twelve games was the first check to the team's Mercedes-like passage through the summer landscape. The Yankees, meanwhile, began to motor in the opposite direction, moving from fourteen games behind to eight behind in the space of eight days. Another thing I didn't know was that Catfish Hunter's fortunes were undergoing a dramatic alteration. Immediately after his appalling outing in Boston, he had been treated by the Yankee physician, Dr. Maurice Cowen, who put him under anesthesia and manipulated his damaged pitching arm; the doctor said later that the popping noise when he broke the adhesions in Hunter's shoulder was so startling that for a moment he thought he had broken the pitcher's arm. Hunter played catch with his son the next day and reported that he had thrown without pain for the first time in two years. A little later, he had a very poor outing against the Indians, but again felt no pain. He then won his next six decisions in a row, and the Yankees' pitching was restored.

Another thing I didn't know was that Billy Martin would resign his job, on July 24th (after some alcoholic and ill-considered words about his employer, George Steinbrenner), and that Bob Lemon, who had been released earlier in the summer as manager of the White Sox, would take his place. No autopsy will be attempted here on this celebrated but moldering cadaver of sports news, or its startling sequel — the announcement by Steinbrenner that Billy Martin would return as the Yankee manager in 1980, with Bob Lemon moving up to the general manager's office. Speculation cannot determine what effect the change of managers had on the Yankees' triumphal course through the rest of the season; for that matter, no one has been able to prove that a manager was ever responsible for winning or losing a single ballgame. What is clear is that the difference between the two men in outward (and perhaps inward) manner is antipodal — a contrast that is perhaps best illustrated by the manner in which each comported himself upon being removed from office. Martin, it will be recalled, broke down before the cameras and reporters during an extempore press conference on the mezzanine of a Kansas City hotel and was led away in tears. Bob Lemon, after being relieved by White Sox owner Bill

Veeck, because the club had gone sour on the field and at the gate, asked his boss if he could speak in private to the Chicago players before he departed. One of those players, the veteran shortstop Don Kessinger, later said to a local writer, "It was something. All he did was talk about us. He thanked us, and told us how good we were. He never mentioned himself once." This seems typical of the man. Bob Lemon is the only contemporary manager I have encountered who always refers to his players as "they," instead of the currently obligatory, Scoutmasterish "we." He also never makes critical comments or jokes about a player in front of his teammates or to members of the press. He is soft-spoken and outwardly gentle and consistently humorous, and since he has moved into his office there, the Yankee clubhouse has become a cheerful and much more youthful place, and a pleasure to visit. In Martin's defense, it should be pointed out that the Yankees won for him last year, when the clubhouse atmosphere was tainted from April until October, and that this year's team had just run off five straight wins when Billy quit. Martin is a tough and resourceful field director, and there is no evidence that sweetness and laughter in the locker room or on the team bus are translated into winning habits on the ball field. I have no idea if he will be in pinstripes next year, but he will be back somewhere.

The last traces of my baseball neutrality disappeared during the month of August, which I passed on vacation in Maine, deep in Red Sox country. Far from any ballpark and without a television set, I went to bed early on most nights and lay there semi-comatose, stunned by another day of sunshine and salt air but kept awake, or almost awake, by the murmurous running thread of Bosox baseball from my bedside radio. I felt very close to the game then — perhaps because I grew up listening to baseball over the radio, or perhaps because the familiar quiet tones and effortless precision of the veteran Red Sox announcers, Ned Martin and Jim Woods, invited me to share with them the profound New England seriousness of Following the Sox. Sometimes, I must confess, I did fall asleep, usually when the team was playing on the West Coast — well past midnight on Penobscot Bay — and when I awoke in the morning to the lap of water under my windows (or, at low tide, to the conversation of gulls and crows on the stony beach) I would spring up, scoreless and anxious, and twirl the dial in search of the news. Whatever the result, the previous night's game was then replayed during the morning and afternoon with my friends and co-religionists at the general store, the post office, and the boatyard, and then again over drinks at the end of the day on somebody's porch overlooking Eggemoggin Reach and, behind Isle au Haut, Fenway Park. I have spent many summers in this part of the world, but this was the first year I could remember when the Red Sox were in first place all through August — a development that seemed only to deepen the sense of foreboding that always afflicts the Red Sox faithful as the summer wanes. First place, I suddenly understood, means responsibility. We Red Sox fans were like a young couple who for years had rented a nice little apartment on the second floor, dreaming and saving in the hope that someday they could afford a house of their own. Now, at last, we had it — Top o' the Hill Cottage — and for the first time we realized that the place was mortgaged, that it had to be painted and kept up and looked after, and that it could be lost. It was almost better the other way.

The Sox entered August five games ahead of the second-place Brewers and finished it six and a half ahead of the second-place Yankees, but it was — in truth as well as in our imagining — an anxious sort of month. Against the Yankees, Boston won a two-day game in which they had once trailed by 5–0, before tying it up in the eighth. Postponed after fourteen innings by rain, the game was resumed the next night, with the Sox winning it by 7–5 in the seventeenth; then they won the other game that night, by 8–1. The team fared less well against easier foes, and one began to notice that several Boston victories were attributable to plain luck. They beat the Indians in the thirteenth inning when one Cleveland infielder dropped a little pop fly and another threw the ball past third base, giving Butch Hobson a hitless inside-the-park homer. They beat the A's when Jerry Remy hit a three-run homer in Oakland just after the home-plate ump had called a foul tip on an apparent third strike — a magical foul tip that Remy himself could not detect. Down a run with two out in the twelfth inning, they beat the Angels when the California third baseman threw wildly past first on a routine play and Jerry Remy was ruled safe at home on a frightful call by the ump. (A lot of American League umpires had hard days at the office this summer.) Luckily, too, the Yankees ran into repeated difficulties with the last-place Mariners. But the Yanks kept coming on now, and a lot of Red Sox regulars were aching or were mired in slumps. George Scott struck out again and again. Bill Lee lost seven straight games and was taken out of the rotation. Lynn and Fisk and Hobson were injured. The bone chips in the elbow of Hobson's throwing arm were so painful at times that he fell into the habit of sprinting toward first base before getting off a peg; he also made a great many errors. Dwight Evans was beaned, and Jerry Remy cracked his wrist. Carl Yastrzemski had an agonizing back-pull and a sore right wrist. (Corseted and bandaged, Yaz came off the bench and went four for six against the Angels.) Somehow, the team won six in a row at home, and it looked as if the mortgage might be safe after all.

I came home tanned and confident, but my real troubles were just beginning, for the Red Sox now fell into a corpselike stillness at the plate. In one game at Baltimore, after Jim Rice hit a three-run homer in the first inning, the next twenty-three Boston batters went out in order, as the Orioles won by 5–3. When the Yankees came into Fenway Park on September 7th, to begin a pair of critical home-and-home series on successive weekends, the Bosox had lost six of their last eight games, while the Yankees had won twelve of their last fourteen. The Boston lead was down to four games. Then it was down to three, as the defending champions thrashed the Sox, 15–3, scoring twelve runs in the first four innings. (This game, by the way, was the rescheduled Fourth of July rainout that I had so magnanimously and insanely wished to see played when the teams were more evenly matched.) The following evening, the Sox committed four atrocious errors in the first two innings while the Yankees were scoring eight runs; eighteen Boston batters went down in order against Jim Beattie, the Yanks' big freshman right-hander, and the Yankees won by 13–2. There were seven Boston errors all told. The Sox had now committed twenty-two errors and given up nineteen unearned runs in their last nine games. Keeping score, I had begun to feel like an accountant for a Wall Street brokerage-firm in the fall of 1929. The cabdriver who took me home from Fenway Park that night said, "I turned that game off three different times on the radio."

The game on Saturday — Eckersley vs. Guidry on a glazy, windy, sharp-shadow day at the Fens — was better, at least for a while. In the fourth, Yastrzemski made a diving, rolling catch of Jackson's drive at the foot of the wall in left, and the relay doubled Munson off first base — the kind of play that sometimes turns a series and a ball team around. A moment or two later, however, with two Yankee base runners aboard, five Boston fielders (not including Remy, who was still benched with his injury) circled and stared and paused and pulled back under Piniella's high, wind-bent fly in short right-center field, allowing it to drop untouched for a double. At once, there came a little flurry of hits and walks, a wild pitch, and a passed ball, and the Yankees had seven runs — and this game, too, was gone. Guidry pitched a two-hitter, so perhaps none of the rest of it mattered. I left after seven innings — my earliest departure ever from Fenway Park, I think. I didn't have the heart to come back the next day, when the Yankees won again, 7–4, and moved into a tie for first place. In the four games, the Yankees had scored forty-two runs on sixty-seven hits, as against the Red Sox' nine runs on twenty-one. Boston had also committed twelve errors, and "The Boston Massacre" had gone into the baseball lexicon.

They resumed the next Friday in New York, with the

Yankees now up by a game and a half and the Stadium hordes yowling into the night like coyotes. Once again, the Red Sox made a trifling mistake in the fourth, and once again the Yankees, with two outs, scored all the runs of the game. Rivers was on second and Randolph on first when Piniella rapped into a round-the-horn double play, on which Rivers took third, and a little more; Yastrzemski (who was playing first base) took the peg and, seeing Mickey ten or twelve feet down the line, fired a hasty throw back across the diamond to Hobson, hoping for an incredible triple play. The throw went wild,

The team at its best is awesome, but it is slow and luck-prone (good and bad) at other times, and at its worst it resembles wet concrete. The Yankees, by contrast, seem capable of playing four or five different kinds of offensive baseball; in the first game of the Massacre, the 15–3 affair, they hit sixteen singles. Finally, I must observe that the Sox appear too restrained or introverted by nature to turn their troubles into a purging anger on the field. The Yankees are raunchy and disputatious and hard for most of us to cotton to, but their scandals and harsh words somehow translate themselves into a cheerful and extremely dangerous pride when the going is toughest. The Red Sox are a team of watchers and quiet talkers, with a few true eccentrics and emotional zombies among them. The leaders, Carlton Fisk and Carl Yastrzemski (Yaz especially), burn within, and sometimes burst into beautiful, fiery deeds on the field, but their finest feats — the impossible late-season batting outburst, the fabled catch, the historic homer — appear as isolated and hallowed events, almost too painful in their personal cost to be emulated or enjoyed. These are decent, lonely men caught up in a dream of one perfect and thus perfectly unattainable season.

The best part of the baseball year was just ahead. The Red Sox recovered their poise after winning that final game in Yankee Stadium, and picked up a game and a half on the league leaders in the next six days, to cut the lead to a single game, with seven to play. The two teams, which had alternated between strength and frailty throughout the year, now steadied to their duties, each winning on six successive days against lesser clubs in their division. The Red Sox had the closest call, pulling out a fourteen-inning affair at Toronto in which the Blue Jays loaded the bases in the eleventh and again in the thirteenth but could not score. The Yankee margin on the last Sunday morning of the season was still one game.

Unable to decide which park to visit, I stayed home that Sunday and frantically manipulated the dials of my television set, like Captain Kirk at the controls of the Starship Enterprise, as I tried simultaneously to bring in the critical plays from the Indians–Yankees game at the Stadium and the Blue Jays-Red Sox game at Fenway Park. Unsurprisingly, I usually clicked away from each field just before some significant moment, but finally, after I had added a radio to my instrument console, the broad messages began to come through. Rick Waits, a left-handed Cleveland curveballer, stifled the Yankee hitters while his teammates were jumping all over Catfish Hunter and several successors, winning by 9–2. Up at the Fens, Luis Tiant threw a masterly two-hitter against Toronto, in a game that the Bosox finally broke open with late homers by Burleson and Rice, and won 5–0. "THANK YOU, RICK WAITS," the Fenway scoreboard said in lights when it was all over. The two clubs were tied at ninety-nine wins and sixty-three losses apiece, and a one-game playoff at Fenway Park would settle it the next afternoon.

Before I departed for the Hub, I thought at length about the Red Sox, whom I had given up on so often in the times of their worst troubles. Here, at the very last, they had won twelve of their final fourteen games, including the last eight in succession, and not only had achieved the tie but had somehow preserved themselves as a team worth our emotion and attention. Anything less, given their horrible earlier fall from grace, would have stamped them for good as character-less losers — in their own minds as well as in the forever hoping, forever doubting mass unconscious of the New England fans — with bitter and unimaginable consequences. The same result would have come, I believe, if the Red Sox had collapsed in the playoff game. But that didn't happen, either.

By every standard, the playoff was a classic — a game that held us spellbound for every moment of its two hours and fifty-two minutes. Omens and citations hailed its arrival. The *Boston Globe* quoted Dickens ("It was the best of times, it was the worst of times . . .") in its pregame story that morning. Ron Guidry, the Yankee starter, could pick up his twenty-fifth victory by winning the game. The team that won it would step onto the marble plinth of one hundred wins for the season — and into the East–West playoffs the next day. Mike Torrez, the Red Sox pitcher, had been a Yankee last year but had quit the club, with considerable bitterness, to become a free agent. The only three pitchers to beat Guidry this year (Caldwell, Flanagan, Willis) were all named Mike. Carl Yastrzemski said, "Today is the biggest ballgame of my life."

It all meant such a lot that nobody in the shirtsleeved, sun-drenched crowd seemed to have much fun. The cheering, when it came, was savage but abrupt, quickly terminated again and again by the weight and anxiety of the occasion. It was a game played for the most part in a profound, crowded silence. The first real noise was an ovation for Carl Yastrzemski — the captain, the nonpareil — as he stepped up to bat in the second inning, and the second, and much louder, explosion of sound came an instant later, when he pulled Guidry's second pitch on a low, precise parabola into the right-field stands, just fair. Fisk and Lynn followed with hard, long outs to the farther reaches of the park, and it was clear that Guidry on this day was a little below his untouchable best. But the Yankees were attacking Torrez, too — a double by Rivers in the third, a frightening line drive out to right field by Jackson — and the strange, waiting silence again fell over the park. No one in the bleachers was moving; in the crowded bullpens, the pitchers and catchers sat immobile in two silent rows, as they stared in, riveted, through the low-lying, glary sunlight. On the mound, Mike Torrez, all emotion, repeatedly kicked the dirt and shook his head as he battled home-plate umpire Don Denkinger for the corners. Then he would heave in a great breath of air and blow it out again, and fire another fastball. When his turn came, Guidry, a little pitching machine, reared and threw, touched his cap, walked backward, did it all over again.

Torrez opened the fifth by walking Roy White, and Brian Doyle, the rookie Yankee second baseman who was filling in for the injured Willie Randolph, rapped the ball to the right side on a hit-and-run, just as he was meant to, moving White to second. Bucky Dent popped up, on a killing Torrez pitch that came in on his fists. Mickey Rivers bounced deep to short, where Rick Burleson, glimpsing Mick flying up the line, wheeled at the last instant and threw instead to Brohamer at third, who tagged White, sliding in, for the third out. Wonderful baseball.

After six innings, Torrez had surrendered only two hits, and in the home half of the sixth Burleson doubled, moved along to third on a bunt by Remy, and came in on Rice's single — hit on sheer muscle off an excellent pitch by Guidry. Rice went to second on Yaz's infield out, and Fisk was passed intentionally. Freddy Lynn worked the count to three and two, and, as the runners flew away, lashed a deep drive to the right-field corner, where Piniella, hunching over and half averting his head against the frightful sunlight, pulled it in on the run — a difficult, crucial chance.

Two runs ahead now, and perhaps feeling more comfortable, Torrez surrendered singles to Chambliss and White. With two out, he threw a high slider on an 0–2 count — only a middling-good pitch at best — to Bucky Dent, the ninth hitter in the Yankee order, and Dent lofted it down the left-field line and just into the netting above the wall, for a three-run homer. The silent, apprehensive crowd had been right after all. Since that day, I have heard some Red Sox fans complain that Dent's minimal wind-lifted blow would have been an easy out at any other park, including Yankee Stadium, but this is unacceptable. Those who live by the wall must die by the wall. And this bitter railing at fate (or at Mike Torrez) does not take into account what the Yankees did next, still with two outs, when Mickey Rivers walked and Thurman Munson, swinging against Bob Stanley, the new Boston pitcher, doubled him home. In the top of the eighth, Reggie Jackson hit a leadoff homer, to make it 5–2 for the Yankees. For me, these deadly secondary shocks are the absolute certifying mark of a champion. You cannot open the door to the Yankees by as much as a centimeter, for they will kick it down.

The Fenway silence after these disasters was blown away for good in the bottom of the eighth, when the Red Sox, down to their last six outs of the year, rallied for two runs. Remy doubled (Gossage was the Yankee pitcher now), and came scooting home on Yaz's single to center. Carlton Fisk battled Gossage interminably, barely fouling off his fastballs again and again, and singled on the tenth pitch. Then Lynn singled, too, to bring it to 5–4. With two out, George Scott stood in ("Boom-ah! Boom-ah! Boom-ah!" the bleachers cried), and struck out, swinging.

I left the press box and went down into the dark, ancient grandstand, standing between home and first among hundreds of clustered, afflicted rooters who had gathered behind the sloping stands for a closer look at the end of it. Peering over shoulders and around heads, I saw Burleson walk, after one out in the ninth. Now Jerry Remy whacked a hard drive to right, and Lou Piniella, paralyzed by the glaring sun, froze in the field with both arms outstretched, unable to see the ball. Suddenly it rematerialized and bounded in front of him, a foot or two to his left but within reach. Backing up, he gloved it on the first big hop — a lucky play, perhaps, but by no means an easy one. Burleson, thundering past second, abruptly threw on the brakes and came back to the base — a final but perhaps fatal bit of Boston conservatism on the base paths. Rice flied out to right, deep enough to send Burleson to third.

Two out, and the tying run on third. Yastrzemski up. A whole season, thousands of innings, had gone into this tableau. My hands were trembling. The faces around me looked haggard. Gossage, the enormous pitcher, reared and threw a fastball: ball one. He flailed and fired again, and Yastrzemski swung and popped the ball into very short left-field foul ground, where Graig Nettles, backing up, made the easy out. It was over.

Afterward, Yaz wept in the training room, away from the reporters. In the biggest ballgame of his life, he had homered and singled and had driven in two runs, but almost no one would remember that. He is thirty-nine years old, and he has never played on a world-championship team; it is the one remaining goal of his career. He emerged after a while, dry-eyed, and sat by his locker and answered our questions quietly. He looked old. He looked fifty.

Later that week, many editorials and sports stories in the Boston papers explained that it was the fate of the Yankees to win always, and the fate of the Red Sox always to wait another year. Emily Vermeule, a professor of classics at Harvard, wrote in the *Globe*, "The hero must go under at last, after prodigious deeds, to be remembered and immortal and to have poets sing his tale." I understand that, and I will sing the tale of Yaz always, but I still don't quite see why it couldn't have been arranged for him to single to right center, or to double off the wall. I'd have sung that, too. I think God was shelling a peanut.

Ward Just

Regroup, Recoup
Retrench, Reinforce, Reward

Boston Globe, October 6, 1986

Retreat After a Lost Battle
In a lost battle the power of an army is broken, the moral to a
greater degree than the physical. A second battle unless
fresh favorable circumstances come into play, would lead to a
complete defeat, perhaps to destruction.
— Carl Maria von Clausewitz, "On War" (Vol. 1, Book IV,
     Chapter XIII)

This was roughly the situation after the murderous Western
campaign in July. The Army had lost its confidence, in a
fortnight losing nine of 12, losing every way it is possible to
lose, and then finding another. It was true that for the season
the Army had won more often than it had lost, was indeed
ahead by four, but the signs of breakdown were everywhere.
As the distinguished correspondent Shaughnessy cabled from
the Oakland salient: "Only the Red Sox can give the appearance of being mathematically eliminated from a pennant race
while they are still in first place."

Herr von Clausewitz, an ensign at 12, protégé of Scharn-
horst, captain and aide de camp to Prince Augustus of Prussia
in the battles of Jena and Auerstadt, military instructor to the
crown prince of Prussia, mercenary with the Russian army in

1812, at 34 chief of staff to General Wallmoden's Russian–German legion, at 35 chief of staff to General Thielmann's Corps, at 41 appointed by Feldsmarschall Graf August von Gneisenau as chief of staff of the army sent to subdue the insurrecton in Prussian Poland, dead that year of cholera, the greatest military writer in the history of Western thought, a pessimist of Himalayan dimensions, the spiritual father of every Chicago Cub fan who ever lived. Von Clausewitz' mordant commentary on the inflated expectations of civilians far from the battle: "Whoever thinks that by a few rapid marches to gain a start, and more easily to recover a firm standing, commits a great error." Exactly so. And in his seminal chapter, "Retreat After a Lost Battle," the great pessimist declares: "Every lost battle brings weakness and disorganization; and the first necessity is to concentrate, and in concentration to recover order, courage, and confidence."

Did General McNamara know this text? There were no marches, rapid or otherwise; and in July no concentration. No order, no courage, no confidence. The general described this as a temporary slump of the sort that comes to any great Army weary of serial victory, but Shaughnessy and others responded with a Bronx cheer. In New York, the great beast was moving its slow thighs, and slouching northeast to be born again, or not, depending on the weakness and disorganization of the Boston Army; and to the south, almost unnoticed in the general disarray Field Marshal Weaver was commencing his wilderness campaign.

The central question remained: Was the strategy an error, or was it a failure of the tactical commanders? This was, after all, a colonel's and captain's retreat. "Regular small battles," according to Clausewitz, fought "by a strong rearguard composed of picked troops, commanded by the bravest generals, and supported by the whole Army at critical moments. . . ." Boyd, so brilliant, so erratic, a kamikaze pilot who combined the humility of General Chuck Yeager with the self-assurance of Wrong-Way Corrigan, cracked under the pressure, insulting his troops, storming out of the command post and retiring to a field hospital with battle fatigue. Army information officers were helpless as correspondents filed bitter dispatches, and civilian morale plunged. Clemens, the stopper who had stood so often alone, standing on his mound as imperious as Napoleon on the hill at Borodino, winning it seemed by sheer force of will (and an outstanding fastball) — winning when it was necessary to win, not when it was merely convenient — throwing a tantrum and removed from command. The comparison to the outrageous Patton was inevitable. Sox lose, 7–2. Seaver, a late acquisition, now serving Boston as the great pessimist had once served Imperial Russia, seeking only to demonstrate his skill, a man now only crafty, experienced, healthy and stable, but lucky as well. Seaver guaranteed the Army a solid seven, retiring then in good order to the CP while a subordinate mopped up. However, in July he did not win. Seaver was 4–10 at the beginning of August, and the headline of a dispatch filed from the Supreme Headquarters told the entire dispiriting story: "Seaver Lacks Support." Somehow, when Seaver led the charge, the Army refused to fight.

This was the text from the great pessimist that was urged on General McNamara: "According to the usual course the retreat is continued up to that point where the equilibrium of forces is restored, either by reinforcements, or by the protection of strong fortresses, or by great defensive positions afforded by the country, or by a separation of the enemy's forces. The magnitude of losses sustained, the extent of the defeat, but still more the character of the enemy, will bring nearer or put off the instant of this equilibrium." So that was it, stoical and fatalistic advice. Great defensive positions afforded by the country? Could Herr von Clausewitz mean Tiger Stadium? Comiskey Park? What, precisely, was meant by "reinforcements"? Would one want to destroy the Army in order to save it? Was the ambiguous phrase "the character of the enemy" a subtle reference to the egomaniacal Steinbrenner, the Mussolini of the American League? In early August, with the monsoon offensive soon to begin, the

Army seemed to have recovered its equilibrium. Seaver was strong, Clemens stronger. The artillery battalions led by Baylor, Rice and Boggs were performing according to doctrine. Still, where were the fresh favorable circumstances? And when would they come into play? The great pessimist was silent on this point, and General McNamara was only left with bromides. "The result of the whole combat consists in the sum total of all partial combats. . . ." Not much, but it would have to do. And for those of us in the stands, as it were, observing the combat with caught breath, there were these words: "No such urgent haste to die is needed yet; and as by instinct the drowning man catches at a straw, so in the natural course of the moral world a people should try the last means of deliverance when it sees itself hurried along to the brink of an abyss." Be of good cheer.

(All quotations taken from *A Short Guide to Clausewitz on War,* edited by Roger Ashley Leonard, G.P. Putnam's Sons, New York, 1967.)

Thomas Boswell

Red Sox–Angels: Once More with Feeling

Washington Post, October 13, 1986

Now, the battle is fairly and fittingly joined. The California Angels and Boston Red Sox will bring all their demons, detractors and dark doubts to Fenway Park tonight. Also on hand for the sixth game of an already historic American League playoff series will be their high hopes for a trip to the World Series and their deep sense that they deserve far better than the bleak reputations they've dragged behind them for years.

What new black magic will unfold at 8:20 P.M. when California's Kirk McCaskill, who grew up in New England worshipping the Red Sox, meets Boston's master of spontaneous combustion, Oil Can Boyd?

Yes, we'll see your Red Sox jinx and raise you an Angel hex. If you Sox can blow a three-run lead in the ninth, then we Halos can come back the next day and do it, too. In fact, we'll top you. We'll go down to the last strike, have the pennant champagne uncorked, and then lose.

Who says Boston always plays heroically, as it did Sunday, until the very end, then loses and breaks your heart all the worse? Forget that Carlton Fisk's homer in Game 6 of the 1975 World Series was followed by Bill Lee's blooper pitch in the seventh game.

Who says the combination of Gene Autry's Angels and
Gene Mauch are like mixing witches' teeth and wolfbane?
Why shouldn't the unluckiest owner of the last quarter-
century and the most star-crossed manager in history get
together and go to the World Series?

Try to forget that, the last time they teamed up, in 1982,
the Angels became the first team in history to lose three
straight to blow a pennant.

By all means, give us more Angels and Red Sox. What two
teams have ever been so perfectly matched? They're both
blunderful wonderful. Goats with laurel garlands on their
brows.

Baseball has had postseason games as good as the fabulous
one here on Saturday and the even better one on Sunday. But
never — not by a light year — has the old sport ever had
more or better excitement in a 24-hour period in October
than it did in Games 4 and 5 of this American League series.

Why? Because baseball may never have shown more
clearly the three basic reasons why it is our best sport. First,
the game has no clock, so every contest must reach its
organic conclusion. Next, the sport is utterly open to inspec-
tion and has a perfect balancing of credit and culpability on
every play. And, finally, in a playoff or World Series, the
batting order rolls 'round, and the breaks of the game revolve
often enough, that every player has ample chances to atone
for sins or to tarnish glory.

On Saturday and Sunday, the clock waited — first 3:50,
then 3:54 — so every twist of fate could be played out. In a
symmetry almost too perfect to believe, both games were
tied in the ninth and won in the 11th. Both managers gambled
and lost when they took out their aces and went to their
bullpens in the ninth. And, above all, within those two games,
every goat redeemed himself. Both teams left the field dig-
nified.

Blunderful wonderful, indeed. We'll never see anything like
this again:

Clank a potential pennant-losing home run off your glove

and over the fence one inning, then, with the season down to one pitch, hit a ball out of the park to save the game and your name.

Meet Dave Henderson. "We're ballplayers, so we fail most of the time. You have to learn to cope with it. But before that last pitch, I had to step out of the box and gather myself."

Throw the worst pitch of your life one night, stay awake until dawn with remorse, then come back 19 hours later and save the day.

Step up, Calvin Schiraldi. "If there had been a rest room out on the mound," he said, "I'd have used it."

Misjudge a fly, overthrow the cutoff man, leave the potential winning run on third with one out, then leap to the top of the fence to pull a homer back in the park and save the next game.

Give us a smile, Jim Rice.

Hit a ninth-inning homer to start the most exciting rally in franchise history one night, then, when a simple fly ball will send you to the World Series, pop up the first pitch.

Say, Doug DeCinces, didn't you let a couple of ground balls go through your legs recently?

"I got no place to sleep tonight," cracked Mauch, "because I bet my house that DeCinces would get that run in from third [to win the pennant]."

Lose a popup in the sun. Get caught off base. Throw a tantrum at your coach in public. Boot grounders a new way every day. Go zero for 10. Then win the game in sudden death.

In Anaheim, they call you "Rags to Griches," but in Boston, you're "The Grich Who Stole the Pennant."

"We may have awakened New England," said Bobby Grich, who almost had the game-winning RBI in both games.

Bring in Gary Lucas to pitch to Rich Gedman one day (strikeout) and look like a genius. Bring Lucas in to face Gedman the next day (hit by the first pitch), and be called a fool.

"Mauch made a big mistake by taking out [Mike] Witt,"

said Boston's Marty Barrett. "I don't know why he did it. To me, that's what cost them the game."

"Mauch made no mistakes," said Reggie Jackson. "It was textbook, man. Hell, Rich Gedman had hit three rockets off Witt, and Donnie Moore is still our man."

And so this playoff flies in to Fenway. Will Bob Boone, Gary Pettis and Gedman, who have done everything conceivable correctly, find a comeuppance awaiting them? Will Moore, Jackson (.118) or Rice (.182) end up doing dances to match those we've already seen from Grich and Henderson? And who, in the last act, will collapse full length on the ground in dismayed disbelief as Bruce Hurst did when his own outfielder knocked a home run over the wall?

In 1975, when Pete Rose came to bat late in that famous sixth game, he said to Fisk, "This is some game, isn't it?" In 1977, when Jackson hit four Series homers in four swings, Steve Garvey applauded into his glove as Jackson ran past him. In 1978, Fisk watched the final popup of the Yankees–Red Sox game and thought, "I hope it never comes down. Neither team deserves to lose."

In the 11th on Sunday, down by first base, Baylor met Grich, his teammate from the minors to the Orioles to the Angels, but now his foe.

"So, whataya think?" said Grich.

"Best I've been in," said Baylor.

"Me, too, pardner," said Grich.

PLAYGOERS

There are a number of theories as to why so many writers are Red Sox fans, not the least of which is that it only seems that way. Some of it may simply have to do with the sheer number of writers who abound in New England because living in Connecticut or teaching at Harvard or vacationing on the Cape is everything any successful writer would want to do. By the same token, there are probably an inordinate number of Wall Street bankers who are Yankee fans and hog butchers who are Cub fans. (There certainly are too many Hollywood producers who are Dodger fans, and if you don't believe it you've probably been sleeping through those *CHiPS* reruns.) But surely there are writers in Seattle and writers in Texas — so where's Larry McMurtry's elegy to his first Rangers game? Perhaps writers are drawn to the Red Sox because the Red Sox, through accident or destiny, so thoroughly inhabit the Ironic Element that's the preserve of the writer's art. Seasons are not simply ends unto themselves but threads in a constantly evolving storyline; steadfast heroes like Yaz struggle valiantly against a shifting cast of venal exhibitionists from New York; the dramatic tension is drawn to ever-excruciating degrees of tautness — *will they finally conquer the ghosts of seasons past and win it all?* Whatever the reason, Sox fans have been fortunate to have such an eloquent roster of champions for the cause. In the pages that follow, three more esteemed members of the literary community — David Halberstam, Geoffrey Wolff, and Stephen King — step forward to give unique expression to our common passion. There's also a welcome encore from John Updike. And your humble editor once again suits up in the persona of Joe Fan to relive a critical game in that 1972 season when the boys lost a pennant by half a game! Only the Red Sox.

Dan Riley

Taking Her Out
to the Ballgame

Another Story

Turbo the Significant was banned from baseball for a year by his mouse wife Nancy who got her nose out of joint after our last foray into Fenway. Aparicio was out with a broken finger then, and Beniquez, the rookie, was generously giving games away at short. Maybe that's what was eating at Turbo when the vending machine off I-93 refused to honor his request for an Almond Joy, and he proceded to dismantle the thing all across the Mass. line and clear into the "Live Free or Die" state.

In any case, Turbo was saving up to pay the Commonwealth back for its machine and wouldn't be accompanying me south for the critical September showdown with the Birds of Baltimore. Easier to replace Aparicio at short, I'll tell you, than Turbo for the two hour trip to Fenway through the New Hampshire mountains. Turbo and I are not exactly Bureau of Land Management kind of guys. We like our planning in the spur-of-the-moment mode. Like, "The game starts in 45 minutes, wanna see if we can bust the land-speed record and make it?" Spontaneity, of course, is not a trait generally associated with New Hampshiremen (that devil-may-care Daniel Webster gent being the exception rather than the rule). All of which helps explain why Turbo was such a rare, good buddy — truly Turbo the Significant. But I like to look for silver linings whenever possible . . . hey, I'm a Sox fan, right? . . . so I made a quick perusal of the countryside for a game companion.

There was a new fem in town — not too bad looking in a Mary Tyler Moorish sort of way — the two of us had gotten tangled up in some mutual embarrassment once or twice down at the general store, eyeing each other over the cracker barrel. Small town, so what the hay? I asked her to the game.

Actually it was two games. Doubleheader. But even with Turbo behind the wheel, there wouldn't have been a snow-ball's chance in Palm Beach of catching the first one. Anyway, the new girl on the block says yes just like that, which got me to wondering a bit what her response would've been if I'd been asking her for a night at the Holiday Inn. I didn't dwell on that too much, though. There was a pennant race going. The Sox had already jumped off to an early lead in the first game. If they swept them both, they'd have a solid one-game lead on the Tigers — and two and a half over the O's. Not to mention the stake they'd be driving through the heart of the stinking Yankees.

When I picked her up, she was wearing the damndest take-me-out-to-the-ballgame outfit I'd ever seen. Color coordinated jacket and pants of alternating fat and skinny, yellow and blue stripes. I'd seen things like that on color television.

"UCLA," I said.

"How'd you guess?" she squealed, all pop eyes and smiles.

I told her there was a blanket in the back seat she might want to take along — for warmth. She checked it out, but said she didn't think so. She may have been put off by the clash of the red plaid with her own choice ensemble. Then again she may have been put off by the dog hairs. Whatever. I decided to drag the damn blanket along myself. Call it a hunch.

When we got to the park, the Sox were polishing off the Birds and setting the stage for a second game match-up of hallucinogenic dimensions between Tiant and Cuellar. Odd team these Sox of '72. What was driving them to play so well? Yaz had just barely achieved mediocrity — 9 homers, .263 at the plate. Except for the blind, dumb luck of finding Tiant under a bushel basket in June, the pitching staff was typical Boston Blah. Sure, a couple of kids like Fisk and Evans were looking good. But if you had to pick an MVP just about anybody'd be eligible, including a guy named Bob Burda who wasn't even with them any more but who'd won a game in July with a homer.

Anticipation hung over the park like Mr. Theodore Samuel Williams himself on a slow breaking pitch just outside the black. This was '67 all over again. A cats-in-heat scramble for the top with three or four teams taking it right down to the wire.

On the first pitch of the night . . . bang! Grich hit a scorcher to Aparicio who gobbled it up and pegged him out at first. Heavens to Don Buddin, an entire career of Little Looey at short and we'd have been up the Pesky Pole in pennants.

"May I have a coffee?" she whispered into my disbelieving ears. Eyeball-wise, I gave her a high, hard one. She was serious. She wanted coffee. And I could tell she wasn't the type of woman you could say "Yeah, later" to. She was the type that was going to harp on the issue 'til she got her way. As I made my way down the runway, Blair rifled a single up the middle.

The coffee line was very, very long, and when I got to the front of it, the guy behind the counter said, "No coffee. Ran out during the first game." Which was totally believable since there probably hadn't been a night so cold since about mid-February.

The news nearly killed her. What nearly killed me was that while I was down in the no-coffee line Young Man Fisk had thrown Blair out at second on an attempted steal.

"Did they have any tea?" she asked.

Tea?

I wanted to shake her delicate little shoulders and shout, "This isn't bleeding Merry Old England, Sweetheart. This is

NEW England. This is the goddamned MAJOR LEAGUES!!!"
But I hardly knew the girl, so I put on the restraints. "I
don't believe they serve tea here," I said, "but you might find
some hot cocoa right through that runway." And I handed her
a buck.

After the offensive skirmishing of the first inning, the game
quickly started settling into the inevitable pitching duel between Tiant and Cuellar. They were both doing full repertoire
stuff, and it was looking more and more like someone was
going to have to scratch for a run to win it.

As my date for the festivities returned to her seat,
clutching two bags of hot, roasted peanuts to the side of her
head like ear muffs, some bare-chested goon about twenty
rows up yelled, "Hey, lady, you look like an *effin* Sunoco
sign." Everyone seven sections around got a real big laugh
out of that, and even she'd been in the East long enough to
figure out the gagging similarity between the blue and yellow
motif of her evening wear and that of those ubiquitous
gasoline pumps.

She quickly gave me a look that clearly expressed a wish
that I do something about the effrontery. But I acted like I
was the only one in the bleachers who didn't quite catch the
fellow's remark. After all, what was I supposed to do? Parade
up there like an usher in a movie theater and flash a light on
the guy? Maybe if Turbo'd been with me, we might've gone
up there and menaced a few donkeys. But Turbo would've
had more sense than to wear blue and yellow stripes to a Red
Sox game.

Anyway, me and 27,000 other cheering fanatics soon had
more important things on our collective mind than the alleged
insult. Griffin did the near impossible getting one by Brooks
"The Human Hoover" Robinson at third. It should've been
down in the corner for two, but the ump at third was asleep
at the wheel, figuring, like everyone else I guess, that if it's
hit on the ground to the left of home plate, Brooks is going to
get it. So as he's dancing around calling the ball fair, it runs up
his leg and caroms off his chest and back to Robinson.

Brooks. Even when he doesn't make the play, he ends up dripping in eau de rose. Give the ump an assist. Give Griffin a single. Give Tiant a sacrifice and the Sox their first legitimate threat against the Junkman of Baltimore. Aparicio delivers a clutch two-out single for the first run of the game.

"Where's this man been all my life?" I'm yelling. "Where's this man been?" We're all delirious . . . we're all smelling pennant . . . all 27 screaming, cheering thousand of us.

No, not quite all of us. The lady in blue and yellow by my side wants to know if we can go now. Her words exactly, "Can we go now?"

I want to know if it's etiquette to ask about mental deficiencies on the first date.

"You like baseball?" I ask instead.

"I like tennis better," she says.

I gave her a look that pretty much summed up the thought processes going on in my brain at the time, which was basically, "Lady, the only friggin' way we'd leave this ball park now is if the Union of Soviet Socialists Republicans decided to drop about 112 intercontinental ballistic missiles right on top of our heads." She read my mind pretty well, wrapped herself up in that damned, dog-haired red-plaid blanket and curled up right there on the bleacher seat.

She stayed that way, too, right through rookie Evans' triple to right and subsequent homer to left. When it was over, the Sox had it 4-zip. We had a raucous good time cheering Tiant who looked like he was on the verge of inventing the automatic shutout.

"Is that it?" asked sleeping beauty.

Is that it?

She piled herself into the backseat of my car, pulled the blanket up around her chin, and, quicker than you could say, "Hell of a game," she was asleep. I made my way out of the happy Hub of the Universe while replaying game highlights in my mind. I found Rt. 93 just where I'd left it in daylight and, as I motorized north, I carefully worked out a scenario for the remainder of the season: next we take 3 out of 4 from

Detroit, we split with Milwaukee and beat the Royals; or, we split with the Tigers and sweep the Brewers and KC; then the Yanks do us a rare favor and do two of three on Detroit before falling on their own ugly faces in Cleveland . . . then the Orioles show up at the wrong park and have to play the Jets in a football game.

There came a little purring sound from the backseat.

But first, I said to myself, I gotta get Turbo the Significant out of house arrest.

John Updike

Loving the Sox

Boston Globe, October 6, 1986

Forty years ago and 400 miles from Boston, I sat in my father's Chevrolet, in the Shillington (Pa.) High School parking lot, and listened to the seventh game of the 1946 World Series, the Red Sox vs. the Cardinals. Eighth inning, score 3–3, Cardinals up, Enos Slaughter on first base, Harry Walker at the plate; there's a hit to center field, Leon Culberson (substituting for the injured Dom DiMaggio) throws to the infield, shortstop Johnny Pesky cuts it off — Slaughter is being waved around third! Pesky hesitates, the throw is late, Slaughter scores!! The Cardinals hold on to win the game and the World Series. I don't know if I cried, sitting alone in that venerable Chevrolet, but I was only 14 and well might have. Dazed and with something lost forever, I emerged into the golden September afternoon, where my classmates were jostling and yelling, nuzzling their steadies, sneaking smokes and shooting baskets in a blissful animal innocence I could no longer share.

What had led me, who had never been north of Greenwich, Conn., and didn't know Beacon Hill from Bunker Hill or Fenway Park from the Public Garden, to attach my heart to that distant aggregation? Ted Williams had made a dent in my consciousness before the war, but it was the '46 Sox that made me a passionate fan. What a team that was! — Ted in left, Dom in center, Doerr at second, Pesky at short, Big

Rudy York having a great twilight season at first, Boo Ferriss and Tex Hughson on the mound. Though the Cardinals squeaked by them in that Series, the Sox looked sure to cruise to pennants at least until I got out of high school in 1950. But in fact they didn't, coming perilously close in '48 and '49 but not quite having it in the clutch. The postwar pattern of thrills and spills was set, and whenever they came to Philadelphia, there I was, hanging by the radio.

With its nine defensive men widely spaced on the field, baseball is an easier game to visualize than a fast shuffle like basketball and hockey, and until girls and a driver's license got me by the throat, I spent many an idyllic summer day indoors huddled on the family easy chair next to the hoarse little Philco. The announcers' voices in their granular shades of excitement, and the wraparound crowd noise, and the sound in the middle distance of the ball being hit (not to mention the uproarious clatter when a foul ball sailed into the broadcast booth) made a vivid picture in ways superior to what I would see when, once or twice a summer, I was bused the 50 miles to Shibe Park's bleachers. I even kept box scores of my audited games, and listened on the rainout days when the play-by-play of some remote and feeble contest like the Browns against the Senators would be verbalized from a teletype whose chattering could be heard in the lulls. The two Philadelphia teams were pretty feeble themselves, and created the vacuum into which my irrational ardor for the Red Sox had flowed.

My barber was a Yankee fan; that was the other choice in Pennsylvania. As his scissors gnashed around my ears and his hair tonic corroded my scalp, he would patiently again explain why Joe DiMaggio was a *team* player, and why as a team the Yankees would always *win*. But they didn't like Roosevelt or Truman at the barber shop either, and I would rather lose with Boston than win with New York. When my college choices came down to Cornell or Harvard, the decision was obvious. And yet, those four years in Cambridge, it rather rarely seemed to have dawned on me that the Red Sox were only two 10-minute subway rides (or, on a sunny day, a nice walk along the river) away. Living in New York, though, I would risk the subway up to the Bronx and from within the cavernous shadows of the Stadium admired the aging Williams as he matched strokes with Mickey Mantle, who had replaced DiMaggio as the hood ornament of the onrolling Yankees. The Fifties Red Sox didn't leave much of a mark on the record book, but they seem to have inspired a quixotic loyalty in me. While it is not entirely true that I moved from New York to New England to be closer to the Red Sox, it is not entirely false either. I wanted to keep Ted Williams company while I could.

Lying in back yards or on the beach, driving in the car or squinting into a book, I listened to the games and internalized Curt Gowdy. That ever so soothing and sensible voice, with its guileless hint of Wyoming twang, relayed popups and bloop hits, blowouts and shutouts to my subconscious; phantom heroes like Clyde Vollmer and Ellis Kinder and Walt Dropo and Sammy White flitted across the airwaves, and Jackie Jensen and Jimmy Piersall glimmered in Williams' lengthening shadow. My wife's parents had a retreat on a far hill of Vermont without electricity or telephone but with plenty of pine cones and bear turds in the woods. We parked our car on the edge of that woods, and there I would go, many an afternoon, to sit in the front seat and tune in the Red Sox. Curt's voice came in strong from (I think) Burlington — so strong that one day the car battery wouldn't turn the starter over, and we were stranded. I must have been the only man in New England who rather than lose touch with the Red Sox, marooned his family in a forest full of bears.

The older you get, the stranger your earlier selves seem, until you can scarcely remember having made their acquaintance at all. Whatever held me there, rapt by the radio, all those precious hours? Ted, of course, who was always doing something fascinating — getting injured, going off to Korea, vilifying the press, announcing his retirement, hitting .388, hitting Joe Cronin's housekeeper with a tossed bat, spitting at

the stands, going fishing when he shouldn't, etc. But the Red
Sox around him had a fascination too; generous-spending
Yawkey saw to it that there were always some other classy
performers, and some hopeful passages in every season. Yet
the wheels inevitably came off the car, or were lubricated too
late in the season, and the Red Sox had that ultimate charm,
the charm of losers.

All men are mortal, and therefore all men are losers; our
profoundest loyalty goes out to the fallible. Chris Evert, for
example, did not win our hearts until Navratilova began to
push her around, and I know a man who to his own evident
satisfaction has been a Chicago Cubs fan for 50 years. Are
the killer Mets of today nearly as much fun as those hapless
teams of post-expansion days, the "Amazing Mets" that New
Yorkers, bored by the Yankees, clasped to their ironical
hearts? As a boy in Pennsylvania, I felt sorry for Mr. Yawkey,
that all his financial goodness couldn't buy a World Series. I
felt sorry for Williams, that he didn't go 5 for 5 every day and
that spiteful sportswriters kept cheating him of the MVP
award. The Red Sox in my immature mind were like the man
in the Hollywood movie who, because he's wearing a tuxedo,
is bound to slip on a banana peel. They were gallantry and
grace without the crassness of victory. I loved them. I might
have loved some other team just as well — an infant gosling
if caught at the right moment, will fall in love with a zoologist
instead of its mother, and a German, if kicked often enough,
will fall in love with a shoe — but the Red Sox were the team
I had chosen, and one's choices, once made, generate a self-
justifying and self-sustaining inertia. All over the country,
millions of fans root and holler for one team against another
for no reason except that they have chosen to. Fanship is *acte
gratuité* hurled in the face of an indifferent (or at least
preoccupied) universe.

Since Williams retired — dramatically, as usual — in 1960,
my Red Sox ardor, with its abuse of car batteries, has cooled.
But I have not been unaware, in the quarter-century since, of
the pennants of 1967 and '75, and, just as in 1946, the
subsequent seventh-game disappointments in the World Se-

ries. I remember, in fact, on a late September Sunday of 1967, crouching with some other suburban men in an inter- ruption of a touch football game, around a little radio on the grass as it told us that the Twins were losing to the Red Sox while the Angels were beating the Tigers, thus allowing our Yastrzemski-led boys back into their first pennant in 21 years. And I remember, as well, another September, in 1978, when my wife and I, heading for a Cambridge dinner date, parked along Memorial Drive and listened to the last innings of the Yankees–Red Sox playoff. We heard about the poky Bucky Dent home run, and we heard in living audio the foul Yastrzemski popup. It was Slaughter rounding third all over again.

The memoirs of a Red Sox fan tend to sound sour, a litany of disappointments and mistakes going back to the day when Babe Ruth was traded. But the other side of this tails-up coin is that time and time again the team, as its generation of personnel yield to one another, has worked its way to the edge of total victory. Yaz' famous popup, for instance, was preceded by a heroic week of solid victories, forcing the Yankees to a playoff, and in the game itself, we (notice the reflexive-possessive pronoun) had fought back from a 5–2 deficit to 5–4 and the tying run on third. In sports, not only do you win some and lose some but 25 competitors, in a 26- team sport, are going to come in lower than first. What makes Boston — little old Boston — up there among the rocky fields and empty mills — think it deserves champion- ship teams all the time? Having the Celtics is miracle enough, perhaps, not to mention a Patriots team that finally won in Miami. The founding Puritans left behind a lingering convic- tion, it could be, that earthly success reflects divine election, and that this city built upon a hill is anciently entitled to a prime share. Certainly the scorn heaped in the Boston columns upon imperfect Red Sox teams approaches the self- righteous — and not just the sports columns, Mike Barnicle.

Now this summer's team, casually relegated by most April prophets to a fourth- or fifth-place finish, has made it to the playoffs. It seems a strange team to us veteran Red Sox watchers — solid, sometimes great pitching, and fitful, even anemic hitting. Where are the home runs of yesteryear? Wade Boggs singled his way to some batting championships, and now Jim Rice has choked-up on the handle and is hitting for average, too. Only Baylor and Armas seem to be swinging from the heels anymore. Heroism has moved from the plate to the pitcher's mound: Clemens so full of the Right Stuff his uniform fairly pops its buttons, and Hurst and Seaver looking just as resolute. Oil Can Boyd emerged from his month in the doghouse with an enhanced charisma; the one thing made clear in that murky episode was how much we need him, his arm and his twitchy self-exhortations and his terrific name. And Sambito and Schiraldi staggered out of nowhere to help the much abused Stanley nail the slippery games down. This nervous-making crew, with its gimpy veterans and erratic infield, has shown toughness and courage and internal rapport, and like last year's Patriots did better than anyone dared to hope. These Sox were spared that burden of great expectations carried by so many of their star-crossed predecessors; now they have nothing to lose but the marbles. Once again, I'm tuned in.

David Halberstam

The Fan Divided
He Gets to Follow Two Teams

Boston Globe, October 6, 1986

I grew up with my soul divided. For I am both a man of New York and of New England. Things as critical as this, the selection of a favored baseball team, are not, as some suspect, a matter of choice; one does not choose a team as one does not select his own genes. They are confirmed upon you, more than we know an act of heredity. By an odd blend of fates and geography, I am somewhat schizophrenic in my baseball loyalties; I think of baseball, and I think American League, and then New York and Boston. The National League has always been a distant shadowy place. I was born in New York in the very borough where the Yankees play; my father, a small-town boy with a small-town obsession about baseball, took me to the Stadium in 1939 when I was 5, having in the previous two years talked almost exclusively about the great DiMaggio. So I began not just with loyalty to a locale, but to a mythic figure, a man worthy of his myth and who did not disappoint. He was to the little boy sitting there that day, pleasure of pleasures excused early from school, every bit as dazzling and graceful as my father had claimed he would be. The Stadium seemed not so much a sports coliseum as a cathedral; never had grass seemed so green, never had any group of men caught my attention; this, unlike the world of elementary school I had just left behind, was real. I departed that day a confirmed Yankee fan. Soon the war came, my father went back in the service, and we moved to Winsted, in northwest Connecticut, which serves as the selected site of my otherwise dislocated childhood. Winsted then was the classic New England mill town of about 8,000, a serious baseball town, its own loyalties somewhat divided between Boston and New York. But it is about 20 miles nearer New York and the magnetic pull of the Yankees was somewhat more powerful then, in large part I suspect because the reception for the Yankee games, WINS-1010 on your dial, Ballantine Blasts and White Owl Wallops with Mel Allen, was stronger than that of the Red Sox.

But we were a divided family; my mother's family had grown up in Boston, and my Uncle Harry, her oldest brother, had become successful in the wholesale paint business. He occasionally visited us in Winsted and was intrigued by the idea of a young nephew whose knowledge of batting averages was so encyclopedic, and who could repeat so faithfully the wisdom of that era's sportcasters. He also had, it turned out, season tickets to the Red Sox games. That seemed almost beyond comprehension to me; it was not that we were so poor, but we were, in those immediate post-Depression years, most assuredly frugal. We lived on a World War II officer's allowance, and something like going to a baseball game was at best a pleasure permitted once a season. Uncle Harry was said within family circles to be something of a dandy; that is, he not only made a lot of money but he was quite willing to spend it. That he could go to all 77 home games, and sit in the very same seats, seemed both miraculous and quite possibly frivolous. We simply did not know people who did grand things like this. It seemed to mark him not so much as a relative, but as someone from another family who had mistakenly wandered into our lives. His seats, he said, were right behind the first base dugout, and he loved them because he could see the ballplayers' faces up close.

They were such clean-looking young men, he said. Could this really be true? Did he have seats this good? If it were, then it struck me that Uncle Harry, if not actually on speaking terms with these distant and vaunted celebrities, was at least on *seeing* terms with them. He seemed to know a great deal about them — Pesky, Doerr, York, the mighty Williams. Pesky's name, he confided, was not really Pesky. It was Paveskovich. Mel Allen, to my knowledge, had never mentioned this. Could I doubt Uncle Harry and his inside knowledge anymore? But it was true; in time the war was over and we were allowed to travel again and we visited Boston and Uncle Harry made good his pledge. He *did* have wonderful seats and I could see the players' faces up close the disappointment after they had grounded out, and turned back toward the dugout. They seemed quite wonderful, so large and powerful, and on that day, against Detroit, with Hal Newhouser (Ron Guidry before Guidry) pitching, I found myself rooting for them.

So it was that my childhood concluded with two conflicting loyalties. The first was one to the Yankees, and most of all DiMaggio. When I think of DiMaggio, I see him, not so much at bat, though the stance was classic, but of him going back on a fly ball, or of running the bases, particularly going around second on his way to third; I have never seen a tall man run with more grace. He was the first of my heroes; my true (and pure) loyalty to the Yankees ends with his retirement. Never in the age of Mantle was I able to summon the commitment and obligation innocence that I had brought to the age of DiMaggio. I was growing older. By the time DiMaggio retired in 1951, I was 17, and it was time to go on to other things.

But even as a young man, the vision and the loyalty were clouded. For there was the other vision, that of the Red Sox, and most of all, of Williams. As DiMaggio seemed so natural in the field, so Williams seemed equally natural at the plate, first seemingly loose, and gangly, and then suddenly bound tightly and perfectly together, the swing at once so smooth and yet so powerful, all of it so completely focused — as if he was destined to do this one thing, hit a baseball and nothing else. Of his talents, there was no lack of admiration among Yankee fans: When I was a boy, there was a constant schoolboy debate not just about the respective merits of DiMaggio or Williams, but of what would happen if each had played in the other's park, DiMaggio with the Green Monster, Williams with the short Stadium right-field porch. It was the ultimate tribute to Williams that had the trade been made, it would have been accepted without complaint by most Yankee fans.

In the summer of 1946, my father had come back from the war, and he had taken my brother and me to the Stadium to see a Yankee–Red Sox game. That was a glorious year for the Red Sox, all their players had come back from the war, and the Red Sox players more than those of the Yankees were making a comfortable readjustment to baseball. Their pitchers were healthy, and by mid-season they held an immense lead over the Yankees. On that day, Aug. 10, 1946 (you could look it up, as Casey Stengel said), Williams hit two home runs, the first of them a truly massive three-run shot off Tiny Bonham that went into the upper deck. The memory of that drive, the hardest-hit ball I have ever seen, remains with me today; I still see the force of it, the unwavering majestic trajectory, the ball climbing as it hit the seats, the silence of the fans, stunned not just that the Red Sox had scored three runs, but that a ball had been hit that hard. Williams seemed that day to a young boy a glorious figure, a hero who did what heroes are supposed to do.

I went on to college in Boston a few years later. There I was, like most visitors to the city, puzzled by the harshness with which the Boston press treated him. He was clearly the greatest hitter of his generation in baseball, he had just returned from his second tour of duty as a combat pilot, he was, it seemed, defying baseball's actuarial tables, and it was a pleasure to go out early to Fenway and watch him taking batting practice, a game within a game. I did not know as much about the media then as I do now, but I knew that the

Boston papers were by and large bad (in fact, they were probably worse than that in the early Fifties), that he was personally victimized by the most primitive kind of circulation wars, and that he, proud, idiosyncratic and unbending, was red meat for newspapers which were desperately trying to survive in a world which no longer needed them. What they did to him seems in retrospect to border on cruelty. It is probably true that he played into their hands, and was his own worst enemy, though his behavior, so much criticized then, seems by the modern Richter scale of athletic behavior mild enough. I did not share that view of the Boston writers that the problem with the Red Sox was Williams. (I suspect that this was why John Updike's piece, "Hub Fans Bid Kid Adieu," has itself taken on such singular importance. It is as if after hundreds of lower courts had ruled unfairly against Williams for all those years, Updike, a writer of skill and knowledge, taking time off from the chronicling of suburban infidelity, became in effect the Supreme Court ruling in favor of him, overturning the lesser judgments of lesser courts). It was not the fault of Williams at all. Quite the reverse: It struck me that the late Forties was a time of marvelous matchups between two almost perfectly equal teams, that the advantage that the Yankees held was one of pitching and depth — the ability to trade for a particular player. For example, in 1946 the Yankees traded additional bench strength for Eddie Lopat. That gave the Yankees a pitching staff of Reynolds, Raschi and Lopat, the core of the strongest pitching staff in the league for the next six years.

The memory of Williams and that special grace lingers. I now think often of him; we live in a nation which seeks heroes and cites as its heroes the kings of celluloid like John Wayne and Sylvester Stallone, each of whom managed to stay out of his generation's war. I am wary of heroes in general, but as I grow older, I have become more and more intrigued by Williams, the man apart. Perhaps it is that wonderfully leathery face, for Ted Williams even looked like what he was and what he did with that William Holden cragginess. Perhaps it is the deeds, that prolonged exquisite career, the willing-ness to go for it on the last day of the .400 season. But finally it is as well the ability to stand apart, crusty, independent, outspoken, true to himself, living to his own specifications, and rules, the frontier man of the modern age. I have a sense of a life lived without regret and I hope that that is true. Grown now, I can still close my eyes and I can see DiMaggio going back on a ball, or kicking the dirt at second base after Gionfriddo had caught the ball in the 1947 World Series; I can as clearly still see these 40 years later Williams swinging, the ball heading for the third tier.

As I grew older, my loyalties softened, and my priorities changed. I went to school in Boston, and I soon was overseas as a foreign correspondent. Other issues clouded the purity of my baseball loyalties. I would root for certain teams based on their special character or my feeling about their cities (I root as a matter of course against all Texas and California teams, and I was deeply disappointed when Houston knocked off the Lakers this year, thus depriving the Celtics of the chance to do it). The real world began to interfere with the fantasy world of baseball; my pull to the Yankees weakened and that to the Red Sox began to grow, for I liked the Red Sox teams of the late Sixties, Yastrzemski-Smith-Conigliaro-Petrocelli. In 1964, just back from two years in Vietnam, I went to Opening Day at the Stadium with my editor and a few other writers, and I remember two things, Ann Mudge, the girlfriend of Philip Roth, refusing to stand for the National Anthem as an antiwar protest, the first I had ever seen, and the sweet swing of a young rookie named Tony Conigliaro. In 1967 I went to an early-season game at Yankee Stadium. On that day a Red Sox rookie pitcher named Billy Rohr was pitching. About the sixth innning, it was obvious that he had a no-hitter going. The fascination grew, the crowd inevitably rooting not so much for a team, but for the event. The seventh and eighth innings passed. Still a no-hitter. In the ninth inning, with one out, Tom Tresh hit a shot to left field. Yastrzemski was playing shallow, if memory serves, and went back, and dove just at the right moment, his body tumbling into a complete somersault as he made the catch. It ranks with the Gionfriddo catch as the greatest I have ever seen, made more remarkable by the fact that it saved a no-hitter. The next batter, Elston Howard, lined a hit into right-center. I thought, as I had of Conigliaro, that Rohr had a great career ahead of him. He was to win two more games in his major league career.

That summer and fall, I was back in Vietnam; it was a bad time for me. The American mission was optimistic (this was just before Tet) and I was pessimistic, convinced that 500,000 men had managed only to stalemate the other side. I hated the futile violence of the war. It was not a face of America I was comfortable with, and the combination of the flawed commitment — so many men and so much hardware to a job which could not be done, and the self-deception which accompanied it had put me in a grim mood. That was also the season of Yastrzemski; that summer and fall when I was not out in the field, I would go over to the AP office. Saigon was 12 hours different from Boston and so the results of the night games would tend to come in about 11 A.M. There was also a man who hung around the AP office, for the same reason: Doc, as he was known. Doc was Dr. Tom Durant, a Boston doctor helping the Vietnamese with their medical training (he is now assistant director of Mass. General), and each morning I would meet him there, bonded by this need to escape, and this common passion, and we would follow the results of a wonderful pennant race and perhaps the greatest one-man pennant drive in modern baseball history by standing over the AP ticker. I felt very close to him; we never agreed in advance to meet at the office but indeed we always did. We would sit there in that small airless room, and we could almost see Yaz as he was in Fenway, the exaggerated stance; it was all oddly exhilarating. Each day the heroics seemed even more remarkable, the box score would come clicking over the printer — Yaz, 2 for 4 with two RBIs — and then, more often than not, the mention of some extraordinary catch as well. In what was for me a bad season, his was a marvelous season and it reminded me of the America I loved, and which otherwise seemed quite distant. I have felt fondly of him ever since, and my affection has weathered even the current hokey hot dog commercials.

That next year I became a citizen of New England again, buying a home in Nantucket, connecting myself once again to Boston sports coverage, which now in modern times seemed to make the Red Sox players larger than life (Williams had played 25 years too soon, I suspected; he should have played in an era of semi-monopoly journalism) and returning to Fenway once again. I had remembered it as a small shabby park, an embarrassment after the grandeur of the Stadium, but now I saw it differently; in an age of antiseptic ballparks, gimmicky electronic scoreboards, fans who cheered every pop fly, it was a real ballpark. Going there was like going back in time, stepping into a Hopper painting. It must have been like this, I thought, when Smoky Joe Wood was ready to pitch. I had rooted for the 1975 team, a glorious and exciting team in a wonderful Series, wondering what might have happened if there had been two Luis Tiants instead of one. Then in 1978, for the last time, I faced the question of divided loyalties, the human heart in conflict with itself, to use Faulkner's phrase. I was no longer an automatic Yankee fan, but that was a good and gritty Yankee team, Munson-Nettles-Chambliss-Piniella-Jackson-Hunter, a Gabe Paul rather than a Steinbrenner team, not yet contaminated by the worst of all baseball owners. I like the chase as much as anything else, and that summer I found myself cheering the late-season New York surge. It was also a very good Red Sox team as well, Rice-Lynn-Yastrzemski-Evans-Fisk, weaker as usual in pitching. The season was as good as any I have ever seen, the early, seemingly insurmountable Boston lead, the feral, almost ruthless late Yankee surge to reclaim part of first place. One hundred sixty-two games played and both teams dead even — that was not a flawed season, that was an almost perfect season. Of that in the bitterness of postmortem charges and countercharges, there was much talk about a Red Sox collapse. I never believed it. The Yankees, as usual, had a demonstrably better pitching staff. Perhaps, I thought, the key moment took place six years earlier when the Red Sox made one of the worst trades of modern times, swapping Sparky Lyle for Danny Cater. Lyle was then young, a proven lefthanded reliever, 53 saves in his last three seasons; Cater was a good, albeit limited, pinch hitter. Lyle was the perfect relief pitcher for the Stadium and he gave an improving Yankees team exactly what it needed, a kind of instant late-inning legitimacy. In seven years as a Yankee, he had 141 saves, and in that year, 1978, when his star was already in descent in New York (Goose Gossage had arrived and Lyle went, said Nettles, from Cy Young to Sayonara in one season), he nonetheless had nine saves and a 9–3 record. In a season where two teams end up with the same record, that was all the difference the Yankees needed.

That team is gone: Piniella as manager and Randolph and Guidry are the only survivors. In the age of narcissus, Steinbrenner is the perfect modern baseball owner now, the bully as owner (if Tom Yawkey was flawed because he loved his players too much, Steinbrenner is flawed because he envies them their talent and youth and fame too much). He has won the tabloids, and lost the team. The 1978 team struck me as one which was bonded together by a mutual dislike of him; now, eight years later, his act has played too long, he is the national bore, and contempt has replaced dislike. It's not easy, in an age of free agency, to screw up owning a baseball team in the media capital of the world, but he has done it. The team is a wonderful extension of him, overpaid, surly, disconnected; the quintessential Steinbrenner player is Rickey Henderson. I do not doubt his talent, indeed his brilliance, but he seems, whenever I watch, in a perpetual sulk, entirely within himself, and watching him is almost as much fun as watching Carl Lewis during the 1984 Olympics. In this year I wish the Red Sox well, I did not think it was a good race, there was too much stumbling around. In a personal sense, if I am pleased for anyone, it is Don Baylor; trashed by Steinbrenner, he gained the sweetest kind of revenge, hitting against righthanders. His trade subtracted character from the Yankees and added it to the Red Sox. And I rooted as well for Tom Seaver, carried in this season as much by a feral instinct to compete as by natural skill, awesome if not in talent anymore then in toughness of mind.

If the Red Sox stumble through, however imperfectly, then I am pleased, for there have been enough very good Boston teams which, playing far better baseball, had their pennants denied. If they win, so be it: The gods owe them one.

Stephen King

'86 Was Just the Ticket
Wrong Formula, Right Result

Boston Globe, October 6, 1986

When I called Dan Casey late last December, after two months of careful cogitation, and asked if he could get me tickets to a block of four good seats on the first or third baseline for the 1986 Red Sox season, there was such a long pause on the line that I thought we'd been disconnected.

Dan is, as far as I'm concerned, one of the two best limo jockeys in the world, and the only one who's a friend. Like any good limo driver, he knows his city, and, if he thinks you deserve the benefit of his expertise (something a mere tip cannot buy), he can find you anything from a place that sells jeans at midnight to one that will trim your hair at 5 A.M. But when he finally spoke, he sounded both cautious and oddly solicitous.

"Steve," he said at last, "seats like that aren't going to come cheap. And the way you go at things, your summer's apt to be more like the Tet Offensive than a vacation. How many games could you actually make? Ten? Fourteen?"

That sounded about right, but I still wanted the tickets.

There was another long pause. Maybe Dan was thinking about the Vegas odds, which had the Sox finishing one place out of the cellar — below Milwaukee and above Cleveland —

two full months before the first spring training warmup lob
would be thrown. At last he said, "Do you know something I
don't, Steve?"

"I hope so," I said.

Two weeks later, I got my tickets — one long computer-
ized printout with perforated fold lines so you could collapse
it into a single stack that looked a little like Myron Floren's
accordion on the old Lawrence Welk show. A note from Dan
was enclosed: "Good seats . . . and good luck. The odds
don't look good."

Want to know the oddest thing about the odds? The people
who make them usually wind up with a set that reflects the
previous season's final standings, no matter what the sport.
They gussy their explanations up with a lot of "insider" jive-
talk, but *the basic oddsmaker's philosophy is What was shall
be, forever and ever, amen.*

If that were really the case, the Yankees would still be
winning the AL championship every year and the Mets would
still be finishing 30 games out.

Want to know my definition of an upset? Large groups of
fans who make the mistake of believing small groups of
oddsmakers who continue to forget that change is the essence and fascination of sport.

Not that I'm any great baseball sachem; I could have just
as easily bought that season's box in a year when the Red Sox
finished five games out of first (which is exactly what I
thought they'd do this year: I had 'em picked like this:
Yankees, Red Sox (five back); Cleveland (six back); Toronto
(eight back). But I had been a good deal more interested in
how the Sox finished the '85 season than in the final standings.
That finish was like watching a Titan-II rocket just reaching
full thrust when, at the instant before it can leave the
launching pad, the guys in the control room hit the shut-down
switches.

I thought that if the entire '86 season was anything like the
last four or five weeks of the '85 season, I just might see staid
old Fenway Park do some rocking and reeling.

And on that one, I feel like I can look anyone in the world straight in the eye and say "I told you so."

I thought the pitching had a chance to be not fair, or "pretty good," but *really* good for the first time since dinosaurs walked the earth — or, at least, since Babe Ruth swapped his red hose for a pair of pinstripes.

I thought Al Nipper would win at least 15 — five on his own, five on the hitting support of his mates, and five on sheer guts (the spiked-at-home injury is something no one can predict, of course), I thought Bob Stanley was worth his high price tag in spite of the Fenway wolfpack that has conceived an irrational dislike for the man who has been Boston's most consistent and dependable pitcher during the lean years, and I thought Sammy Stewart would be . . . well, a little better than he has been. As for Bruce Hurst and Oil Can Boyd — well, I thought the two of them might just turn out to be the 1986 equivalent of "Spahn and Sain and pray for rain."

Clemens?

Guy had arm surgery, didn't he?

With strong front-line pitching for a change and a bullpen that looked a good deal stronger than many of the experts were giving it credit for (Calvin *who?* isn't he some guy with the Pawsox?), I thought the Red Sox could win a lot of games . . . probably not enough to win the division, but, yes, maybe even that. An outside shot, granted, but a *shot.* After all, they would really clobber the ball — all those heavy hitters, you know (Jim *who* is choking up on the bat?) — and that alone would win them some games the pitching couldn't.

Well, the hitting turned out to be a lot lighter than I thought, maybe because I overlooked something I hope the Red Sox management won't (although, in light of the Seaver trade, you have to wonder): this team is not getting any younger. Guys like Tony Armas, who were not just hitting that left-field wall two years ago but angling bank shots off it, now seem a little less able to catch up with the ball; a lot of 1984's bank shots have been 1986's foul balls rolling back down the screen behind home plate. I have wondered a couple of times how many Rocket Roger might have struck out if it had been the Red Sox he'd been facing on that night when he . . . well, never mind. Some things are best not thought of.

So the hitting's been a little off, but when the Sox have absolutely needed the right hit at the right time, someone — a Baylor, a Barrett, a Gedman, and, time after time, a Boggs — has been able to supply it.

As for myself, I don't regret the dough I spent for that box of mine one little bit, I regret the games I missed — most of all Clemens' 20-K masterpiece (that one I heard on the radio) — but that's all. Because no matter how it turns out, the Red Sox have had a *fabulous* season and have put on a fabulous show. I'm glad I was around to dig it, and hey, Dan: if you're reading this, maybe I did know something last December. Or had a brain-wave. Or just got lucky.

But . . . *Clemens?* Can't expect too much from a guy with a retooled pitching arm, even if he *is* from Texas. He might win five, I suppose . . . maybe even seven. . . .

Geoffrey Wolff

No El Foldo Foils Fandom

After All, Someone Has to Win

Boston Globe, October 6, 1986

Oh, woe! Break, my heart! I "cheer" for the Red Sox. It
hurts so bad? I'm a "fan." Woe is me! What can I do? I live in
New England. Medic! Why are they so mean to me? They're
only division champions!

Am I crazy? Wasn't this supposed to be fun? To "root" for
the home team (I'd been told) was to shout yourself hoarse
with huzzahs, to yell hey, hooray! What is this? Greek
tragedy? Seven months of freezing rain? Beirut? I thought
that ball*players* were sports who *play* a ball*game* watched by
sports. I'd underestimated *Schadenfreude,* an emotion so
complexly perverse (the leap of one's heart at another's bad
luck), only the Germans can contain it in a single word. I'd
counted out self-importance, the conviction that a stranger
who takes a mighty cut at a fastball and misses has violated a
contract with me, myself and I, has failed the "heartbroken"
moi-même. I'd overlooked the good news on the newsstand
of bad news.

Consider, please:

You're up to here with being told Fenway Park is a "jewel
box," but it is. The fence may or not be "friendly," but it sure
is interesting. Last time I tasted it, the beer was cold, and

worked well. I eat Fenway Franks at home, from choice. I'm glad Boston has lost only one major league club since my years riding the pine as outfielder-wannabee for the Old Lyme (Conn.) Elementary School baseball team. You can spin a radio dial in Newport, N.H., or Newport, Vt., and hear the course — not merely the outcome — of the Red Sox' play. In Newport, R.I., you can hear them, and Presque Isle, Maine, in Florida even, and I wouldn't have it any other way.

"Is this a plain old slump or the advance guard of the collapse?"
   — Art Turgeon, *Providence Journal*, Aug. 10

It is true that they have only the second-best record in major league baseball. And as every Boston fan and sports journalist seems to know, there's Numero Uno, and there's all the rest.

"But they are No. 1," whispers a moron kid in Woonsocket.

"For the moment," says a sourpuss savant, *"for the time being."* The savant began exercising his sense of history on May 12, when the Red Sox climbed into first place, and waited for El Foldo, The Slide, The Great Tumble, The Choke.

What is it with New England? What a gang of hanging judges and long-faced sad sacks. Is it the Yankee heritage? (And speaking of *them*. . . . no, let us not speak of them.) This isn't the 17th century, or even the 19th; New Englanders are too various, too comfortable with pleasure to hang crepe like a corporation of gravediggers, or bankers.

We're not bankers, and the Red Sox don't owe us a nickel. From "our" baseball team we can hope for:

Our money's worth of fun. Fun might be the product of a few sweet plays in a losing game, or a Roger Clemens fastball, or Gedman's grand slam against Detroit, a lefthand poke off a lefthand pitch, a winner. ("Bosox Barely Escape Tigers," in the exemplary judgment of my local newspaper.) And if the Red Sox don't bring "us" the pennant, let alone the

Series, this team has delivered this year all it owes, and plenty more.

What are we? Little League parents? Such figures of contempt as those lard-assed geezers driving Cherokees or Blazers, who heap contumely on the tyke thrown out trying to steal second, the mite who God forbid goes down on a called third strike, who boots a grounder idling down the third base line. These hapless children are *their* children, of course, those unlucky girls and boys who hear their failures reviewed at dinner ("You took your eye off it . . . you let me down . . . you broke my heart, again . . ."), or foretold at breakfast ("You'll take your eye off it . . . drop it . . . choke . . . let me down again . . .").

How would you like to hear it in barber shops on talk shows? Now your kids read it in the paper, day after day: *"He was a good rookie cabbie, but now? — el foldo! His move on the exact-change basket at Callahan Tunnel last night seemed . . . tentative."* Or: *"For the second consecutive day of a losing streak that began yesterday, B. failed to close a sale of a home entertainment center. Reliable sources have begun alluding to a trade, or release on waivers: 'He's lost a step.'"*

I write books. It has been known that critic both professional and amateur have failed to appreciate the excellence of the books I have written. I cast my bread upon waters publicly held. I tell myself I'm fair game. I pretend to stand up well to a trimming. But the worst I've had to take is the contempt of a reader for a book. Critics rarely accuse a writer of being brain-dead, or a coward, or too old and fat to write, or of beginning with *this* piece of work a long and inexorable slide from first place (on the List? as winner of Nobel? Pulitzer?) to disgrace and oblivion.

It doesn't require a long memory to recall New England's disgrace two years ago when the Lakers beat the Celtics (and Jack Nicholson — whose knees won't give him pain for the rest of his life, who never went one-on-one against The Chief — won nothing; neither was he owed that Los Angeles victory, nor paid with it), or more recently when the Bears chomped on the Pats. The disgrace belongs not to two local teams who were beaten by better teams — who lose, merely — but to bravos who shouted names at athletes from the safety of a newsroom or the 13th row of a public arena.

What's wrong with us is probably a disease of a country wild for a condensed and polluted version of Darwinian combat (feral Ty Cobb, all spikes and hate and good box scores), the American Dream of eternal progress. Every day in every way, better and better. Slip and you fall. Fall and you're dead. Dead, you're a bum. Color me pink and yellow but I never really understood the apercu of that philosopher-king, Vincent of Green Bay: *"Winning isn't everything; it's the only thing."* Huh?

(How about a possible dream, American as get-out? A dreamy fly hit long to Dewey on a dreamy afternoon. A dream of a throw rifled to second just in dreamy time to nip the baserunner who dreamed in vain of tagging up, of sliding in safe.)

No. 1 gives me the creeps. It's what babies do when they go potty. Twenty-five major league baseball teams will not be No. 1 Dare I ask, "So what?" Does this efface all that pleasure given all that time between April and October? Do you really want each of "our" batters, at the plate *right now,* now, in the moment, in fact thinking about *this pitch,* to contemplate the great reckoning come October? I mean, if the Red Sox were really to think what we seem to think they think, why bother? The game — the real game, who's No. 1? — is over. History says so.

In fact, thank God, there's considerable evidence that what "fans" and inklings think ballplayers think are thinks un-thought. Gedman says, and I believe, that his mind was clear when he pinch hit that grand slam, against historical proba-bilites.

If the choke exists, it's nurtured rather than natured. To fail under pressure is not the most notable genetic component of a professional athlete's makeup, but to read in the newspa-pers and hear on radio talk shows that he *will* fail under pressure is surely one of the principal experiences of a New England athlete's professional destiny.

On July 26, 1986, with the eleventy-zillionth recapitulation of Bucky Dent's homer off Mike Torrez, Oct. 2, 1978, with the Red Sox three games up, fans want to read that "the emotional scars left by the 1978 season are being rubbed raw this year as the once-powerful Red Sox are in a horribly reminiscent slump" (Steven Krasner, *Providence Journal*).

Poor babies: With those emotional scars "rubbed raw," no wonder the fans are choking.

Like deploring Polish jokes to tell them (for example, *"This makes me sick, there's this Polish first baseman . . ."*) sports reporters and columnists in our quadrant of America love to quote what the enemy propagandists say about "our" boys: "Baseball's accordion franchise," "Boston G-g-g-gag Sox." Don Baylor, who is no stranger to a bedeviled team (and how would you like to have the Yankees to root for? Like US Steel, remember?), has said, with no little wonder, I hope: "You can see it; they expect us to choke, just like they expect the Celtics to win." (Except when the Celts didn't win The Big One — Numero Uno — the pansies.)

It's a sorry business, the perversion of the heart's investment in game-players, feelings of kinship yielding to proprietary rights. We don't own this or any franchise, and the people who do don't own Rice or Evans or Boggs. (They sure as hell don't own Lynn or Fisk, which is another and truly sad story.) And if we did own them, could oblige them to mow our lawns or hit homers 10 for 10, we shouldn't make them read and hear what "our" players have to read and hear.

A bad book review is one thing. "Brain-dead" is another. If Oil Can Boyd got taken out behind the woodshed by his manager — who defined precisely what a player owes "his" fans, the recognition that men and women in the bleachers and even the boxes would trade a vital organ to be in a starting pitcher's uniform and on the mound at Fenway — no one, forget an 11-game winner, merits the treatment that man got. The stories about Boyd's troubles, which have been troubles since he was a kid, which *he* says have been troubles, were sadistic, and the worse for being unctuous. It was like watching a bully shed crocodile tears while he pulls the wings off a fly.

The bear-baiting has gone way over the edge. It's bush league, the way Jack Nicholson's cheap connection with the Lakers, bought at no more cost than of free time and tax-deductible tickets, is bush. Yikes, we're even beating up on Boomer again, six — what is it, seven? — years later. I read in the *Providence Journal Sunday Magazine* in July a caption to a photograph: "Right, George Scott — too fat to swing a heavy bat, too fat to run fast — is forced at second base in a 1979 double play."

A final word about that article, a single symptom of *Schadenfreude*: two days before it ran, the newspaper apologized for it: "It seemed like a good idea at the time. . . . The timing seemed perfect (in June); the Sox were soaring. . . . However, there is this little problem. The Sunday Journal Magazine is printed ahead of time. In this case, it was printed before the Sox began to, ahem, fall like a rock. So on Sunday morning read 'Pennant Fever' in the *Magazine* and see how the pennant race *should* be going. Just blame the Red Sox for reality." (If "we're" in the World Series, think of the hedged bets! No lead time at all to bet on a sure thing.)

Reality was, of course, the Red Sox were then in first place. Winners. But reality's rewrite guy was *Schadenfreude*, who sang of "the fall of 1972, my first autumn of despair (not my last) as a Sox fan."

What profession other than sports keeps score so brutally, with a win or loss at the close of each performance? Not only are the rest of us — teachers, actors, farmers — not summed by a scorecard, we do not answer a calling in which the people with whom we work try their damnedest to louse up our performance. It is true that some writers, for example, use the metaphor of sports to determine the question of whether Mailer could go 15 rounds against Hemingway, whether Hemingway could get a split decision against Tolstoy, whether Tolstoy or Dostoevsky was No. 1 in the Czar's league. These questions get asked by some writers, some industrialists, many barflies, but they are ignoble questions, with silly answers.

Look: Someone is always younger, faster, better than someone else. The older, or slower, or worse player is not always, or often, a bum. To hear New England "fans" speak and write, an athlete might forget this. An athlete, hearing often enough that he will choke because once upon a time other athletes from the Boston area choked, which they didn't either, might come to believe such a prophecy. It might make playing games seem less pleasurable than not playing them.

Remember the baseball strike? These Red Sox, this baseball team everyone loves to call quitters . . . let's imagine they read and hear the line on them, they get together to study 1949, and 1974, they watch the replay of Bucky Dent's homer in 1978 and Yaz' pop fly (this wouldn't be the first the team heard of these years and plays), they talk it over and come to a conclusion; they make an announcement:

"You're right. We're quitters. We quit."

That would be tragic, because then *my* fun goes in the toilet, No. 2.

NOTICES

Ah, I knew there had to be a Harvard classics professor in here somewhere — Emily Vermeule will have the next-to-last word as she properly puts the fine point on the Sox-as-Greek-heroes myth. First, however, Charlie Pierce and Peter Gammons, who've striven to cover the Sox with their heads rather than their hearts for years, let it all hang out in their respective pieces. Then with deep satisfaction there comes an essay by my boyhood pal Mike Blowen, who grew up with me as a Sox fan in Connecticut, a border state in the bloody Sox–Yanks civil war. Those were days spent deep in the jaws of Second Division Hell. No one knew then that those floundering Sox of the '60s were but one act in a myth in the making. This is our revenge.

Charles Pierce

History's Sad Lesson

A Sports Writer Struggles with a Fan's Heartbreak

Boston Herald, November 9, 1986

There are still stories worth telling about the 1986 baseball season. These are only two of them.

Guy calls his wife, right? He's a lifelong Red Sox fan, and he has an 11-month-old son. Before the sixth game of the World Series, he tells his wife that if the Sox are leading with two out in the ninth inning she should wake up the baby and hold him up in front of the television set, because there is no guarantee that the baby will see Boston win another world championship in his lifetime.

She complies. So do the Red Sox. Bob Stanley winds and delivers to the backstop against Mookie Wilson. Tie game. Wilson's grounder turns Bill Buckner into the city's most famous turnstile. Ball game. The child is marked now. He will meet someone from Boston in his sociology class and they will complain about That Sixth Game, and it will be 2007.

Or he will grow up to be Sydney Schanberg, Pulitzer Prize winner, *Newsday* columnist, and subject of the remarkable movie *The Killing Fields*. Schanberg is also a Red Sox fan of deep and abiding loyalty. He attends a World Series game at Fenway. The fellow sitting next to him has a vision:

There is a field of bones bleached white by the sun. Men are firing automatic weapons, and tropical birds scream hotly from the distant jungle. The world is ending all the way to the horizon. Sydney Schanberg is there, cooly taking notes, counting the rounds of ammunition being fired over his head. He turns to his Cambodian interpreter. "Hey, Pran," Schanberg says. "You get the Sox score last night?"

The first time I ever heard a certain important curse word, I was sitting on my grandfather's lap, and the word was directed against Frank Malzone, who used to play third base. I recall thinking the word was a very important one, because it brought my mother and my grandmother scurrying in from the kitchen.

I don't recall if Frank Malzone deserved what my grandfather called him. The Red Sox were so bad then that it hardly mattered. The best thing about Red Sox telecasts were the Elaine May and Mike Nichols commercials for Narragansett Lager Beer — "Hi, Neighbor!" — that popped up every half-inning. The commercials are still the most positive contribution that television has ever made to baseball.

It was such a comfort back then, being 52–110. No one cared. Famous authors wrote their books; they didn't seem compelled to draw the unavoidable historical parallel between Aeneas and Roman Mejias.

People noticed that Fenway Park was cramped and impossible to get to, not that it was some sort of cultural relic. Of course, this was before they started building ballparks round, and plastic, and dull. These were the joys of back-running, and only the oldest fans remembered the 1946 Series, or the 1948 Playoff game.

That was the way I learned my baseball: a context in which the actual playing of the game was very secondary to the grass, and the bright blue sky, and the 'Gansett commercials. There didn't seem to be much point in caring a great deal whether Dave Morehead could hold down the Indians.

If matters had stayed that way — if there had been no 1967, or 1972 or 1975, or 1978 or 1986 — a happy balance would have been achieved. If there had been no possibility of a championship between 1946 and this season, then the players would have been spared relentless questions about their team's "history." They still don't know the answers, because they don't understand the questions.

"I can appreciate what the fans are going through," said Bruce Hurst. "But we're the guys who have to suit up."

Players are mercenaries now. This is not entirely a bad thing; the reserve clause was a pernicious evil that deserved to be abolished. Nevertheless, teams do not stay together long enough for players to become absorbed in the life of the community that they ostensibly represent. Bill Buckner does not go to the Museum of Fine Arts, or stroll through the Public Gardens on a fine spring afternoon. Don Baylor — the much-celebrated "spiritual leader" of this year's Red Sox — is playing for the fourth team of his career. Don Baylor does not ride the Swan Boats.

Consequently, none of the players ever understood that the obsession with the past has nothing to do with who hits behind which runner, or who pitches fourth in the rotation.

"What's going to happen when we win it?" wondered Joe Sambito. "What's everybody going to talk about?"

The same thing they always talk about here. The thieves on Winter Hill, and the thieves on Beacon Hill. The changeable weather. Haunted questions of race and class, handed down through the years, laced with a Puritan's zest for righteous penance.

And the Red Sox. The doom-fattened Boston bleeping Red Sox, who always blow it. No Red Sox player understands that that simple fact has more to do with James Michael Curley than it has to do with Bill Monbouquette. There's brigandage at City Hall, and the snow has stalled the MBTA, and the Red Sox will blow it. They don't understand the connection, because they don't understand their city.

It was fascinating to watch this team use its catastrophic history even while denying that history's relevance. In Baltimore, very early in the season, Barrett addressed the question. The Red Sox were leading the division, and playing very well.

"I don't understand why people expect us to fail," Marty Barrett said. "We're playing real good ball right now. Why can't people just enjoy that? Why dwell on the negative things in the past? Why not just blink those things out?"

There were times in which they seemed to do that. David Henderson was the greatest sports hero in Boston's history — step aside, Bill Russell; jump back, Bobby Orr — for about 20 minutes. He was mystified by it all.

"People are coming up to me on the street," he says. "They're telling me how happy I made them."

My baseball season began inauspiciouly. Somebody tried to sink my boat in Baltimore harbor. There I was, puttering around the harbor in my little electric dinghy, and suddenly it's PT 109. I should have been warned.

I do not like covering baseball. Which is not the same thing as not liking baseball itself. I enjoy going to baseball games, because the sport is so undemanding. It doesn't force itself into the consciousness, at least not in parks that have avoided the temptation of DiamondVision.

From the perspective of grandstand woolgathering, it's a charmer. From the perspective of the clubhouse, it's often like being trapped in the worst football frat in the Southeastern Conference. In fact, the reason that so many people have taken to becoming baseball essayists, rather than baseball reporters, is because essayists do not have to deal with the overwhelming number of rude and stupid people who play the game.

Thus, there was a certain four-way split in what I was doing. I liked the game, but not the players. And I liked the Red Sox, but not the members of the team. I was a fan long before I took this job, and I'll be one long after I leave it. I was from the *Herald,* but I grew up near Worcester.

There is no trouble in finessing the latter question. All it takes is the basic reporting skill of looking at a tree and not writing that it is a frog. If the Red Sox play well, write that they play well. If they play like cementheads, write that too. Simple.

Being from the *Herald,* I knew that I would have to hear Rich Gedman say, "Let's not get too dramatic," and Dwight Evans opine that "That's a ridiculous question," and Jim Rice's stony one-word answers. Being from Worcester, I knew that all of these guys were putting up a season that brought bubbles to the 'Gansett in Slattery's, and the Kelley Square Yacht Club, and Breen's.

Being from the *Herald* meant believing that they might be different, that *this* time they might change history. Being from Worcester meant knowing there was no chance. They were answering karma with starting pitching, trying to deal rationally with irrational events.

They won games in new ways, and they won games that they should have lost. They took this as proof from Above that they were different. The *Herald* duly noted this. Worcester cocked its eyebrow.

There was some danger in dismissing what had gone before, and the players knew it. There was no season wilder than 1967, with four teams after a real pennant until the last day. In 1967 they lost the World Series four games to three.

They came back from the absolute dead against California, and took it as destiny. But destiny predates September. It goes back farther than Anaheim Stadium. It is older than Bobby Grich. That the same situation came up in the mirror in Game Six should have been a sign.

It *was* a sign, to anyone who had watched this team for longer than six months. Which doesn't include a lot of the players. So, when they somehow managed to give it away, the players were shocked. Hardly anyone else was. Nothing ever happens to the Red Sox by accident.

The Red Sox players and their fans were talking at cross-purposes the entire season. The players insisted that history didn't matter, that it was an invention of those wretches with the minicams and the VDTs. Of course, this devalues the disappointment felt at the failures of the past 68 years.

It also makes light of the fact the Red Sox are a major civic institution, just like the *Herald,* the Pops, and the Metropolitan District Commission. Institutions are common goods, owned in part by those whose faith is invested in them. The Red Sox are an institution with an unparalleled record of spectacular failure under ultimate pressure. There is no way to divorce them from the legacy, and, if there were, it certainly wouldn't be by denying that it exists at all. The end of the 1986 World Series is part of the job for every player who puts on a Red Sox uniform from now until they finally win another world championship. John Williams has to live with Arthur Fiedler and Bill Buckner has to live with Denny Galehouse.

It was a dilemma not entirely dissimilar from my own. Together, there was the 14-year-old kid sneaking a transistor radio past the Xaverian Brothers and listening to the second game in 1967 and the 32-year-old reporter who had to look at things with a properly dispassionate mien. (And they mean it, too. "This is a working press box," the PA intones before every game, sounding very much like *Animal House*'s Dean Vernon Wormer announcing, "No more fun of any kind." And, while no cheering in the press box is a noble and laudable rule, two other disrespectful scribes and I were once soundly rapped this year for the offense of laughing too hard at the Cleveland Indians. To paraphrase the late Bill Veeck, there aren't many things in this life you can do spontaneously anymore, but laughing at the ballpark in the afternoon ought to be one of them.)

Logic in this season was so steadily undermined that, when it finally surfaced, nobody was prepared for it. The Red Sox lost because their middle relievers were hash, and everybody knew it. Bob Stanley is a Victim, and that's all there is to it.

But at an instinctive level, the Red Sox lost the World Series because that is what the Red Sox do, just as the Pops do the *1812 Overture.* The 14-year-old kid — an earplug running up the sleeve of his suitcoat — knew that. The 32-year-old, shivering in an open press box at Shea Stadium, had forgotten it. When the lead went up to 3–0, it was the 14-year-old who turned to the respected columnist and asked, "Okay, how's it going to happen?"

At the end of it, the players were still answering the same questions that were being tossed at them in the fatter times of August. There remained a sense that one party or the other was speaking Chinese.

"Nobody picked us to win it, and nobody thought we'd finish higher than fifth," said Marty Barrett, who had the greatest World Series of any Red Sox player since Babe Ruth. "I don't think this club has anything to be ashamed of."

Nobody was saying that. No one is ashamed of the Red Sox. No one is ashamed of the Green Line when it stalls in Allston. You're mad at it, or you laugh about moving to Melrose, but you're not ashamed to be riding it.

Still, nobody was cutting the 1986 Red Sox any slack for having surpassed even the franchise's stunning history for spotlit buffoonery. "Who are those guys?" asked Bruce Hurst, with considerable heat. "What do they have to do with me?" The great Bob Dylan line popped to mind: "Cursing the dead, who can't answer him back."

There's a question that they ask you when you're new on the beat: Whaddya know about baseball? It's as though the game were nuclear physics (and if it was, Davey Johnson and John McNamara would have blown up Queens). Late on the night that the World Series ended, liquid scribes were tossing around the famous George Santayana line about studying history.

Well, George, whaddya know about baseball, anyway?

Even those who study the past are condemned to repeat it.

Peter Gammons

Living and Dying with the Woe Sox

Sports Illustrated, November 3, 1986

How will it feel? For years we had asked ourselves, "How will it feel if the Red Sox ever win?" How will it feel if there are two outs and none on in the bottom of the 10th with a 5–3 lead in Game 6 of the World Series? How, in God's name, will it *feel?*

"Warm," my brother Ned had predicted. His relationship with this team dates back to the '30s, and all he knew was that he wouldn't yell or jump up and down or run to a local bar, because it is a private relationship. "It will be a special family matter," Ned said last Saturday afternoon, "and we New Englanders don't share such things with strangers." He thought he would have a glass of champagne, then fall into "a wonderful sleep." That is almost exactly what Ted Williams had said he would do at his house in Citrus Hills, Fla. "I'm going to watch the game with some friends," said Ted, "and if we win, we'll raise our glasses and say a toast. Then I'll go to sleep with a warm feeling."

The story was warm, too: David Henderson, the Seattle exile whose playoff homer two weeks before had saved the day and redeemed so many past sins, broke the 3–3 tie with a home run at 11:59 P.M., reaching the dugout precisely as the Shea Stadium clock read midnight. But reality can never fulfill expectation, and, after all, we all grew up with the Red Sox' annual tide of hope receding into disappointment and rising back to hope. To relinquish that feeling after 68 years might be as much of a loss as a victory. Ron Darling, the Mets pitcher who grew up with the Sox, had wondered before the Series began if a Red Sox victory "might not alter the way New Englanders view the world." When Boston's second lead had been lost in the eighth inning of Game 6, journalist Clark Booth turned to me and said, "Jonathan Edwards, Melville and Ethan Frome are part of us, which is why that part of us loves living this ongoing Calvinistic tragedy."

Gary Carter singled with two outs in the 10th, but that still didn't change the burgeoning conviction that the Red Sox were going to do it, they were going to win the World Series. CONGRATULATIONS BOSTON RED SOX momentarily — and mistakenly — flashed on the electronic message board at Shea Stadium as Calvin Schiraldi prepared to pitch to Kevin Mitchell. I thought of the NBC pregame show on which 92-year-old Dick Casey, a chronicler of the '18 series, said, "Every day since, I've prayed to God that the Red Sox would win one more World Series before I die, so now I guess I'm going to die soon."

Mitchell singled. "They're going to do it," a friend said, nudging me. "Just when we thought that we had been freed at last, they're going to create a way to again break our hearts that goes beyond our wildest imaginations. Stephen King wouldn't be what he is today if he'd grown up anywhere else." I thought of the New Haven bar owner who, after the '78 playoff, said, "They killed our fathers, and now the sons of bitches are coming to get us."

And when the ball went through Bill Buckner's legs, 41 years of Red Sox baseball flashed in front of my eyes. In that one moment, Johnny Pesky held the ball, Joe McCarthy lifted Ellis Kinder in Yankee Stadium, Luis Aparicio fell down rounding third, Bill Lee delivered his Leephus pitch to Tony Perez, Darrell Johnson hit for Jim Willoughby, Don Zimmer chose Bobby Sprowl over Luis Tiant and Bucky (Bleeping) Dent hit the home run. Booth went downstairs to find Mike Torrez, the man who had given up the homer to Dent, and when he found him, a giddy Torrez shouted, "I'm off the hook!" Then when Booth's TV crew turned off the lights, Torrez unloaded the poltergeist that he had carried for eight years by yelling, "——— Boston!"

Bart Giamatti, the new National League president, abandoned his public allegiance and confessed to a feeling of rage. Beside him, a stranger in a Red Sox cap shouted, "McCarthy, Johnson, Zimmer and now McNamara. How could he not hit Baylor for Bucker against Orosco with the bases loaded when all Buckner has done is end innings and strand runners in scoring position? Why wasn't Stapleton at first base in the 10th?" After the fan's diatribe came his lament, "What if Roger Clemens doesn't come up with a blister. . . ." Now I could feel the wounds opening up again. What if Williams hadn't hurt himself before the '46 Series; what if Larry Barnett had called interference on Ed Armbrister in '75; what if the wind hadn't shifted just before Dent came up in '78 . . . what if . . . what if . . . Enough already.

Mike Barnicle, the *Boston Globe* columnist, Booth and I were in the since-razed Abbey Feare Pub in January of 1976 watching a Bruins game. At the end of the bar, an elderly gentleman washed down 25-cent drafts, staring straight ahead for most of the game. When the Bruins game ended, he turned in our direction. "How the hell could he have taken out Willoughby?" he mumbled, then passed out on the bar.

Last Saturday night, after the clubhouses had cleared out and emotional exhaustion set in, the whole thing seemed to make sense. We in New England dwell on history because we are brought up with the English notion that we are what we are because of who and what came before us. The 10th inning of this sixth game was part of something bizarre and supernatural that is bigger than any of us. "Maybe they are going to win, maybe even Buckner will end up the hero," I told a friend. "But before we could find out what it feels like to win, we have to be made to suffer one last, excruciating time."

Red Sox players and their families don't understand Red Sox fans. They come from places like California and Mississippi. But Sherry Gedman grew up 40 miles from Boston, so she knows. That is why she was the only Red Sox wife who remained seated while Schiraldi pitched to Carter.

"Baseball is not a life and death matter," Barnicle once wrote, "but the Red Sox are." My very first recollection is my mother ironing and listening to the '48 playoff. I still vividly recall my first entrance into Fenway Park on June 28, 1952 (Ike Delock, Ray Scarborough and Dizzy Trout pitched in the 5–1 loss to Washington), and how when first I went up the ramp to the right of home plate the green picture and the dank atmosphere gave me the feeling that I had been placed in a forest after a night of warm rain. I walked up that ramp before every postseason game in 1975 and 1986. At the Groton Elementary School, Opening Day was a legal excuse to leave at 10:30, and my father's desk, on which I did my homework, bore the holes of a compass my brother had driven into it in the ninth inning of the seventh game in '46. I listened to Billy Martin's catch in the '52 World Series in the barber's chair of a Red Sox fan named Billy Sambito, whose nephew Joe now pitches for Boston, and when I got home from school one May day in 1957, my mother, bless her heart, had written down all the names involved in the Dean Stone–Bob Chakales deal with the Senators.

I sat in the traffic jam in '67 when someone refused to enter the Sumner Tunnel until Reggie Smith finished his at bat with the bases loaded, and I was in Fenway the night Tony C was beaned. I found a strong enough radio in my Chapel Hill fraternity to get WTIC in Hartford just in time to hear Yaz hit the homer off Mike Marshall in the ninth in Detroit after we had already used up a car battery listening to the first six innings of the game.

The last time my brother Ned and I spoke to our father before he died in 1981, he said to us, "The Red Sox will win in your lifetime."

Michael Blowen

The Perfect Ending to a Perfect Season

Boston Globe, October 29, 1986

"It's a wrong ending to the story book year," said Dave Henderson after the Red Sox defeat in the seventh game of the 1986 World Series — an event that echoed the final game losses in both 1967 and 1975. "I expected it to end with me doing something right and everything going great. It just didn't end that way. . . ."

Henderson is wrong. But he can be forgiven because he hasn't spent an entire season as a member of the most fascinating professional baseball franchise in American history.

It was a perfect ending to a perfect season. They might have lost but the fans didn't.

Let's suppose, for the moment, that the Red Sox defeated the New York Mets in the seventh game and Henderson did "something right" such as hitting a grand slam. After the champagne, trophy presentation, and big parade, which wouldn't have been any bigger than the one they had yesterday, and the temporary, off-season bragging rights that come with a world championship, what would be left except the emptiness that immediately follows hollow joy.

The obvious has finally occurred to me after 35 years of

following the Sox, during which time I selected my college (Boston University) based on its proximity to Fenway Park.

What finally occurred to me is not that the witches of Salem control the team's fate or that there's some sort of curse woven into the fabric of their uniforms but that, in a society based on the oversimplified logic of mathematical wins, losses and profit margins, the Boston Red Sox represent the kind of classicism that Aristotle might envy.

Although, as fans, we often think that winning brings eternal gratification, it doesn't.

James Dickey, the poet-novelist, was once asked why he wrote so many depressing poems.

"Some of them are depressing," he replied, "but I hope it's the type of depression that you leap up from, renewed."

All fans of the Red Sox should take his advice to heart because what we have here is not simply a baseball team, like the Mets, but one of the most artistic companies ever to take the stage. Burdened by forces beyond their control, they perfectly conform to the Aristotelean dramatic ideal. They fulfill the requirements of the rising action of the Greek drama by being elected to finish fifth, winning the division and the pennant. They saved an entire season's worth of falling action for the final two hours.

Bruce Hurst, the man who would be MVP, claimed over and over again that he wasn't part of the team that lost in 1967 and 1975, therefore implying that he shouldn't be burdened by the past. However, like the generations of actors who played Lear — Barrymore, Olivier, Welles — the cast may change but the play's the same. It's the Red Sox.

The Red Sox transcend the individuals who wear the uniforms, the various managers who direct the different casts each year, and even the game itself.

Despite attempts to trivialize this team on television with sentimental songs played against slow-motion shots of familiar faces and performances, they will persevere.

As a movie critic who's regularly exposed to failed art, it is clear that this baseball team combines elements of comedy and tragedy in such an innocent, yet sophisticated, way that playwrights and film-makers who fail to even come close to this team's artistry must be infuriated.

The final image of the stoic Wade Boggs, baseball's best hitter, sitting motionless in the dugout with a single tear rolling down his cheek is surely as evocative as Ingrid Bergman's departure in *Casablanca*. New York can have the Mets. They're just another ballclub.

Emily Vermeule

It's Not a Myth —
They're Immortal

Gallant Red Sox Didn't Really Fail

Boston Globe, October 1978

The Red Sox did not fail, they became immortal. The classic tale of their summer, and autumn, could not have matched the great dramatic literature of the past had it ended any other way.

They were worthy of the Sophoclean stage, actors in traditional and poignant myth, in the long conflict between the larger-than-life hero and inexorable time, native brilliance and predestined ruin, the flukiness of luck, tyche, set against the hardest striving of the individual. It was life in the miniature, and not so small at that.

Following the purest form of individual and collective tragedy, that is, a traditional tale with a tough unforgettable ending, the Red Sox passed through the ancient cycle of olbos, koros, hubris and ate, and then some.

Olbos: The initial state of happiness and prosperity, in which a man seems blessed to himself and his fellows; so Remy, Torrez and Eckersley were bought for us with fine gold, at the cost of characters we loved on the mound, in the field and in the office, and life looked good.

Koros: Too much of a good thing almost, when a man feels superior to destiny; Tiant and Lee were pitching marvelously,

Yaz had drunk of the Fountain of Youth; Scott, Burleson, Lynn and Evans were fielding better than ever if that were possible, and we had three catchers uninjured.

Hubris: A kind of dangerous physical and spiritual arrogance; did we suffer that phase? Of course, and *The Globe* warned against it early, in the editorial of July 26, "Thinking the Unthinkable in Boston," when we were 14 games ahead of Them. In this stage of physical euphoria we ripped legs stealing second, hurtled down enemy dugouts, gave our hands to be spiked and our heads to be beaned and challenged the metal stands with our slender ribs. We lived in pain and wondered about our new stepparents, who sold Carbo myopically for mean cash. Recognition of truth inevitably followed.

Ate: A mix of blind fumbling against destiny and distorted perception, leading to ruin; Bob Bailey looking at a called third strike over his belly. Ate leads the hero along a dubious path and leaves him desolate (in a) place, but has the classic function of confirming him as hero, the proud soul with head erect as all the darts of a dark fate are thrown against him.

Every ballplayer is alone on stage as he faces Fate on the mound. He is totally exposed. It is amazing, and could happen in no other sport, that from the first greening of the willows to the reddening and dropping of the leaves, and the most exciting, despairing game of many seasons on Monday in Fenway Park, nothing was decided until the last out of the last of the ninth.

Then the hero took his proper stance, which is loss and immortality. Astronomers wept, judges blinked hard, truckdrivers sped around town trying to change the radio news, children crept under the bed; but they were wrong. Our hearts were with the Trojans in that war, and with the Sox in this. The hero must go under at last, after prodigious deeds, to be remembered and immortal and to have poets sing his tale.

That so few gallant, striving men on the brilliant green stage of Fenway stirring so many souls for so long, and lost by such a small, inevitable twist at the last second, made the Red Sox a theme of song for a century to come.

Epilogue

In truth had it not rained after the sixth game of the 1986 World Series, I don't think I could've come back for the seventh game. I know it's a baby-out thing to say, but I just didn't have the emotional stamina to do it. As I write this, the champagne and the pain from that gut-wrenching loss still sit on ice in my fridge. But as I sat nearly comatose while Dwight Evans and Rich Gedman hit home runs to stake the Sox to an early three-run lead in game seven, Gillian, my youngest daughter, who was just beginning to master the intricacies of the game, turned to me in puzzlement and asked, "Isn't this good?" To which I meekly replied, "It could be." To which she asked, "So why aren't you cheering?" To which I said, "I can't. I just don't have it in me." To which Older Daughter Meagan, who at first had become a baseball fan out of sympathy for my sonless state and then became a fan out of love for the game, said, "This isn't going to be any fun to watch if you're not going to be jumping up and down screaming."

She was right of course. When all the wondrous words have been written, and all the wondrous writing's been read, having fun is what it's all about.

Go Sox.